Working Backwards

Working Backwards

Insights, Stories,
and Secrets from
Inside Amazon

Colin Bryar and Bill Carr

St. Martin's Press
New York

First published in the United States by St. Martin's Press, an imprint of St. Martin's Publishing Group

www.stmartins.com

Design by Meryl Sussman Levavi

Library of Congress Cataloging-in-Publication Data

Names: Bryar, Colin, author. | Carr, Bill, 1967- author.
Title: Working backwards : insights, stories, and secrets from inside
    Amazon / Colin Bryar and Bill Carr.
Description: First edition. | New York : St. Martin's Press, 2021. |
    Includes bibliographical references and index. |
Identifiers: LCCN 2020037477 | ISBN 9781250267597 (hardcover) |
    ISBN 9781250275714 (international, sold outside the U.S., subject
    to rights availability) | ISBN 9781250267603 (ebook)
Subjects: LCSH: Amazon.com (Firm)—Management. | Electronic
    commerce—Management. | Leadership. | Corporate culture. |
    Decision making. | Success in business.
Classification: LCC HF5548.32 .B795 2021 |
    DDC 381/.14206573—dc23
LC record available at https://lccn.loc.gov/2020037477

Our books may be purchased in bulk for promotional, educational, or business use. Please contact your local bookseller or the Macmillan Corporate and Premium Sales Department at 1-800-221-7945, extension 5442, or by email at MacmillanSpecialMarkets@macmillan.com.

First Edition: 2021

10 9 8 7 6 5 4 3 2 1

To Sarah and Lynn

Contents

Part Two
THE INVENTION MACHINE AT WORK

Introduction

To say that Amazon is an unconventional company is an understatement. Its most significant initiatives have often been criticized and even derided as folly. One business pundit dubbed it "Amazon. toast."[1] Time and again, Amazon has proved the doubters wrong. Established competitors and aspiring newcomers have studied the company from the outside, hoping to uncover the secrets of its success and build upon them. Though many have adopted one or more of its famous principles and practices, even Amazon's most fervent believers haven't managed to duplicate the culture of innovation that continues to drive the company further into the lead.

Of course, the company has also come under scrutiny, even under fire, for some of its business methods. Some take issue with its impact on the business world and even on our society as a whole.*

---

* In his shareholder letter of April 16, 2020, shortly after the outbreak of the coronavirus pandemic, Jeff Bezos did address Amazon's impact on multiple fronts. He described the company's efforts to answer the increased demand on Amazon's services by people in lockdown. He described safety measures at fulfillment centers, an accelerated Amazon program to ramp up testing, and the

These issues are obviously important, both because they affect the lives of people and communities and because, increasingly, failure to address them can have a serious reputational and financial impact on a company. But they are beyond the scope of what we can cover in-depth in this book, which is primarily about showing you some of the unique principles and processes at Amazon with enough detail that you will be able to implement them if you choose to.

We spent a combined total of 27 years at Amazon, and we were there for some of the most pivotal moments of its development and growth. Any time either of us mentions that we worked at the company, we are immediately asked some version of a question that tries to get at the essential causes of its singular success. Analysts, competitors, and even customers have tried to sum it up in terms of the Amazon business model or corporate culture, but the simplest and best distillation is still that of founder Jeff Bezos (hereafter referred to as Jeff): "We have an unshakeable conviction that the long-term interests of shareowners are perfectly aligned with the interests of customers."[2] In other words, while it's true that shareholder value stems from growth in profit, Amazon believes that long-term growth is best produced by putting the customer first.

If you held this conviction, what kind of company would you build? In a talk at the 2018 Air, Space and Cyber Conference, Jeff described Amazon this way: "Our culture is four things: customer obsession instead of competitor obsession; willingness to think long term, with a longer investment horizon than most of our peers; eagerness to invent, which of course goes hand in hand with

---

partnership of Amazon Web Services with the WHO and other health organizations. He announced a two-dollar increase in Amazon's minimum wage, and the doubling of its overtime pay. The letter also outlined the company's Climate Pledge—to move to 80 percent renewable energy by 2024 and to achieve net zero carbon by 2040. For details on these and other efforts by Amazon to improve the lives of its workers, its customers, and the human population in general, see https://blog.aboutamazon.com/company-news/2019-letter-to-shareholders.

failure; and then, finally, taking professional pride in operational excellence."

That description has held true since Amazon's earliest days. In its first shareholder letter back in 1997, Amazon's first year as a public company, you'll find the phrases "Obsess Over Customers," "It's All About the Long Term," and "We will continue to learn from both our successes and our failures." One year later the term "Operational Excellence" entered the discussion, completing the four-faceted description of Amazon's corporate culture that endures today. Over the ensuing years, the wording has been tweaked to reflect lessons learned and scars earned, but Amazon has never wavered in its commitment to these four core principles. And they are in large part the reason that in 2015 Amazon became the company that reached $100 billion in annual sales faster than any other in the world. Remarkably, that same year Amazon Web Services (AWS) was reaching $10 billion in annual sales—at an even faster pace than the one Amazon had set.[3]

Of course, these four cultural touchstones don't quite get at the "how," that is, how people can work, individually and collectively, to ensure that they are maintained. And so Jeff and his leadership team crafted a set of 14 Leadership Principles, as well as a broad set of explicit, practical methodologies, that constantly reinforce its cultural goals. These include: the Bar Raiser hiring process that ensures that the company continues to acquire top talent; a bias for separable teams run by leaders with a singular focus that optimizes for speed of delivery and innovation; the use of written narratives instead of slide decks to ensure that deep understanding of complex issues drives well-informed decisions; a relentless focus on input metrics to ensure that teams work on activities that propel the business. And finally there is the product development process that gives this book its name: working backwards from the desired customer experience.

Many of the business problems that Amazon faces are no different from those faced by every other company, small or large. The difference is how Amazon keeps coming up with uniquely Amazonian solutions to those problems. Taken together, these elements combine to form a way of thinking, managing, and working that we refer to as *being Amazonian*, a term that we coined for the purposes of this book. Both of us, Colin and Bill, were "in the room," and—along with other senior leaders—we shaped and refined what it means to be Amazonian. We both worked extensively with Jeff and were actively involved in creating a number of Amazon's most enduring successes (not to mention some of its notable flops) in what was the most invigorating professional experience of our lives.

Colin

My first job out of college was designing and building database applications at Oracle. After that, I co-founded a company called Server Technologies Group with two colleagues. We wanted to use our experience in large-scale database systems to help companies move their business activities to the then-nascent Web. Our customers included Boeing, Microsoft, and a small company called Amazon. We recognized that Amazon was something special, and in 1998 we moved to Amazon, where I worked for 12 years as an executive, two of them in a role that brought me into the room with Jeff during an extraordinary period in Amazon's growth and innovation. Those two years began in the summer of 2003 when Jeff asked me to become his technical advisor, a role that is known colloquially as "Jeff's shadow," and is similar to a chief of staff role at other companies.

The position had been formalized about 18 months earlier when Andy Jassy, now CEO of Amazon Web Services, became Jeff's first full-time technical advisor. It had two main responsibilities. One was to help Jeff be as effective as possible. The other was, as Jeff put it to me, to "model and learn from each other" so that the person who held the position could eventually move on to a bigger role in the company.

Both Jeff and Andy made it clear that this was not the role of an observer or auditor, nor was it a training role. I would be expected to contribute immediately: to come up with ideas, take risks, and be a sounding board for Jeff. Before I took the job, I asked for the weekend to think about it and called a couple of friends—one had a comparable role assisting the CEO of a Fortune 10 company, and another was the right-hand man of a prominent government official. They both said, in effect, "Are you crazy? This is a once-in-a-lifetime chance. Why didn't you take the job on the spot?" They also told me my schedule would not be my own, and that I'd learn more than I could possibly imagine. One of them told me that while he learned a huge amount on the job, it was not exactly fun work.

Most of what my friends told me was true of being Jeff's shadow, with the notable exception that my job actually *was* a lot of fun. Once, we were traveling to New York for a series of meetings and events, including a tennis exhibition in Grand Central Terminal to promote Amazon's new apparel store. On the flight, Jeff asked me if I'd mind hitting some tennis balls with him when we landed so he could practice for the event, as his game was a bit rusty—he'd last played two years earlier in a charity event with Bill Gates, Andre Agassi, and Pete Sampras, "and before that, who knows?" I told him I'd played two weeks earlier at the local park with my buddy John. "So you have me beat on the A-list tennis partners," I said, "but I've got you on recency. I'm calling it a push. We'll have to settle the rest on the tennis court this evening." Jeff laughed and said it was a deal.

This story is atypical—95 percent of the time I spent with Jeff was focused on internal work issues rather than external events like conferences, public speeches, and sports matches. But it's typical in that he faced challenging situations such as this one—playing a sport he almost never practiced in front of a big crowd—with optimism, humor, and his well-known infectious laugh. This is the same spirit with which he faced his daily business decisions that were bigger than most people make in their whole careers. He truly embodies the Amazon motto, "Work hard, have fun, make history."

I worked with him during his regular office hours from ten in the morning to seven in the evening. Most days entailed between five and seven meetings with product or executive teams. Before and after Jeff's office hours I worked with those teams to help them prepare for their interactions with him so they'd be more productive for everyone. I already knew what it was like to be on the receiving end of an endless flood of ideas from him and then be asked to accomplish things quickly and with standards that could seem unreasonably high. I was often asked, "How do you think Jeff will respond to this idea?" My standard answer was, "I can't predict what he'll say, but these are the principles that typically inform his response. . . ."

During my time with Jeff, several pivotal Amazon businesses came to life, including Amazon Prime, Amazon Web Services, Kindle, and Fulfillment by Amazon. Several Amazon business processes, now firmly entrenched in *being Amazonian*, were introduced, including writing narratives and using the Working Backwards process.

I was aware of my good fortune and the rare opportunity my job afforded me to work side by side with Jeff and the Amazon senior leadership on a daily basis for over two years. I was determined to take advantage of every minute. I'd view activities such as car rides, lunches, and walking to meetings as precious learning opportunities I did not want to miss. One time a friend saw me writing down a long list of items in a notebook and asked what I was doing. I responded, "Well, I have a five-hour flight to New York with Jeff later this week and I want to make sure I have at least five hours' worth of questions and topics in case there's any free time." When I write about what led to Jeff making key decisions in this book, I can do so because I often directly asked him for his specific thinking behind his insights, as the reasoning behind them was often more illuminating than the insights themselves.

Bill

My path to Amazon was circuitous. After college I worked in sales for a few years before getting my MBA. I then took a sales job at Procter & Gamble before becoming one of P&G's account analysts for Kmart. Wanting to work in technology, I left P&G for a job at a software startup called Evare. In May 1999, at the suggestion of a college friend, I interviewed for a position at Amazon. The company was still housed in a single building on Second Avenue in Seattle. Space was so cramped that one of my interviews was conducted in a break room where, on the other side of a cubicle divider, people were getting coffee and chatting. I was offered a job as product manager in video (VHS and DVD), and remained at the company in various roles for the next 15 years.

For the first five years of my tenure, I worked in Amazon's largest business at that time, the U.S. physical media group— books, music, video—where I rose through the ranks to director. In January 2004, just a few months after Jeff invited Colin to become his technical advisor, my manager and good friend Steve Kessel dropped a similarly unexpected bombshell on me. He was going to be promoted to senior vice president and, at Jeff's request, take over the company's digital business. He told me that I was to be promoted to vice president and that he wanted me to join him.

Steve informed me that Jeff had decided the time was right for Amazon to start enabling our customers to buy and read/watch/ listen to books/videos/music digitally. The company was at a cross-roads. Though the books, CD, and VHS/DVD business was Amazon's most popular, changes in internet and device technology, as well as the emergence of Napster and Apple iPod/iTunes, made it clear that this would not last. We expected that the physical media business would decline over time due to the shift to digital. We felt we had to act right away.

Jeff often used an analogy in those days when describing our efforts to innovate and build new businesses. "We need to plant many seeds," he would say, "because we don't know which one of those seeds will grow into a mighty oak." It was an apt analogy. The oak is one of the sturdiest and longest-living trees in the forest. Each tree produces thousands of acorns for every one tree that eventually rises to the sky.

In retrospect, this was a renaissance era at Amazon. The seeds Amazon planted beginning in 2004 would grow into the Kindle e-book reader, the Fire tablet, Fire TV, Amazon Prime Video, Amazon Music, Amazon Studios, our voice-activated Echo speaker, and the underlying Alexa voice assistant technology. They would become some of Amazon's strongest and fastest-growing new businesses and value drivers. By 2018, these business units had created devices and services used daily by tens of millions of consumers around the world, generating tens of billions in annual revenue for Amazon.

I was fortunate enough throughout the decade to sit in either the driver's seat or a passenger seat (with a great view) for these new product initiatives. My role would evolve over the years, and I would become the owner and leader of Amazon's worldwide digital music and video business and engineering organizations. My team and I led the launch, development, and growth of the services that are known today as Amazon Music, Prime Video, and Amazon Studios. Through this experience, I had the opportunity to observe, participate in, and learn from the development and invention not only of these new products but also of a set of new Amazon processes, the combination of which would propel the company's second stage of growth, which has made it one of the most valuable companies on earth.

Working Backwards on an Amazon Book

We became friends through my wife, Lynn, and Colin's wife, Sarah, who became close friends when they both landed on the Amazon Toys category team in 2000 after earning their MBAs. Our friendship grew through our mutual love of golf and regular trips to play Bandon Dunes. We decided to write this book in 2018, when we observed two trends. The first was that Amazon's popularity had exploded, having become omnipresent in the media. People clearly craved to learn more about Amazon. The second was that Amazon was consistently misunderstood, which we experienced during our years on the inside. Wall Street analysts couldn't comprehend why Amazon didn't make a profit, as the company reinvested its cash in new products to drive future growth. And the press was often baffled by and critical of each new Amazon product, including Kindle, Prime, and Amazon Web Services.

Both of us moved on from Amazon to pursue new endeavors—Colin in 2010 and Bill in 2014—but we were forever shaped by our Amazon experiences. We worked with a variety of companies and investors in venture capital. Typical of the kind of thing we heard in our work was this remark by the CEO of a Fortune 100 company: "I don't understand how Amazon does it. They are able to build and win in so many different businesses from retail, to AWS, to digital media. Meanwhile, we have been at this for more than 30 years, and we still haven't mastered our core business."

We realized that there was a gap in the marketplace. There was no source, no book to answer the questions and explain Amazon's peculiar behavior and how it has produced exceptional results. We know the answers to those questions, and that is what we will share with you in these pages.

Since leaving Amazon, we have both introduced many of its elements to our new organizations, to great effect. But we find that when we talk to colleagues about introducing Amazon's principles to their workplace, they often respond with some version of, "But you had a lot more resources and money, not to mention Jeff Bezos. We don't."

We're here to tell you that you do not need Amazon's capital (in fact Amazon was capital constrained for most of our years there), nor do you need Jeff Bezos (though if he is available to work on your project, we'd highly recommend him!). Amazon's concrete, replicable principles and practices can be learned by anyone and refined and scaled throughout a company. After reading this book, we hope you'll see that *being Amazonian* is not a mystical leadership cult but a flexible mindset. You can take the elements that you need as you need them, then tweak and customize them as conditions warrant. The concept also has a wonderful fractal quality, meaning it can add benefit at any scale. We have witnessed the successful adoption of these elements across companies ranging from a ten-person startup to a global enterprise with hundreds of thousands of employees.

Here we will guide you toward *being Amazonian* in your own way, within your own organization. We'll offer specific, practical advice expressed through some of our favorite Amazon lore: the events, stories, conversations, personalities, jokes, and more that we have accumulated over the years.

We don't claim that *being Amazonian* is the only way to build a high-performing organization. As Jeff has written, "The world, thankfully, is full of many high-performing, highly distinctive corporate cultures. We never claim that our approach is the right one—just that it's ours . . ."[4]

Now it can also be yours.

Part One

Being Amazonian

Introduction to Part One

In the first half of this book, we will lay out in detail some of the crucial principles and processes that define *being Amazonian*. These ways of working—patiently honed over the years—have enabled Amazon's remarkable efficiency and its record-breaking growth. They have made Amazon's culture one in which invention thrives and delighting customers is highly prioritized. We will tell some of the origin stories of these principles and processes to demonstrate that they were solutions to problems that were impeding our ability to invent freely and satisfy our customers consistently.

The Amazon Leadership Principles are the main focus of chapter one. In the very early days of the company, when it consisted of a handful of people working out of three small rooms, there were no formal leadership principles because, in a sense, Jeff was the leadership principles. He wrote the job descriptions, interviewed candidates, packed and shipped boxes, and read every email that went out to customers. Taking part in every aspect of the business allowed him to communicate the Amazon philosophy informally to the relatively small group of employees. But the company expanded so quickly that it was soon impossible to communicate it that way anymore. Thus, the need for the Leadership Principles. We tell the story of the process by which they were created—itself a quintessentially Amazonian story—and we describe how they are infused into every capillary of the company's operation.

Hand in hand with the Leadership Principles go the mechanisms, which we also discuss in chapter one. These are the consistent, repeated processes that ensure the Leadership Principles are reinforced year to year and day to day in the company. We enumerate the method by which Amazon generates its yearly plans and goals for each individual team and for the company as a whole, and how it creates alignment between the team goals and the company goals. We also describe Amazon's distinctive compensation policy, which reinforces collaboration and long-term focus over intramural competition and orientation toward short-term gains.

In chapter two, we discuss the Bar Raiser, Amazon's unique hiring process. Like the Leadership Principles, we created the Bar Raiser because the company was growing extremely fast. One of the major pitfalls of needing to hire a lot of new people very quickly is urgency bias: the tendency to overlook a candidate's flaws because you are overwhelmed with work and need bodies. The Bar Raiser provides teams with methods to make the strongest hires efficiently and quickly, but without cutting corners.

In a company known for its inventiveness, separable, single-threaded leadership has been one of Amazon's most useful inventions. We discuss it in chapter three. This is the organizational strategy that minimizes the drag on efficiency created by intra-organizational dependencies. The basic premise is, for each initiative or project, there is a single leader whose focus is that project and that project alone, and that leader oversees teams of people whose attention is similarly focused on that one project. This chapter is as much the story of how we arrived at single-threaded leadership as it is a description of it: we outline the problems it was created to solve, and the imperfect solutions we developed before we came to the one that really works. We'll also discuss how and why we had to completely change the way we built and deployed technology in order to make separable, single-threaded teams a reality.

We also found that what really works in meetings is not what most companies do in meetings. As much as we respect PowerPoint as a visual communication tool and speaking aid, we learned the hard way that it's not the best format to communicate complex information about initiatives and ongoing projects in a one-hour meeting. We found, instead, that a six-page narrative written by a given team is the method that best enables everyone in a meeting to get up to speed quickly and efficiently on the project that team is working on. At the same time, the process of composing that narrative requires the team itself to reflect on the work they've been doing or propose to do, and to articulate it clearly to others, thereby sharpening their own thinking about that work. We discuss the details of this genre of narrative—and give an example of one—in chapter four.

In chapter five, we discuss how new ideas and products are developed at Amazon: Working Backwards from the desired customer experience. Before we start building, we write a Press Release to clearly define how the new idea or product will benefit customers, and we create a list of Frequently Asked Questions to resolve the tough issues up front. We carefully and critically study and modify each of these documents until we're satisfied before we move on to the next step.

The customer is also at the center of how we analyze and manage performance metrics. Our emphasis is on what we call controllable input metrics, rather than output metrics. Controllable input metrics (e.g., reducing internal costs so you can affordably lower product prices, adding new items for sale on the website, or reducing standard delivery time) measure the set of activities that, if done well, will yield the desired results, or output metrics (such as monthly revenue and stock price). We detail these metrics as well as how to discover and track them in chapter six.

Part one does not comprise an exhaustive list of principles

and processes developed at Amazon. We selected the ones that we think best illustrate what it means to be Amazonian. We will show you how we arrived at each one of them. And we will give you concrete, actionable information that will help you hone the methods by which your company or organization, big or small, can maximize its potential to serve its customers.

1

Building Blocks

Leadership Principles and Mechanisms

The development of the 14 Amazon Leadership Principles. How they're infused into everyday work. Checks and balances (mechanisms) reinforce them. Why they confer a significant competitive advantage. How they can be applied in your company.

* * *

Amazon.com opened for business in July 1995, staffed by a handful of people handpicked by Jeff Bezos. In 1994, Jeff had read a report that projected annual internet usage growth at 2,300 percent. He was then a senior vice president at D. E. Shaw & Co., a New York hedge fund specializing in sophisticated mathematical models to exploit market inefficiencies. He decided that getting in on the growth of the Web was a once-in-a-lifetime opportunity, so he gave up his lucrative and promising career and drove west with his wife, MacKenzie, to start an internet business.

Along the way to Seattle, he wrote his business plan. He identified several reasons why the book category was underserved and well suited to online commerce. He outlined how he could create a new and compelling experience for book-buying customers. To begin with, books were relatively lightweight and came in fairly uniform sizes, meaning they would be easy and inexpensive to warehouse, pack, and ship. Second, while more than 100 million books had been written and more than a million titles were in print in 1994, even a Barnes & Noble mega-bookstore could stock only tens of thousands of titles. An online bookstore, on the other hand, could offer not just the books that could fit in a brick-and-mortar store but any book in print. Third, there were two large book-distribution companies, Ingram and Baker & Taylor, that acted as intermediaries between publishers and retailers and maintained huge inventories in vast warehouses. They kept detailed electronic catalogs of books in print to make it easy for bookstores and libraries to order from them. Jeff realized that he could combine the infrastructure that Ingram and Baker & Taylor had created—warehouses full of books ready to be shipped, plus an electronic catalog of those books—with the growing infrastructure of the Web, making it possible for consumers to find and buy any book in print and get it shipped directly to their homes. Finally, the site could use technology to analyze the behavior of customers and create a unique, personalized experience for each one of them.

The first Amazonians worked elbow to elbow in three small rooms, upstairs from a converted basement filled mostly with overstock from the army surplus store across the street. Desks, including Jeff's, had been fashioned out of doors affixed to four-by-fours with metal angle brackets. A padlocked plywood door in that basement secured the first Amazon "distribution center," a room measuring perhaps 400 square feet that had last served as the practice space for a local band whose name was still spray-painted on the door.

In such close quarters, Jeff could take the pulse of the company—from software development to finance and operations—by turning his chair around or poking his head through the doorway of an adjoining room. He knew everyone who worked for the company and, apart from writing the all-important software, he had done each of their jobs alongside them while they learned the ropes. And, never shy about how he wanted things done, he began to instill guiding principles, like customer obsession and unrelentingly high standards, into every step his small team took.

From the tone of customer emails to the condition of the books and their packaging, Jeff had one simple rule: "It has to be perfect." He'd remind his team that one bad customer experience would undo the goodwill of hundreds of perfect ones. When a coffee-table book arrived from the distributor with a scratch across the dust jacket, Jeff had customer service write to the customer to apologize and explain that, since coffee-table books are meant for display, a replacement copy was already on order, but shipment would be delayed—unless time was of the essence and they preferred the scratched copy right away. The customer loved the response, and decided to wait for the perfect copy while expressing their delight at receiving this surprise consideration.

Jeff also proofread customer service emails that dealt with any new topic. One day a prominent technology columnist wrote to ask a series of penetrating and challenging questions about the business, credit card security, and more. Jeff read his team's response to the columnist, seemed to read it a second time, and then said, "That's perfect." After that, apparently satisfied that customer service had now internalized the core principles he insisted upon, he checked in far less frequently.

Another of Jeff's frequent exhortations to his small staff was that Amazon should always underpromise and overdeliver, to ensure that customer expectations were exceeded. One example of this principle was that the website clearly described standard shipping as U.S. Postal Service First-Class Mail. In actuality, all these shipments were sent by Priority Mail—a far more expensive option that guaranteed delivery within two to three business days anywhere in the United States. This was called out as a complimentary upgrade in the shipment-confirmation email. Thank-you emails for the upgrade included one that read, "You guys R going to make a billion dollars." When Jeff saw it he roared with laughter, then printed a copy to take back to his office.

The job description he wrote for his very first employee said, "You must have experience designing and building large and complex (yet maintainable) systems, and you should be able to do so in about one-third the time that most competent people think possible."[1] In his very first letter to shareholders, in 1997, Jeff wrote, "When I interview people I tell them, 'You can work long, hard, or smart, but at Amazon.com you can't choose two out of three.'"[2]

In those days, the spirit of Amazon meant that most Amazonians embraced Jeff's challenging standards. People worked a minimum of 60 hours per week, with music blasting in the office late at night, and did whatever was needed to satisfy customers. Every afternoon, Jeff would join everybody in the basement to pack customer orders, at first working on hands and knees on the concrete floor. A wide variety of orders came in ever-increasing numbers from all over the world. It quickly became clear that something very special was happening, and it was exciting to be a part of it.

The growth that followed was historic and virtually unprecedented, and it meant changes in the company. Months after moving into its first office, door desks crowded every space, so the company moved to a vastly larger office down the street. They soon burst the seams again and moved a second time. During the first critical years, Jeff could transmit the strength and clarity of his message directly to the small leadership team through daily and weekly interactions; he could be present for decisions big and small; and he could formulate and apply principles like customer obsession, innovation, frugality, personal ownership, bias for action, and high standards. But new employees—who in the beginning had each been hired personally by Jeff—quickly reached numbers that demanded new layers of leadership. By the late 1990s, the organization had grown from tens to more than 500. This fantastic growth began to limit Jeff's ability to be fully involved in hiring leaders and inculcating them with his values. His standards could be maintained only if the company itself, from top to bottom, somehow committed to keeping them at the forefront.

In this chapter, we'll discuss how Amazon established a set of principles and mechanisms, enabling the company to grow from a single founder to several hundred thousand employees[3] while remaining stubbornly true to its mission of obsessing over customers to create long-term shareholder value. Some of these methods are well known and have been widely adopted. Some are probably unique to Amazon.

What distinguishes Amazon is that its Leadership Principles are deeply ingrained in *every* significant process and function at the company. In many cases, the principles dictate a way of thinking or doing work that is different from the way that most companies operate. As a result, newly hired Amazonians go through a challenging multimonth period of learning and adapting to these new methods. Because these processes and practices are embedded in every meeting, document, decision, interview, and performance discussion, following them becomes second nature over time. And any employee who violates them draws attention to themselves like a person loudly scratching their fingernails across a chalkboard. If, for example, a person spoke up at a meeting and suggested an idea that was obviously geared toward short-term considerations and ignored significant longer-term ones, or proposed something that was competitor- rather than customer-centric, there would be an uncomfortable pause before someone pointed out what was on everyone else's mind. While this practice may not be unique to Amazon, it is a defining element of its success.

By the late 1990s, there was a set of Amazon core competencies that every Amazonian was expected to exhibit, as well as an additional set of competencies that all managers were expected to master and employ. When I (Bill) first read through the long list of competencies as a new hire in 1999, I recall feeling a mix of inspiration and intimidation thanks to the combination of super-high standards applied across such a breadth of disciplines. I thought, "I will have to work harder and smarter than I have ever worked if I am to live up to these."

In 2004, human resources head Mike George and his colleague Robin Andrulevich made an observation: the company had grown like a weed, adding many leaders who were inexperienced and in need of some formal management and leadership training. So Mike asked Robin to create a leadership-training program. Robin asserted that doing so would first require clearly and succinctly codifying what leadership meant at Amazon. Such an exercise would certainly delay the rollout of the program, but, after much discussion, everyone agreed it would be a worthy undertaking.

In the 2015 shareholder letter, Jeff wrote, "You can write down your corporate culture, but when you do so, you're discovering it, uncovering it—not creating it."[4] This was the assumption on which Robin had been operating when she set about to codify the Leadership Principles. She interviewed people throughout Amazon who were effective leaders and who embodied the essence of this burgeoning company. What she thought would be a two-month project took nine months to complete. But by the time she was finished, her effort had gone a long way toward identifying many of the elements that would make the company what it is today.

This initial set of Leadership Principles was basically an articulation and synthesis of the ethos of the people Robin interviewed. In a few cases, a principle was based on the leadership activities of a single person. For instance, Jeff Wilke, then SVP of Worldwide Operations and now CEO of Amazon's Worldwide Consumer business, insisted on data-driven decision-making and frequent auditing from everyone he worked with, and this became the basis of the leadership principle Dive Deep.

Robin would review each draft with Mike and the HR leadership team. Veteran HR leaders Alison Allgor and Kristin Strout, in particular, provided valuable feedback. They'd debate each principle with a critical eye as to whether it belonged on the list. Some were jettisoned altogether if they sounded generically corporate or weren't universally relevant. Robin and Jeff Wilke met frequently to review progress and refine the list, sometimes bringing other leaders—including Rick Dalzell, Tom Szkutak, and Jason Kilar—into the process. Robin also checked in regularly with Jeff and Colin.

I (Colin) remember one particularly intense debate that centered on the proposed phrase "Leaders do not believe their body odor smells of perfume" in the Apolitical/Vocally Self-Critical principle. Was it okay to use quirky language when communicating with a wide audience? Would people take the principles seriously if we did? In the end, we concluded that although the phrase was unconventional, it was devastatingly effective at providing clarity. Body odor stayed.

In late 2004, after months of discussion and debate, Robin

emailed what she thought was the final list of nine leadership principles to Jeff. It felt like a lot at the time, but each one seemed essential, and we could not agree to strike any.

In early 2005, with the principles completed, Jeff sent an email to all managers at Amazon, formally announcing the ten Amazon Leadership Principles. Thanks to Robin, who did a superb job collecting these powerful principles, they were expressed in an actionable and distinctly Amazonian way. For example, the Insist on the Highest Standards leadership principle is described like this: "Leaders have relentlessly high standards—many people may think these standards are unreasonably high." The words "relentlessly" and "unreasonably high" are distinctly Jeff-ian and therefore Amazonian ways of thinking and speaking.

Another important Amazonian phrase often appears alongside the Amazon Leadership Principles and key tenets: "Unless you know better ones." This reminds people to always seek to improve the status quo.

Over the following years, some of the original ten principles underwent modification, and more were eventually added. Even today the principles are questioned and refined from time to time, adapting along with the company as new understandings and new challenges arise.

Amazon now has 14 Leadership Principles—notably more than most companies have. They are displayed right on the Amazon website along with this explanation: "We use our Leadership Principles every day, whether we're discussing ideas for new projects or deciding on the best approach to solving a problem. It is just one of the things that makes Amazon peculiar."[5]

People often ask, "How do you remember all 14 principles?" The answer is not that we are particularly good at memorization. In fact, if a company's principles must be memorized, it's a warning sign that they aren't sufficiently woven into the fabric of that company. We know and remember Amazon's principles because they are the basic framework used for making decisions and taking action. We encountered them every day, measured ourselves against them, and held one another similarly accountable. The longer you work at Amazon, the more these 14 principles become part of you and how you look at the world.

If you expose the workings of any major Amazon process, you'll see these principles playing a prominent role; employee performance evaluations highlight this perfectly. Much of the peer and manager feedback used in these evaluations focuses on how a person exhibited, or fell short of exhibiting, the Amazon Leadership Principles during the review period. Similarly, every candidate who interviews for a job at Amazon is evaluated in light of the Leadership Principles. Interviewers spend the better part of an hour vetting the candidate according to selected principles, and each candidate typically goes through five to seven interviews. Add in a 30–60 minute debrief meeting attended by each interviewer, multiply that by the number of open positions—10,000 in Seattle alone at the time of this writing—and you begin to understand why Amazon people know the principles intimately. Far from being mere catchphrases on a poster or screensaver, Amazon's Leadership Principles are the company's living, breathing constitution.

Amazon's Leadership Principles[6]

1. **Customer Obsession.** Leaders start with the customer and work backwards. They work vigorously to earn and keep customer trust. Although leaders pay attention to competitors, they obsess over customers.

2. **Ownership.** Leaders are owners. They think long term and don't sacrifice long-term value for short-term results. They act on behalf of the entire company, beyond just their own team. They never say, "that's not my job."

3. **Invent and Simplify.** Leaders expect and require innovation and invention from their teams and always find ways to simplify. They are externally aware, look for new ideas from everywhere, and are not limited by "not invented here." As we do new things, we accept that we may be misunderstood for long periods of time.

4. **Are Right, A Lot.** Leaders are right a lot. They have strong judgment and good instincts. They seek diverse perspectives and work to disconfirm their beliefs.

5. **Learn and Be Curious.** Leaders are never done learning and always seek to improve themselves. They are curious about new possibilities and act to explore them.

6. **Hire and Develop the Best.** Leaders raise the performance bar with every hire and promotion. They recognize exceptional talent, and willingly move them throughout the organization. Leaders develop leaders and take seriously their role in coaching others. We work on behalf of our people to invent mechanisms for development like Career Choice.

7. **Insist on the Highest Standards.** Leaders have relentlessly high standards—many people may think these standards are unreasonably high. Leaders are continually raising the bar and drive their teams to deliver high-quality products, services, and processes. Leaders ensure that defects do not get sent down the line and that problems are fixed so they stay fixed.

8. **Think Big.** Thinking small is a self-fulfilling prophecy. Leaders create and communicate a bold direction that inspires results. They think differently and look around corners for ways to serve customers.

9. **Bias for Action.** Speed matters in business. Many decisions and actions are reversible and do not need extensive study. We value calculated risk-taking.

10. **Frugality.** Accomplish more with less. Constraints breed resourcefulness, self-sufficiency, and invention. There are no extra points for growing headcount, budget size, or fixed expense.

11. **Earn Trust.** Leaders listen attentively, speak candidly, and treat others respectfully. They are vocally self-critical, even when doing so is awkward or embarrassing. Leaders do not believe their or their team's body odor smells of perfume. They benchmark themselves and their teams against the best.

12. **Dive Deep.** Leaders operate at all levels, stay connected to the details, audit frequently, and are skeptical when metrics and anecdotes differ. No task is beneath them.

13. **Have Backbone; Disagree and Commit.** Leaders are obligated to respectfully challenge decisions when they disagree, even when doing so is uncomfortable or exhausting. Leaders have conviction and are tenacious. They do not compromise for the sake of social cohesion. Once a decision is determined, they commit wholly.

14. **Deliver Results.** Leaders focus on the key inputs for their business and deliver them with the right quality and in a timely fashion. Despite setbacks, they rise to the occasion and never settle.

The nature of the Amazon Leadership Principles is borne out in processes and practices throughout the company. For example, the six-page narratives that the company uses in place of PowerPoint decks to present quarterly and yearly business updates require both the writer and reader to Dive Deep and Insist on the Highest Standards. The Press Release/Frequently Asked Questions process—aka PR/FAQ—reinforces customer obsession, starting with customer needs and working backwards from there. (See chapters four and five for a detailed discussion of both the six-pager and the PR/FAQ.) The Door Desk Award goes to a person who exemplifies Frugality and Invention. The Just Do It Award is an abnormally large, well-worn Nike sneaker given to employees who exhibit a Bias for Action. It usually goes to a person who has come up with a clever idea outside the scope of their job. What's peculiarly Amazonian about the award is that the idea doesn't have to be implemented—nor does it have to actually work if it is—in order to be eligible.

The stories we tell in part two of this book about the long, hard road to launching some of Amazon's most successful services— Kindle, Prime, and Amazon Web Services—will provide in-depth examples of the Leadership Principles in action.

Still, even though the Leadership Principles are embedded

into the fabric of the company, they cannot effectively enforce themselves—that's the job of something that Amazonians call *mechanisms*.

Mechanisms: Reinforcing the Leadership Principles

There's a saying often heard at Amazon: "Good intentions don't work. Mechanisms do." No company can rely on good intentions like "We must try harder!" or "Next time remember to . . ." to improve a process, solve a problem, or fix a mistake. That's because people already had good intentions when the problems cropped up in the first place. Amazon realized early on that if you don't change the underlying condition that created a problem, you should expect the problem to recur.

Over the course of many years, Amazon has put in place mechanisms to ensure that the Leadership Principles translate into action. Three foundational mechanisms are: the annual planning process; the S-Team goals process (the S-Team consists of the senior vice presidents and direct reports to Jeff Bezos); and Amazon's compensation plan, which aligns incentives with what's best for customers and the company over the long term.

Annual Planning: OP1 and OP2

Amazon relies heavily on autonomous, single-threaded teams (more in chapter three). These teams keep the company nimble, moving quickly with a minimum of external friction, but their autonomy must be paired with precise goal-setting to align each team's independent plans with the company's overarching goals.

Amazon's planning for the calendar year begins in the summer. It's a painstaking process that requires four to eight weeks of intensive work for the managers and many staff members of every team in the company. This intensity is deliberate, because a poorly defined plan—or worse, no plan at all—can incur a much greater downstream cost.

The S-Team begins by creating a set of high-level expectations or objectives for the entire company. For example, in previous years, the CEO and CFO would articulate goals like "Grow revenue from $10 billion to $15 billion" or "Reduce fixed costs by 5 percent." Over time, Amazon refined such broad goals into a longer list of increasingly detailed objectives. Examples have included: revenue growth targets by geography and business segment; operating leverage targets; improving productivity and giving back those savings to customers in the form of lower prices; generating strong free cash flow; and understanding the level of investment in new businesses, products, and services.

Once these high-level expectations are established, each group begins work on its own more granular operating plan—known as OP1—which sets out the individual group's "bottom-up" proposal. Through the narrative process (described in chapter four), Amazon aims to evaluate about ten times as much information as the typical company does in a similar time frame. The main components of an OP1 narrative are:

- Assessment of past performance, including goals achieved, goals missed, and lessons learned
- Key initiatives for the following year
- A detailed income statement
- Requests (and justifications) for resources, which may include things like new hires, marketing spend, equipment, and other fixed assets

Each group works in partnership with its finance and human resources counterparts to create their detailed plan, which is then presented to a panel of leaders. The level of those leaders—director, VP, or S-Team—depends on the size, impact, or strategic importance of the group. The panel then reconciles any gaps between the bottom-up proposal and the top-down goals the group has been asked to meet. Sometimes a team may be asked to rework its plan and re-present it until there's agreement between the top-down goals and bottom-up plan.

The OP1 process runs through the fall and is completed before the fourth-quarter holiday rush begins. In January, after the holiday season ends, OP1 is adjusted as necessary to reflect the fourth-quarter results, as well as to update the trajectory of the business. This shorter process is called OP2, and it generates the plan of record for the calendar year.

OP2 aligns each group with the goals of the company. Everybody knows their overall objectives, including targets for revenue, cost, and performance. The metrics are agreed upon and will be supplied as part of every team's deliverables. OP2 makes it crystal clear what each group has committed to do, how they intend to achieve those goals, and what resources they need to get the work done.

Some variances are inevitable, but any change to OP2 requires formal S-Team approval.

S-Team Goals

During OP1, as the S-Team reads and reviews the various operating plans, they select the initiatives and goals from each team that they consider to be the most important to achieve. These selected goals are called, unsurprisingly, *S-Team goals*. In other words, my (Bill's) team working on Amazon Music might have had 23 goals and initiatives in our 2012 operating plan. After reviewing our plan with us, the S-Team might have chosen six of the 23 to become S-Team goals. The music team would still have worked to achieve all 23 goals, but it would be sure to make resource allocation decisions throughout the year to prioritize the six S-Team goals ahead of the remaining 17.

Three notably Amazonian features of S-Team goals are their unusually large number, their level of detail, and their aggressiveness. S-Team goals once numbered in the dozens, but these have expanded to many hundreds every year, scattered across the entire company.

S-Team goals are mainly input-focused metrics that measure the specific activities teams need to perform during the year that, if achieved, will yield the desired business results. In chapter six, we will discuss in more detail how Amazon develops such precise and specific metrics to ensure teams meet their business objectives. S-Team goals must be Specific, Measurable, Attainable, Relevant, and Timely (SMART). An actual S-Team goal could be as specific as "Add 500 new products in the amazon.fr Musical Instruments category (100 products in Q1, 200 in Q2 . . .)," or "Ensure 99.99 percent of all calls to software service 'Y' are successfully responded to within 10 milliseconds," or "Increase repeat advertisers from 50 percent to 75 percent by Q3 of next year."

S-Team goals are aggressive enough that Amazon only expects about three-quarters of them to be fully achieved during the year. Hitting every one of them would be a clear sign that the bar had been set too low.

S-Team goals for the entire company are aggregated and their metrics are tracked with centralized tools by the finance team. Each undergoes an intensive quarterly review that calls for thorough preparation. Reviews are conducted in multihour S-Team meetings scheduled on a rolling basis over the quarter rather than all at once. At many companies, when the senior leadership meets, they tend to focus more on big-picture, high-level strategy issues than on execution. At Amazon, it's the opposite. Amazon leaders toil over the execution details and regularly embody the Dive Deep leadership principle, which states: "Leaders operate at all levels, stay connected to the details, audit frequently, and are skeptical when metrics and anecdotes differ. No task is beneath them."

The finance team tracks the S-Team goals throughout the year with a status of green, yellow, and red. Green means you are on track, yellow means there is some risk of missing the goal, and red means you are not likely to hit the goal unless something meaningful changes. During the periodic reviews, yellow or red status draws the team's attention where it's needed most, and a frank discussion about what's wrong and how it will be addressed ensues.

The OP planning process aligns the entire company on what's truly important to accomplish for the year. S-Team goals refine that alignment by giving top priority to the company's biggest or most pressing objectives. The review cadence helps maintain alignment, no matter what happens along the way. This structure ensures that every goal that's important to the company has someone—an accountable owner—working on it.

Last, as Amazon has grown, the planning process has evolved with it. While the overall structure remains the same, there are now separate leadership teams for the retail business and AWS—and even separate teams for the large businesses within those parts of the company. Each of these parts of the company has its own version of "S-Team goals," just with a different label. As your organization grows, you can follow this recursive process too.

Amazon Compensation Reinforces Long-Term Thinking

Even the very best of all these preparations can still be subverted by other factors—the most insidious of which is a certain type of "performance-based" executive compensation that's all too common elsewhere. No matter how clear your leadership principles and yearly plan may be, they speak softly in comparison to financial incentives. Money talks—if your leadership principles, your yearly plan, and your financial incentives are not closely aligned, you won't get the right results.

Amazon believes that the "performance" in performance-based compensation must refer to the company's overall performance, that is, the best interests of shareholders, which in turn are perfectly aligned with the best interests of customers. Accordingly, the compensation of Amazon S-Team members and all senior leaders is heavily weighted toward equity earned over a period of several years. The maximum salary itself is set well below that of industry peers in the United States. When we were there, the maximum base salary for any employee was $160,000 (indications are that this remains true). Some new executive hires may receive a signing bonus, but the bulk of their compensation—and the potentially enormous upside—is the long-term value of the company.

The wrong kind of compensation practice can cause misalignment in two ways: (1) by rewarding short-term goals at the expense of long-term value creation, and (2) by rewarding the achievement of localized departmental milestones whether or not they benefit the company as a whole. Both can powerfully drive behaviors that are antithetical to the company's ultimate goals.

In other industries, such as media and financial services, a large percentage of executive compensation is doled out in annual performance bonuses. These short-term goals (and yes, a year is definitely short term) can generate behaviors that are detrimental to creating long-term value. In seeking short-term targets to maximize compensation, some may intentionally push revenue from one time period to the next, cannibalizing future results and obscuring current challenges. Others might overspend marketing funds to boost sales for the current quarter and thus hit a short-term sales goal, even at the expense of future quarters or long-term sales. Some might be tempted to defer expenses, put off maintenance, or cut back on hiring in order to hit a quarterly cost-containment target—all with negative longer-term implications. A few may even drag their feet if asked to take on an important new role in the company until their bonus is "in the bank," delaying some important company initiative. Long-term stock-based compensation incentives, by comparison, eliminate such selfish and costly decisions by making them nonsensical.

Many companies set entirely independent goals for key players at every level. All too often this gives rise to infighting, information withholding, and hoarding of resources, as each leader is incentivized to undermine the other. Amazon's compensation is, by contrast, simple and oriented toward the long term. As one is promoted at Amazon, the ratio of cash to equity compensation becomes more and more skewed toward long-term equity. The Frugality leadership principle makes the reason very plain: "There are no extra points for headcount, budget size, or expense."

One clear downside to this approach is that other companies with deep pockets can try to hire away your best employees with big cash offers. It's true, some employees leave for a short-term jump in their cash compensation. But on the positive side, Amazon's approach reinforces the kind of culture it seeks to develop. Sometimes it is okay to lose people who have a short-term focus while retaining those who are in it for the long term.

Amazon uses a similar long-term equity structure in order to prevent potential conflicts of interest in its wholly owned subsidiaries, including IMDb, Zappos, and Twitch. Executives in those companies are compensated in the same manner as other Amazon executives, primarily with a base salary and a heavy emphasis on Amazon equity, which encourages collaboration.

* * *

There's no magic number of principles and mechanisms that every company will need. The magic lives in the moments when the principles are put into practice. You'll develop the number that's right for you, provided that you focus on how these principles will give clarity to your company's vision and drive the right behaviors to create meaningful value for your shareholders and stakeholders over the long term—even when the CEO is not in the room.

It's important too to allow your principles to evolve when necessary—to revise, cut, and add as the company grows and changes. Learn and Be Curious was the most recent addition for Amazon. Being Vocally Self-Critical was dropped, with much of its content merged into Earn Trust. Adding, subtracting, and modifying your principles in response to change or deeper understanding is a sign that you're probably doing things right.

Strong leadership principles represent a company's vision and enable good and fast decisions throughout the company. Codifying those principles is a huge step forward, as we've seen, but there is another step that is equally important: to embed them into every one of your company's core processes, including hiring, performance management, planning, operating cadence, and career development.

2

Hiring

Amazon's Unique Bar Raiser Process

The importance of hiring and the steep cost of slapdash hiring processes. The failings of conventional approaches, shown in a fictional example at the "Green Corp." The development of the Bar Raiser process and how it consistently improves the level of skill and talent throughout the company. How the Bar Raiser process can be adapted to your company.

* * *

A former vice president at Amazon told us about the time he applied for the position of COO at a multibillion-dollar global tech company. The CEO interviewing him began with a string of unrelated questions, not one of which was designed to reveal anything of use. The kicker, following an unusually long pause: "Tell me something about yourself that isn't apparent by reading your résumé." You might as well just say, "Look, I don't know what I'm looking for or how to find it, so can you please help me out?"

At Amazon, rapid growth meant we *had* to develop a rigorous process to raise our hiring game, but it didn't happen immediately. Our early emphasis on finding people with high SAT scores who could answer hard questions like "How many windows are there in Seattle?" produced people who were smart, but the process didn't tell us whether they would thrive at Amazon. Jeff often said in those days, "We want missionaries, not mercenaries." We have all encountered mercenaries in our career. They are in it to make a fast buck for themselves, they don't have the organization's best interests at heart, and they don't have the resolve to stick with your company through challenging times. Missionaries, as Jeff defined the term, would not only believe in Amazon's mission but also embody its Leadership Principles. They would also stick around: we wanted people who would thrive and work at Amazon for five-plus years, not the 18–24 months typical of Silicon Valley. And so, in 1999, we set about to develop a hiring process to help us identify and hire people who fit this description.

It is impossible to quantify how successful this process, which we called the Bar Raiser, has been or to establish its importance, relative to other factors, in Amazon's rapid growth. What we can say is that it was common for experienced newcomers to assert that the Bar Raiser process was (a) unlike anything they had ever seen and (b) one of Amazon's secret weapons. We don't claim that this process is the only good one, or that it will entirely eliminate poor hiring decisions. What we can promise is that it is significantly better than the methods (or lack of methods) many companies rely on, and that it will likely raise your ratio of hits to misses *significantly*. We can also point to countless examples of leaders whom we would hire externally, place them immediately into strategically critical roles, and watch them thrive and in many cases stay with the company for ten-plus years.

* * *

When you consider the potential positive and negative impacts of an important hire, not to mention the precious time dedicated to it, it is shocking to consider how little rigor and analysis most companies put into their hiring process. The stakes are high. If he were to have landed that COO position, our friend would have been making strategic decisions that would directly affect the success of the company for years to come. Imagine if the CEO had to make a different decision of similar importance—whether to invest millions of dollars on a new product line or factory, for example—in a single, one-hour meeting. No doubt the CEO would get help from his leadership team and insist on conducting extensive analysis. He would think deeply about what information would be needed to make the right decision and what questions he should ask his team to help make it. He would spend many hours preparing for the meeting.

But at the global tech company where our colleague sought the COO job, the CEO conducted the interview as if he had not spent any time preparing for the meeting and had not given much if any thought to the specific information he would need to decide whether the candidate was a good choice. And this failure didn't just cost him the chance to evaluate his candidate, it *lost* him his candidate. Based in part on this experience, our colleague decided not to pursue the job.

We will make this point again and again: Amazon has faced many of the same problems all companies face. The difference is that Amazon has come up with novel solutions that deliver a significant competitive advantage, and this is true of its approach to hiring. The Bar Raiser process was one of Amazon's first and most successful scalable, repeatable, and teachable operational practices.

* * *

To understand why the Amazon hiring process has worked well, let's first look at what's wrong with the conventional approach. Interviewers who lack a rigorous model for their role in the hiring process leave themselves open to a range of pitfalls, many of which readers may find uncomfortably familiar. Even the smartest interviewer can wander off script and ask questions that lack a clear objective, leading to answers that reveal nothing about a candidate's likely job performance. Interviewer feedback is often communicated to the broader team with insufficient clarity and unintentional bias. Focusing on candidate qualities that don't reliably predict performance can also skew decisions in the wrong direction. Unstructured hiring decision meetings can give rise to groupthink, confirmation bias, and other cognitive traps that feel right at the time but produce poor decisions.

Let's look at the hiring process used by Leah, who headed up the digital media business at a fast-growing company that we'll call Green Corp. Her team had started to fall behind on its performance goals because a key product management position had been open for several months. Under pressure, Leah had been pushing hard to fill the role, and at last her recruiter had identified a promising candidate named Joe who worked for their competitor, Red Corp. Joe had a stellar résumé, with work experience in the exact space owned by Leah's team. He was interested in the job and willing to relocate to Green Corp.'s headquarters. The night before the interview, Leah felt a rush of excitement and relief that the right candidate had finally arrived. Or so it seemed.

Joe arrived at Green Corp. for a day of interviews, known as the "interview loop," which included meetings with four different members of Leah's team, one of whom, a long-standing and well-respected member named Carson, was the most influential. As each interviewer handed off Joe to the next team member, they went back to their desks and excitedly talked about how impressed they'd been with the candidate. Over coffee at the end of the day, Leah conducted a final interview with Joe, which confirmed what she had already heard that day from her team: Joe seemed like an excellent candidate.

Two days later, Leah met with her team to debrief about their interviews with Joe. She arrived with cautious optimism that she'd finally be able to fill this important role, and that Joe was the guy who could help her team get back on track to meeting their goals. The entire team looked and felt less beleaguered than they had a week earlier: they'd finally have a full team.

They started the meeting by reading three evaluations written by the interviewers. They were about the same length and similar in substance and sentiment, which is to say, positive, without being terribly specific. Brandon, a product manager, had the following to say:

> I am inclined to hire Joe for the product management position. He has a solid background owning and driving strategy for Red Corp. and two other relevant companies. He came across as having a good understanding of the unique challenges that face our business space, and he demonstrated a firm grasp on the ways that our company should enter a market segment that is quickly evolving. His experience at Red Corp. will be useful in evaluating/analyzing companies to partner with or acquire. I liked his passion for the industry throughout his career.

After reading the other nearly identical reports, Leah turned to Carson, the one person who hadn't written a report on his interview. He apologized—he hadn't had time to write up his feedback because he'd been putting out fires. He was overstretched, since he had essentially been doing the work of the missing product manager in addition to his own.

Carson was brief; he said that his observations jibed with the feedback of the rest of the team. However, something had left Carson feeling vaguely uneasy about the candidate. But since he didn't have his notes with him and he'd been so busy and overwhelmed since the interview, he couldn't remember what it was. And, given the enthusiastic buzz that had been building in the office, along with the glowing written evaluations, he decided to trust his colleagues' assessments.

At last it came to decision time. They went around the table, and each person stated their hire/no-hire recommendation. Enthusiasm built as each person recommended the hire. Carson, the last to speak, sealed the deal with his hire vote. Leah told the group she'd make an offer to Joe by the end of the day.

Several significant flaws appear in this hiring process. First, the fact that the team members shared their thoughts after each interview increased the likelihood that subsequent interviewers would be biased. And Carson's failure to immediately write up his assessment meant that the group was deprived of the wisdom of its most experienced and insightful team member.

Carson's behavior—uncharacteristic for him—was just one result of the *urgency bias* that affected the whole process. With a key position glaringly open, and a critical employee doing double duty to cover, the whole team felt time pressure that compelled them to accentuate the positive and to overlook some shortcomings in the process.

One of these was the quality of the written evaluations. Brandon's evaluation, for example, showed that his interview questions had *lacked specificity and purpose*. He commented that Joe "has a solid background owning and driving strategy" but did not provide any detailed, credible examples of what Joe actually had accomplished in that regard. How could the group tell if his past experience would portend that he would be a high-performing Green Corp. employee?

The group had also succumbed to some serious *confirmation bias*—the tendency for people to focus on the positive elements that others identify and ignore the negatives and contradictory signals. At every handoff during the loop, the interviewers had engaged in conversation in the team room. The positive comments from the interviewer who had just completed the meeting with Joe influenced the next interviewer to also look for those positive characteristics and to emphasize them in their evaluation. The feedback meeting itself had been relatively unstructured, which had given rise to *groupthink* among a team that valued each other's approval and wanted to help solve the problem by making a hire.

Leah also made a significant mistake that, while not related to Joe's hiring, would probably impact her team's long-term performance. Everybody knew that Carson had not performed as expected by not providing written interview feedback. Yet Leah failed to call him on it. She missed an opportunity to emphasize why the written feedback was essential to the process and that being too busy did not give one a free pass to skip such a crucial element. In not insisting on high standards (one of the Amazon Leadership Principles), she was in fact lowering them.

Every bad hiring decision comes at a cost. In the best cases, it quickly becomes apparent that the new hire is not a good fit, and the person leaves shortly after joining. Even then, the short-term cost can be substantial: the position may go unstaffed for longer than you'd like, the interview team will have wasted their time, and good candidates may have been turned away in the interim. In the worst case, a bad hire stays with the company while making errors in judgment that bring a host of possible bad outcomes. Along the way, a bad hire is a weak link who can bring the entire team down to their standards, a long-term cost that lingers long after they leave the company. Whatever the long-term cost of hiring Joe, Leah and her team will pay a price for their mistake.

And, in fact, they did. Because Joe turned out to be a poor fit, the team members still had to put in extra hours to do the work Joe proved unable to do—and to fix the mistakes he made. Six months after the hire, Leah and Joe agreed that it wasn't working out, and Joe left the company. Still time-pressed and now a little wary of making further mistakes, the team had to go through the whole process again.

The Effects of Personal Bias and Hiring Urgency

There are other types of cognitive biases that affect the hiring process. Another harmful one is *personal bias*, the basic human instinct to surround yourself with people who are like you. People have a natural desire to hire those with similar characteristics: educational background, professional experience, functional expertise, and similar life experiences. The middle-aged manager who holds a degree from the University of Michigan, worked at McKinsey, lives in the suburbs with a partner and kids, and plays golf will tend to be attracted to candidates with similar attributes. From the stack of résumés, such managers will likely pick those candidates who seem most like themselves, and carry positive expectations about them into the interview room. The problems with this approach are obviously (1) that such superficial similarities typically have nothing to do with performance, and (2) hiring for them tends to make for un-diverse workforces with a narrower field of vision.

Urgency in any realm can bring benefits, as we focus on those things that are essential. But in the realm of hiring, as we saw with Leah and her team, it can produce a sense of desperation that leads to taking shortcuts and ignoring essential processes, with devastating results. Imagine you are managing a team within a fast-growing division at Amazon, and you are working on a project of high importance and with multiple S-Team goals. You know you will be unable to meet the goals unless you hire new people. Your staff is overstretched, and morale is suffering. Now, on top of the work that you are struggling to get done, you have to write job descriptions, coordinate activities with recruiters, review résumés, conduct phone and in-person interviews, write and read interview feedback, attend debrief meetings, and then entertain, sell, and close the selected candidates. You also have to ask your already stressed team to give up hours they can't spare to interview people. The urgency is even greater and the work more intense when you're trying to fill a highly in-demand role such as a software development engineer or machine learning expert. According to Sequoia Capital, the average startup in Silicon Valley spends 990 hours to hire 12 software engineers![1] That's more than 80 hours per hire, and all that time taken away from a team that's already understaffed and working on deadline only adds to the urgency to staff up.

It takes almost no time to spot the superstars and to weed out the duds, but the majority of candidates, alas, falls somewhere in between, and that is when biases tend to kick in. If you just pick people who have known characteristics, who already feel familiar, they seem likely to work out. The fact that they sometimes do succeed only makes matters worse, as it reinforces the notion that your process is good enough.

Another force that works against successful hiring is the *lack of a formal process and training*. Startups and rapidly growing companies are particularly likely to hire new people without a process in place, though all too many more-established companies have the same problem. A manager who has been on the job for just two weeks may be expected to quickly hire a new team of ten people. Working without the framework of a formally defined interview and hiring process, managers will often be driven by urgency, biases, and convenience rather than purpose, data, and analysis.

This can have devastating consequences for the fast-growing company. Over a short period of time, say a year, the number of employees can leap from 50 to 150 in a startup, or from 150 to 500 or more during a later phase of rapid growth when the business model is promising and the funding is in the bank. Seemingly overnight, the new employees can vastly outnumber their predecessors, and this dynamic can *permanently* redefine the corporate culture. Brent Gleeson, a leadership coach and Navy SEAL combat veteran, writes, "Organizational culture comes about in one of two ways. It's either decisively defined, nurtured and protected from the inception of the organization; or—more typically—it comes about haphazardly as a collective sum of the beliefs, experiences and behaviors of those on the team. Either way, you will have a culture. For better or worse."[2]

In a period of torrid headcount growth, founders and early employees often feel that they're losing control of the company—it has become something different than what they set out to create. Looking back, they realize that the root cause of the problem can be traced to an ill-defined or absent hiring process. They were hiring scores of people who would change the company culture rather than those who would embody, reinforce, and add to it.

Hiring at Amazon Before the Bar Raiser

Amazon was not immune to these forces. In the company's early days, Jeff handled all the interviewing and hiring himself. Infamously, he would ask the candidate for their SAT scores, even if the candidate was interviewing for a job in customer support or at the distribution center, where the score wasn't relevant. Jeff has high academic standards and a bias for people who are similarly academically accomplished. As company lore has it, Jeff also liked to ask random quiz questions, such as "How many passengers fly through LAX in a year?" or "Why are manhole covers round?" As a result, many of the early hires at Amazon had advanced degrees from highly regarded universities and were good at devising answers to left-field questions. (There are several reasons manhole covers are round. One is that round covers can't fall into round holes. Another is that they're easy to roll.) It gradually became clear that questions like these could be helpful in assessing a candidate's raw intellect and ability to think on their feet, but they aren't good indicators of how well an individual will perform in a given job or how effectively they will lead inside your organization.

As the number of employees at the Seattle headquarters increased, Jeff could no longer participate in every interview loop. It was up to the heads of the various departments to run their hiring process and make the decisions within their respective teams.

One early Amazon employee and a co-worker of mine (Colin), John Vlastelica, put it succinctly when he said to me, "We had new people hiring new people hiring new people."

In 1999, the two co-leaders of the software teams were Joel Spiegel and Rick Dalzell. With the exception of the CTO Shel Kaphan, all the product development employees, including me, eventually reported to either Rick or Joel. Virtually every software team had aggressive hiring goals. And if a team wasn't able to hire fast enough, they likely would not be able to complete the work they had committed to do for the year.

During this time, we hired a director from a much larger and more established retail company and tasked him with building out several new teams. His first new hires were managers from his prior company, and they in turn began hiring people on their own. To say we worked in close quarters at the time would be an under-statement. We'd fill up an office with two, three, or four door desks until there was no more room. If the hallway was wide enough, we'd line up door desks along one wall. When you are working literally side by side with your co-workers, it doesn't take long to know who is flourishing and who is struggling. It quickly became apparent that the talent level of these new hires was much lower than the talent level of the rest of the software teams. With each new hire in the new director's organization, the overall talent level of the Amazon product development group was going down, not up.

The standard company response to such a problem might be for Rick or Joel to push the new director to "do a better job at hiring smart, talented engineers," that is, rely on good intentions. The issue was that not only did the new director have no way of knowing what Amazon considered a worthy hire, but there was also no oversight or process to teach him or prevent him from filling his team with subpar talent. Good intentions were not going to solve the hiring problem at a company growing as rapidly as Amazon, which jumped from roughly 600 employees in 1997 to 9,000 in 2000, and then to 100,000 by 2013 (as of this writing, in 2020, Amazon is approaching one million employees). But a mechanism would. To Joel and Rick's credit, they saw back in 1999 that even if they corrected this individual situation, they would almost certainly face it again as the company continued its rapid growth.

Rick, Joel, and John Vlastelica, who then headed up technical recruiting for the company, set out to codify a process for hiring high-level talent that matched Amazon's culture. From the start, they fixated on the core problem of maintaining a consistent hiring standard as the company grew. Thus, contrary to common lore, the Bar Raiser program, as it later came to be known, wasn't a top-down initiative from Jeff but rather a response to a specific problem that needed to be addressed. Even in these early days of the company, we can see the Leadership Principles beginning to develop. Rick, Joel, and John identified a problem and devised a scalable solution, originally called the Bar Keepers program, but renamed Bar Raiser shortly afterward. They presented it to Jeff, who enthusiastically supported the idea and suggested a few improvements. After this meeting, twenty original Bar Raisers were named, a few of whom, as of this writing nearly 21 years later, still work at Amazon. The Bar Raiser program proved so successful once it started running that it was quickly adopted and made a requirement for all the other corporate departments at Amazon.

The Bar Raiser Solution

The Amazon Bar Raiser program has the goal of creating a scalable, repeatable, formal process for consistently making appropriate and successful hiring decisions. Like all good processes, it's simple to understand, can be easily taught to new people, does not depend on scarce resources (such as a single individual), and has a feedback loop to ensure continual improvement. The Bar Raiser hiring process became one of the earliest and most successful components of the *being Amazonian* toolkit.

As we've discussed, many traditional interviewing techniques rely on the "gut feel" of interviewers working in an informal structure, allowing bias to creep in. It is true that an excellent interviewer will have a keen instinct for who might make a great hire, as well as the ability to ignore biases that arise during the interview process.

The problem with relying on a few gifted interviewers is that it doesn't scale and it's hard to teach. These traits are far from universal and, in the absence of a formal framework, you can't ensure that everyone involved will know how to conduct an excellent interview. Amazon's Bar Raiser process was designed to provide that framework, minimize the variability of ad hoc hiring processes, and improve results.

"Bar Raiser" is the name of both a larger process and the group of individuals—Bar Raisers—central to that process. In formulating the concept of Bar Raisers, Rick, Joel, and John drew inspiration from Microsoft, where Joel had worked prior to joining Amazon. For many—but not all—hires, Microsoft assigned a so-called "as-app" (short for "as appropriate") interviewer, a seasoned interviewer who conducted the final interview. The as-app's role was to make sure that only quality hires were made. They would not be penalized if the role went unfilled, and thus their decisions were unlikely to be influenced by urgency bias.

Amazon Bar Raisers receive special training in the process. One participates in every interview loop. The name was intended to signal to everyone involved in the hiring process that every new hire should "raise the bar," that is, be better in one important way (or more) than the other members of the team they join. The theory held that by raising the bar with each new hire, the team would get progressively stronger and produce increasingly powerful results. The Bar Raiser could not be the hiring manager or a recruiter. The Bar Raiser was granted the extraordinary power to veto any hire and override the hiring manager.

Amazon's first Bar Raisers were handpicked by Rick, Joel, and John for their interviewing skills, ability to assess talent, adherence to high standards, credibility with peers and hiring leaders, and leadership capability.

This program would meet more than its fair share of resistance over the years. There were countless times when a hiring manager was desperate to meet a goal set by Jeff or another leader and couldn't get the people they needed quickly enough. The concept of a Bar Raiser with veto power was seen by shortsighted managers as an enemy standing in the way of their progress. It was bewildering at first to many experienced leaders new to the company. Many would ask if exceptions could be made. But of course, this was part of the problem—hiring almost always felt urgent. We know of no instances where managers were allowed to take shortcuts. Successful managers would quickly realize that they had to devote a considerable amount of their time to the process and would redouble their efforts to source, recruit, and hire candidates who were Amazonian. Managers who failed to put in the time (in addition to their day job) to recruit and interview didn't last. There is no substitute for working long, hard, and smart at Amazon.

The idea worked: of the hundreds of processes developed at Amazon over more than twenty years, Bar Raiser is perhaps the most widely used and enduring.

There are eight steps in the Bar Raiser hiring process:

Job Description
Résumé Review
Phone Screen
In-House Interview
Written Feedback
Debrief/Hiring Meeting
Reference Check
Offer Through Onboarding

Job Description

It is difficult, if not impossible, to make the right hire without creating a well-defined and clearly written job description (JD), which the interviewers use to evaluate the candidates. At Amazon, it is the hiring manager's responsibility to write the description, which the Bar Raiser can review for clarity. A good job description must be *specific and focused*. While some of the requirements, such as meeting the Amazon Leadership Principles, will be standard across all positions, most requirements are specific to the job. The JD for a sales manager, for example, might specify the type of sales (inside or outside), whether the sales are enterprise-related or more trans-actional (i.e., long lead time, high dollar value vs. one-call close, lower dollar value), and the level of the role (e.g., senior man-ager, director, or VP). For a software development engineer, the JD might specify that the candidate must have the ability to de-sign and write computer code for highly available, scalable systems that are easy to maintain. For other roles, the JD may specify the ability to successfully negotiate with vendors or to manage cross-functional teams. If the JD is for a new position, members of the interview loop often begin by meeting with the hiring manager and Bar Raiser to review the description and ask clarifying ques-tions. Typically, this process reveals aspects of the job that the hir-ing manager has failed to identify.

Again, most hiring managers are desperate to get the process started, and without this review process, they tend to get fuzzy and/or out-of-date job descriptions. It is very hard to recover from this mistake. The hiring process will inevitably run into trouble—even fail—if the JD does not clearly articulate the job responsibil-ities and required skills. The people doing the phone screens and in-person interviews need to be clear on the JD so they can ask the right questions to collect the information required to make their decision. We have participated in many debriefs in which a poorly written job description created a conflict between the interview-ers, who were looking for one set of skills, and the hiring manager, who was expecting something different. This can become especially challenging as a company grows quickly and the number of differ-ent kinds of roles you need to fill grows with it.

Résumé Review

Once your JD is set, it's time to zero in on the candidates you want to interview. The recruiter—usually but not always an Am-azon employee—and the hiring manager search for candidates by networking, using LinkedIn, and reviewing the résumés collected in response to a job posting. The recruiter selects the most worthy candidates based on how their résumés fulfill the job requirements as defined in the JD. If the candidates the recruiter selects meet the hiring manager's expectations, that's a sign that the JD is clearly written and specific. If the selected candidates are off target, the JD probably needs work. For example, during the period when we were transitioning to autonomous teams (more in chapter three), we sought to hire fewer people in coordinator roles while ramping up our search for builders and inventors. That required new and more specific language in the JDs. Until the JDs were revised, we received too many résumés from people whose skills included such things as "coordinated between teams," and these would be discarded.

Phone Screen

Once the candidates have been selected from the résumé pool, the hiring manager (or their designate in the case of technical roles) conducts a one-hour phone interview with each person. During the phone screen, the hiring manager describes the position to the candidate in detail and seeks to establish some rapport with them by describing their own background, and why they chose to join Amazon. Roughly 45 minutes of that hour should consist of the manager questioning the candidate and following up where necessary. The questions, formulated in advance by the hiring manager, are designed to solicit examples of the candidate's past behavior ("Tell me about a time when you . . .") and focus on a subset of the Amazon Leadership Principles. Typically, the final 15 minutes of the call are reserved for the candidate to ask questions.

After this detailed phone screen, the hiring manager decides whether they are inclined to hire the candidate based on the data they've collected so far. If so, then the candidate will be invited for an in-house interview. Sometimes the hiring manager isn't sure about a candidate but still invites them to go through the interview loop, hoping that this will assist in the hiring decision. This is a mistake. In most cases, the questionable candidate will not get the job, and a lot of time will have been wasted in the process. The hiring manager should not bring a candidate in for the time-consuming and expensive interview loop unless they are inclined to hire them after the phone interview. There are many variables (the role, the hiring manager, the volume and quality of candidate résumés screened) that affect the rate at which candidates pass the phone screen and are brought in for the in-house interview, but one in four is a reasonable average. Amazon tracks and reports on the volume and rate at which candidates pass through the entire recruiting funnel and uses these data to make process changes as well as to coach and train recruiters and hiring managers. This is the hallmark of a well-run recruiting process.

In-House Interview Loop

The in-house interview loop takes five to seven hours to complete and requires the participation of several people who undoubtedly have many other responsibilities and tasks on their plate, so this step must be carefully planned, prepared, and executed. The hiring manager constructs the interview loop. They decide how many interviewers should be on the loop, as well as the mixture of roles and disciplines, job levels, and types of expertise that should be represented. Typically, the most effective loops consist of five to seven interviewers. The company has found that the returns on having more people than that involved tend to diminish, and that when there are fewer people involved, there are often gaps in knowledge about the candidate. Whatever the exact number of participants, the loop always includes the hiring manager, the recruiter, and a Bar Raiser.

There are a few important qualifications for the loop participants. First, everyone must have been properly trained in the company's interviewing process. Amazon runs a half-day course on how the interview process works and how to conduct an interview (more on this shortly). After training, the interviewer is required to pair up with an experienced senior interviewer to jointly conduct at least one real interview before they do one on their own.

Second, no loop participant should be more than one level below the level of the position the candidate will hold. Nor should there be an interviewer who would become a direct report of the candidate. People often want to have a say in hiring their manager and may be upset if they are excluded from the process, but it is a mistake for direct reports to interview a prospective boss. It's uncomfortable for the candidate during the interview, and the direct report will learn about the candidate's weaknesses, and other employees' views of those weaknesses, during the debrief—which could lead to problems for the future functioning of the team. Also, nothing good happens if a future direct report is not inclined to hire the candidate and you hire that person anyway.

In the early days, before the Bar Raiser was created, one of our former colleagues was, in fact, a member of the hiring process for the person who would be his manager. He wrote strong no-hire feedback, but the candidate was hired anyway. The recruiter then showed the new person the negative feedback our colleague had written. In their first meeting together, the newly hired boss slid the feedback document across the desk to our colleague, as if to challenge him. The whole situation was, in the words of our colleague, "super weird." The boss was gone within a year.

There are two distinctive features in an Amazon in-house interview loop: behavioral interviewing and Bar Raiser.

1. Behavioral Interviewing

As noted, in the early days at Amazon there was not much formal instruction or guidance on how to conduct an interview. Managers and interviewers asked whatever questions made sense to them.

Eventually the most important goals of the interview process became clear: to assess how well a candidate's past behavior and ways of working map to the Amazon Leadership Principles. Managers and interviewers soon learned that the basic information about the candidate—the details of education and employment—are less reliable predictors of the candidate's ability to work in accord with the Amazon principles.

We assessed job-specific functional skills using methods that are probably pretty common, such as asking a software engineer candidate to write software code on the whiteboard. However when assessing how well a candidate exhibits the Amazon Leadership Principles, we adopted a technique called Behavioral Interviewing. This involves assigning one or more of the 14 Leadership Principles to each member of the interview panel, who in turn poses questions that map to their assigned leadership principle, seeking to elicit two kinds of data. First, the interviewer wants the candidate to provide detailed examples of *what* they personally contributed to solving hard problems or how they performed in work situations like the ones they will experience at Amazon. Second, the interviewer wants to learn *how* the candidate accomplished their goals and whether their methods align with the Amazon Leadership Principles. General, open-ended questions such as "Tell me about your career" or "Walk me through your résumé" are usually a waste of time and will not produce the kind of specific information you're after. When asked such questions, most candidates will take the opportunity to deliver a positive, perhaps slightly glorified narrative of their career.

Instead the questions are mapped to their assigned principles. For example, if the interviewer owns the principle of Insist on the Highest Standards, they might ask, "Can you give me an example of a time when your team proposed to launch a new product or initiative and you pushed back on their plan because you didn't think it was good enough?"

After the candidate answers, the interviewer probes further. Each follow-up question is designed to acquire specific information, which is particularly important in determining exactly what role the candidate played in some past accomplishment. Some candidates conflate or exaggerate the importance of their role versus the team's accomplishments in a successful endeavor. More humble candidates understate their role because they don't want to look like they are bragging. In both cases, it's crucial that the interviewer probe carefully for the truth.

The method that Amazon interviewers use for drilling down goes by the acronym STAR (Situation, Task, Action, Result):

"What was the situation?"

"What were you tasked with?"

"What actions did you take?"

"What was the result?"

A good interviewer continues to ask questions until they feel they have a good understanding of what the interviewee personally accomplished versus what the team did. Other questions that can reveal this information include "If you were assigned to work on a different project instead of Project X, what would have changed about Project X?" and "What was the toughest call on Project X, and who made it?"

Some of the interviews may focus on specific functional skills that are necessary for the role. For example, when interviewing for a technical position, such as a software development engineer, interviewers might ask the candidate to write software code, solve a design question, develop an algorithm, or demonstrate knowledge of a relevant subject area.

Interviewers are also trained to maintain control of the interview. We've all been in a situation where the candidate, perhaps seeking to avoid a question, goes on long detours designed to deflect. Or perhaps they are just nervous, and speaking aloud is their way of calming their nerves. In such cases, interviewers know to politely cut the candidate short and move on to the next question.

We mentioned the process of developing a rapport with the interviewee on the phone. This is something that continues at the in-person meeting. Amazon interviewers are reminded to keep in mind that every candidate—whether qualified for the job or not—is a potential customer of the company and a source of leads. Assume they will tell their friends and co-workers about their interview experience. Sometimes that will be difficult, especially if you've determined the candidate is not right for the role or company, but it must be done.

(See the appendix for tips on the process.)

2. The Bar Raiser

The Bar Raiser is involved in every interview loop, and ensures the process is followed and bad hiring decisions are avoided. They are also there to set a good example for other interviewers. In addition to conducting one of the interviews, the Bar Raiser coaches others on interviewing techniques, asks probing questions in the debrief, makes sure that personal biases do not affect the hiring decision, and determines whether the candidate meets or exceeds the hiring bar set by the company.

Bar Raisers are trained to become experts in every aspect of the interviewing process. There is a group of senior Bar Raisers that manages the program, known as Bar Raiser Core, composed mostly of VPs and directors (Bill served in this group). Members of the core typically have been part of the program for many years, have participated in hundreds of interviews, and have demonstrated their mastery of interviewing, managing debriefs, making decisions, and teaching and training other Bar Raisers.

Potential new Bar Raisers are identified by current Bar Raisers and by Bar Raiser Core team members. They are reviewed by the core group and, when provisionally approved, they participate in a training session that is usually led by a core member. They are then paired with a Bar Raiser who will shadow and mentor them, and their work is reviewed again by the Bar Raiser Core. Not all candidates are approved. They may not be able to put their training into practice. They may not be skilled enough at interviewing. They may not be able to properly lead and facilitate the debrief meeting.

It's important to emphasize, however, that the skills of the Bar Raiser can be learned by nearly everyone. Not everyone is naturally a great interviewer, but given good instruction and mentoring, people can learn to be very effective at asking pointed questions and probing follow-ups.

There is no extra merit pay or bonus for becoming a Bar Raiser, and you retain all the duties of your day job. The only public recognition you get for being a Bar Raiser is an icon next to your name in the online company directory. But it's a coveted role, because Bar Raisers directly participate in the process that helps ensure Amazon hires the best.

We should also note that the Bar Raiser process, like other Amazon processes, has evolved. To manage the hiring demands for a company of almost a million people, there are now multiple Bar

Raiser Core teams. This is another example of how Amazon's processes are designed, from the outset, to scale.

Written Feedback

As noted in the Green Corp. example earlier, written feedback is essential to an effective hiring process, and this means that every interviewer must take detailed notes—as close to a verbatim record as possible. Some interviewers create a document with the questions, which they use to record notes. Some enter the notes in their computer, while others write them longhand on paper or on the back of the candidate's résumé. (At the start of the meeting, you may want to explain to the candidate that you will be taking notes and why.) The notes are the record of the data you gather in the interview, and you will use these notes to develop the written feedback you'll give to your fellow interviewers. If you do not take complete and detailed notes, expect a visit from your Bar Raiser.

Written feedback is expected to be specific, detailed, and filled with examples from the interview to address the Leadership Principles assigned to the interviewer. The feedback should be written shortly after the interview is complete to ensure that nothing of value is forgotten. We found it wise to block out fifteen minutes immediately afterward to complete the feedback. The write-up should be thorough and clear enough that the author need not be present for their conclusions to be understood. Again, this is not an optional exercise at Amazon: oral feedback offered in lieu of the written is simply unacceptable.

The written feedback includes the interviewer's vote on the candidate. There are only four options—strongly inclined to hire, inclined to hire, not inclined to hire, or strongly not inclined to hire. There is no "undecided" option. No waffling, provisos, or caveats are allowed—nothing like, "I am inclined to hire but I had the lunch interview slot and couldn't do a full interview," or "I'm on the fence and want to hear what others say before making my final choice." In some cases, it would be acceptable to say, "I am inclined to hire the candidate at a senior manager level but not as a director." In general, the job level should have been established in the job description, but there are circumstances where a hiring manager is open to hiring multiple levels, and this should be indicated in the JD. To avoid bias, the interviewer may not see or discuss other members' votes, comments, or feedback until their own feedback has been submitted.

Debrief/Hiring Meeting

Once the in-house interviews are complete and the written feedback and votes have been collected, the interviewers get together in person or via video conference to debrief and make the hiring decision. The Bar Raiser leads the meeting, which should be held as soon as possible, usually no more than a few days after the interviews have been completed. The meeting begins with everyone reading all the interview feedback. Afterward, the Bar Raiser may kick off the meeting by asking the group, "Now that everyone has had a chance to read all the feedback, would anyone like to change their vote?" The reason for this is that each interviewer submitted their vote based on only the data that they gathered in their interview. In a five-person interview loop, this means that the initial vote is given while in possession of one-fifth of the data. Now that each interviewer has read all the interview transcripts and commentary, they have four times more information on which to base their decision. This additional data may either confirm an initial vote or lead to a change in vote. Either outcome is valid and appropriate; there is no shame in changing your vote based on the presence of additional data.

Another method for the Bar Raiser to help get the meeting started is to create a two-column list on a whiteboard of the Leadership Principles where the candidate meets the bar in one column and falls short in the other. The hiring meeting is more than just tallying votes, otherwise it wouldn't be necessary unless there were a tie. The effective Bar Raiser uses the Socratic method, asking questions that jump-start the critical thinking process, to lead and guide the dialogue with the goal that everyone, or at least the majority, will arrive at the same conclusion about the candidate. The meeting is concluded with a decision from the hiring manager (validated by the Bar Raiser) to hire or not hire. If the hiring manager or Bar Raiser feels that they don't have enough information to make a decision, then there was a failure in the process upstream (e.g., one or more of the interviewers failed to properly assess the candidates on one or more of their assigned leadership principles).

It is extremely rare for a Bar Raiser to exercise their veto power. We know this from our own experience and from an informal poll of interviewers who collectively conducted some 4,000 interviews over the course of 15 years. We've only been able to identify three instances in which the veto was exercised. One of them came during the early days of the process in 1999. The other two involved hiring managers who were new to Amazon and had not yet adapted to the organization. Instead, an effective Bar Raiser shares the right examples from the interview transcripts and asks the right probing questions of the interview panel and hiring manager to help them see why a candidate doesn't meet or raise the bar.

The Bar Raiser process, and the debrief meeting in particular, can take some getting used to—we have witnessed countless hiring meetings in which a new hiring manager becomes visibly uncomfortable in their first debrief run by a Bar Raiser. They are accustomed to a more conventional approach, in which they (as hiring manager) or the recruiter runs the meeting. Furthermore, a new hiring manager's impulse is to sell the room on the candidate. At Amazon, the hiring manager soon learns that they do not lead the meeting and they should not seek to sell the other interviewers. The role of the interviewers is to help the hiring manager gather data and make an informed decision, not to block the hire. The best practice for the hiring manager is to listen and learn and to speak infrequently. The process is designed to prevent urgency and bias from negatively affecting the decision, which could result in wasted time and months of agony.

It's worth noting that many companies do not have a debrief meeting. Instead, the recruiter and the person making the hiring decision review the written feedback and discuss it between the two of them. The Amazon debrief meeting is an opportunity for each interviewer to learn from others and to develop their ability to assess talent. As we've said, one of the roles of the Bar Raiser is to teach and coach the other interviewers on every loop. If the Bar Raiser observes something amiss with the process, they are expected to give real-time coaching and feedback and help get things back on track. A good Bar Raiser sometimes spends more time coaching and teaching in a debrief meeting than assessing the candidate.

Reference Check

The Reference Check has been de-emphasized in today's Bar Raiser process since it has rarely affected a hiring decision, but for completeness we'll briefly cover how it was originally implemented. When the interview panel decides that the candidate is a hire, the process is not complete. The hiring manager or recruiter next asks the candidate to supply four or five references. Ideally, the references will include former managers, peers and subordinates, and others who have worked directly with the candidate, possibly for many years.

The hiring manager, not the recruiter, then calls the references to further explore and confirm the candidate's skills and past performance. One question that often gets a telling response is, "If given the chance, would you hire this person again?" Another is, "Of the people you have managed or worked with, in what percentile would you place this candidate?"

The reference calls should validate the hiring decision and add to the manager's understanding of the person they will be working with and counting on to help the group achieve their important work goals.

Offer Through Onboarding

What happens once the team has decided to offer the job to the candidate? At many companies, the hiring manager has the recruiter make the offer. This is another mistake. The hiring manager should personally make the offer and sell him/her on the role and company. You may have chosen the candidate, but that doesn't mean the candidate has chosen you. You must assume that good employees are being actively pursued by other companies, including their current employer. There is always the risk that you could lose the candidate. Nothing is certain until the day they report to the office.

This is why the hiring manager and team members must remain involved in this part of the process. It's important to keep the candidate excited, not only about the company but also about the team members they'll be working with. They'll be spending the majority of their waking hours with that team, possibly for years to come. There is still a lot that the team can do to ensure that the investment you've made in getting to the point of making the offer will pay off.

After the offer is made, a team member should check in with the candidate at least once a week until he or she makes a final decision. The contact can be as simple as an email saying how excited you are about the candidate joining the team. Sometimes we would send a "book bomb" to a candidate—a stack of books we thought they would like—or a handful of their favorite DVDs. It could be a coffee or lunch. What matters is that the gesture be sincere and personal.

The goal in this final phase is to get to know the candidate better and to figure out what key factors will affect their decision on the offer. Sometimes you'll be surprised by what you learn. The candidate may be sold on the role and compensation, but their spouse or partner may have reservations about some aspects of the job. If you're hiring a recent college grad, their parents may have a voice in the decision. In your conversation with the candidate after you've made the offer, seek to uncover any issues standing between them and accepting the offer, then seek to address and resolve them.

It may be useful to enlist other people to help close the deal. Perhaps you have a current employee who came over from the same company as the candidate, who attended the same school, who knows someone who overcame similar reservations, or who had the same questions about compensation, work style, or whatever else you know is holding your candidate back. Don't be afraid to ask your VP or CEO to get involved by making contact in some way. An email or a quick phone call from a person outside the hiring team, especially a person high up in the organization, may help seal the deal.

Variations on the Bar Raiser

As with many of the Amazon processes we discuss in this book, Bar Raiser has evolved. While the core elements have remained the same as Amazon has grown, many teams have tweaked parts of the process to address specific issues. Don't be afraid to do likewise.

For example, when one group at Amazon needed to hire several entry-level software development engineers, they found that the percentage of candidates getting a no-hire decision after the interview loop exceeded that of other Amazon teams. They theorized that this was because too many candidates were being invited to continue the process after successfully completing the phone screen. To test the theory, they decided to conduct *two* phone screens prior to flying a candidate to Seattle for the interview loop. Regardless of whether this approach improved the process, the motivation was correct: the team realized they had a problem with the process, based on their benchmarking of the hiring metrics to other Amazon teams.

In another case, a simple tweak to the Bar Raiser process generated surprisingly positive results. One director wanted to increase the gender diversity of the team. Over the ensuing quarters, the efforts were so successful that they were noticeable outside the department. When asked how they did it, the team revealed their very simple solution: every résumé received from a female applicant automatically led to a phone screen. It's important to say that this solution did not lower the hiring bar, nor did it favor unqualified candidates on the basis of gender. If the candidate did not pass the phone screen, they would not move forward to the next step in the process.

This technique made it clear that when a candidate's name

implied the gender as female, an unconscious bias had been affecting the résumé screening. The result was that well-qualified female candidates were apparently being rejected too early in the process. This director's insightful solution provides a great example of how simple enhancements to the hiring process can improve outcomes without damaging the core principles that it was designed to protect. It's also a good reminder to always be on the lookout for those places where bias can go undetected and undermine your results.

Bar Raiser and Diversity

As of the completion of this book (June 2020), the Black Lives Matter movement is bringing issues of racism, diversity, equity, and inclusion to the forefront of our national conversation in unprecedented ways. Achieving a diverse workforce that operates in an equitable and inclusive manner has become one of the most important goals for any company or institution today. Because there is no proven process or roadmap that we know of to achieve this, we don't purport to offer a solution in this book. We would submit, however, that the Bar Raiser process can be an effective component of a holistic, long-term plan to achieve diversity, equity, and inclusion.

The Bar Raiser process is designed to minimize personal bias and maximize making data-based hiring decisions based on the substance of each candidate's work and how that work maps to a set of principles. As discussed earlier in this chapter, personal biases naturally occur in an unstructured interview and hiring process. Bar Raiser process steps such as preparing a set of behavior-based interview questions in advance of the interview, insisting on written transcripts of the interview, rereading the transcript post interview (before making an assessment), conducting debriefs, basing debriefs on the interview transcripts, and making assessments based on well-understood principles are all steps that seek to eliminate individual biases. Having a diverse group of people involved in the process obviously reduces the chance of unconscious bias worming its way in.

This is not to say that Bar Raiser is a recipe for your organization to achieve a diverse workforce. Doing so requires long-term and holistic thinking, beginning with your organization's principles and reexamining every step of the hiring process including candidate sourcing, the language in your job descriptions, the composition of the group of people who interview candidates, and your principles or criteria for hiring. If a diverse workforce is your desired output, then you will need a process to ensure that you achieve it, and Bar Raiser can be a component of that process.

Hire and Develop the Best

The Amazon Bar Raiser process has been instrumental in reinforcing a key Amazon leadership principle: Hire and Develop the Best. It has proved to be a scalable way to identify and attract leaders who themselves become instrumental in growing and expanding Amazon across the globe.

Of great importance, the Amazon hiring process has a flywheel effect—it pays greater and greater dividends the longer it is used. Ideally, the bar continues to be set higher, so much that, eventually, employees should be able to say to themselves, "I'm glad I joined when I did. If I interviewed for a job today, I'm not sure I'd be hired!"

3
Organizing

Separable, Single-Threaded Leadership

Why coordination increases and productivity decreases as organizations grow. How Amazon combated this tendency by shifting to "separable teams with single-threaded leadership." Why creating an organization of such teams can take time, especially in a large enterprise. How to untangle dependencies so teams can work independently.

* * *

"The best way to fail at inventing something is by making it somebody's part-time job."[1]

Scene: A conference room. Jeff and several S-Team members sit across the table from the leadership team of a large Amazon business unit, including its VP, two other VPs who report to her, and several of their directors. It's their quarterly business review, and they're discussing an initiative that has been stuck in "Status Red" for the past two quarters. Someone asks, "What blockers are stopping you from making progress?"

DIRECTOR X (*the most knowledgeable person for the new initiative*): As you know, this project has many moving parts. We've identified five unsolved issues so far that are slowing us down. They are—
JEFF (*interrupting*): Before we get to those issues, would someone please tell me who's the most senior single-threaded leader for this initiative?
BUSINESS UNIT VP (*after an uncomfortably long pause*): I am.

JEFF: But you're in charge of the whole business unit. I want you focused on your whole group's performance, and that includes a lot more than this one initiative.

VP 1 (*trying to take one for his team*): That would be me, then.

JEFF: So, this is all that you and your team work on every day?

VP 1: Well, no. The only person working on it full time is one of our product managers, but we have lots of other people helping part time.

JEFF (*impatient now*): Does a PM have all the skills, authority, and people on their team to get this done?

VP 1: Not really, no, which is why we plan to hire a director to head it up.

JEFF: How many phone screens and in-house interviews have you conducted so far for this new director?

VP 1: Well, it's not an open position yet. We still need to complete the job description. So the answer is, zero.

JEFF: Then we're kidding ourselves. This initiative won't go "green" until the new leader is in place. That is the real roadblock this initiative is facing. Let's remove that one first.

VP 1 dashes off a terse email to head recruiter titled, "Open director role for project X leader . . ."

* * *

Speed, or more accurately velocity, which measures both speed and direction, matters in business. With all other things being equal, the organization that moves faster will innovate more, simply because it will be able to conduct a higher number of experiments per unit of time. Yet many companies find themselves struggling against their own bureaucratic drag, which appears in the form of layer upon layer of permission, ownership, and accountability, all working against fast, decisive forward progress.

We are often asked how Amazon has managed to buck that trend by innovating so rapidly, especially across so many businesses—online retail, cloud computing, digital goods, devices, cashierless stores, and many more—while growing from fewer than ten employees to nearly one million. How has the company managed to stay nimble, not stuck struggling to find common ground, as happens with most companies of such size?

The answer lies in an Amazon innovation called "single-threaded leadership," in which a single person, unencumbered by competing responsibilities, owns a single major initiative and heads up a separable, largely autonomous team to deliver its goals. In this chapter we'll explain what these terms mean, how they came to be, and why they lie at the heart of the Amazon approach to innovation and high-velocity decision-making.

The single-threaded leadership model emerged at the tail end of a long, zigzag journey of well-informed trial and error. We asked ourselves a difficult question, then responded with bold critical thinking, experimentation, and relentless self-critique that helped us double down on successful ideas and jettison the failures. You won't find an "aha moment" in this chapter. The path from that first hard question to single-threaded leadership took almost a decade, in large part because it required that we first untangle our monolithic software architecture and the organizational structures that had grown alongside it, then replace both, step by step, with systems designed to support rapid innovation.

Growth Multiplied Our Challenges

First, a bit of background. From 1997 through 2001, Amazon's revenue grew more than twenty-one-fold from $148 million to over $3.1 billion.[2] Growth of the number of employees, customers, and pretty much every other measurement had similar trajectories. Innovations were being rolled out at a furious pace too. Amazon rapidly transformed from a small company that sold only books—and only in the United States—into a multinational company with logistics operations in five countries, selling almost anything that one could buy online.

During this phase, we became aware of another, less positive trend: our explosive growth was slowing down our pace of innovation. We were spending more time coordinating and less time building. More features meant more software, written and supported by more software engineers, so both the code base and the technical staff grew continuously. Software engineers were once free to modify any section of the entire code base to independently develop, test, and immediately deploy any new features to the website. But as the number of software engineers grew, their work overlapped and intertwined until it was often difficult for teams to complete their work independently.

Each overlap created one kind of *dependency*, which describes something one team needs but can't supply for itself. If my team's work requires effort from yours—whether it's to build something new, participate, or review—you're one of my dependencies. Conversely, if your team needs something from mine, I'm a dependency of yours.

Managing dependencies requires coordination—two or more people sitting down to hash out a solution—and coordination takes time. As Amazon grew, we realized that despite our best efforts, we were spending too much time coordinating and not enough time building. That's because, while the growth in employees was linear, the number of their possible lines of communication grew exponentially. Regardless of what form it takes—and we'll get into the different forms in more detail shortly—every dependency creates drag. Amazon's growing number of dependencies delayed results, increased frustration, and disempowered teams.

Dependencies—A Practical Example

Let me take you back to March 1998, when I (Colin) started working at Amazon, to show how dependencies had already proliferated. At that time, the company had two large corporate divisions, one for business and one for product development. The business division was organized into operating groups defined by business function—retail, marketing, product management, fulfillment, supply chain, customer service, and so on. Each of the operating groups on the business side would request technical resources from the product development department, mainly software engineers and a small team of technical program managers (TPMs), which included me.

I got a taste of Amazon's dependency problem in my first week on the job. Our group, led by Kim Rachmeler, was responsible for project and program management for large initiatives that required coordination of activities across multiple teams in order to achieve a key business goal. Projects this group ran included launching our music (CDs) and video (VHS/DVD) businesses, launching new websites in the United Kingdom and Germany, and some other large, internal projects.

My first assignment was to work on the Amazon Associates Program, which to date had not received much attention from the product development team. This program allowed third parties, commonly referred to as affiliates, to place links to Amazon products on their websites. For example, a site about mountain climbing might include a curated list of recommended mountain-climbing books with links to Amazon. When a visitor clicked on one of the links on the affiliate website, they were taken to the book detail page on the Amazon site. If the visitor bought that product, the owner of the affiliate website would earn a fee—known as a referral fee. Amazon was one of the pioneers in affiliate marketing and, when I got involved, we were still trying to figure out exactly what we had with this new program and how big it could become. Although it was growing, it was not widely viewed as core to the business. I guess that's why I, as the new guy, got the assignment.

As I learned more about the Associates Program, I quickly saw that this had the potential to be a very lucrative business. At the time there were already 30,000 affiliates, and the program was growing fast. The affiliates had been creative with a very basic set of tools we had given them and were driving an ever-growing percentage of overall traffic and sales for Amazon. I believed the Associates Program could become an even bigger contributor to the business, but we would have to make several changes to it to realize its huge potential.

Preparing to Dive In

My first task was to manage an initiative to improve a nuts-and-bolts aspect of the program: the process we used to track and pay referral fees. At the time, we paid a referral fee only on the specific item that the affiliate website linked to. We wanted to change the program to pay referral fees on all purchases a visitor made in that shopping session. We did this because associate links were sending many customers to Amazon who didn't purchase the recommended item but did decide to order something else during their visit. So compensating the associates for those purchases seemed only fair—it would strengthen our relationship with them, and it would encourage them to link to Amazon even more. It did not sound like a particularly complicated task. My initial assessment of the project was that we'd quickly make the minor changes to the website software and database to implement this feature, but the majority of the effort would be in the reporting, accounting, and payment software changes, and in the marketing and communication work to announce the feature to our affiliates.

Wrong. That is when I experienced firsthand the extent of dependencies at Amazon—in this case, technical dependencies. At that time, Amazon's website software was monolithic, meaning that its functionality resided in a single massive executable program named Obidos. Its namesake is a village in Brazil along the fastest stretch of the Amazon River. As Obidos grew in size and complexity to support an ever-expanding suite of features and functionality, it began to exhibit the flip side of that once-cheerful analogy. Obidos is the fastest part of the river because it's also the narrowest. Our entire website still flowed through one huge, growing block of code that presented a steadily rising barrier of dependencies. Obidos had become, in effect, Amazon's bottleneck.

Technical Dependency Number One:
Gotchas in Shared Code

Each team whose features also connected to creating a product page, putting the product in the shopping cart, finalizing an order, tracking a return, and so on represented a technical dependency for the Associates team. We had to coordinate every small step with each team because a single mistake on our part could affect their work or, even more catastrophically, could introduce a bug that would take the whole website down. Similarly, we had to dedicate our own time to reviewing *their* changes in this part of the code to ensure that our own functions were not impacted.

Technical Dependency Number Two: Protectors of the Database

Software code was not the only kind of technical dependency that we faced. We also needed to make changes to the underlying relational database (a database structured to recognize relations among stored information such as customers, orders, and shipments) upon which all of Amazon's operations depended. The database was named acb, short for amazon.com books. If acb were ever to go down, the majority of the company's operations would stop—no shopping, no orders, no fulfillment—until we could roll back the change and restart.

As a vital safeguard, a steering group had been set up to review every proposed change to acb, approve the proposal (or reject it), and then figure out the best time to implement it. This group was known colloquially, and accurately, as "DB Cabal" and comprised three senior executives—the CTO, the head of the Database Administration team, and the head of the Data team.

The Cabal reviewers were understandably protective of acb and did a good job at overseeing this important company asset. Anyone who wanted to make a change to acb would have to undergo an intimidating, if well-intentioned, design review. Given the tangled state of our technical architecture, the stakes were high and many things could go wrong, so we needed these skillful, cautious gatekeepers.

To gain their approval, you would have to demonstrate that the proposed change was low risk, the design was sound, and the payoff worth it. At the end of the review, the Cabal might approve the request or require some changes. If the latter, you would have to make the modifications, get back in the queue, and return for another review. The cycle time was maddeningly slow since this august body generally met only a few times each month, and because there were lots of other groups queueing with their own changes.

The project did launch successfully. But I noticed that in the areas where we controlled our own destiny—that is, the reporting, accounting, and payment changes, as well as our marketing plan—we were able to move fast. And in the areas where we had to make very minor changes to Obidos and acb, we moved painfully slowly. Why was that? Dependencies.

The variations in technical dependencies are endless, but each one binds teams more tightly together, turning a rapid sprint into a stumbling sack race where only the most coordinated will cross the finish line. When a software architecture includes a large number of technical dependencies, it is said to be *tightly coupled*, a bad thing that frustrates all involved when you are trying to double and triple the size of the software team. Amazon's code had been designed in such a way that it became more tightly coupled over time.

Organizational Dependencies

Our organizational chart created extra work in a similar fashion, forcing teams to slog through layers of people to secure project approval, prioritization, and allocation of shared resources that were required to deliver a project. These organizational dependencies were just as debilitating as the technical ones.

The org chart had ballooned as we created teams for each new product category, geographic location, and function (e.g., Consumer Electronics, Amazon Japan, Graphic Design). When the company was smaller, you could enlist help or check for possible conflicts by just asking around—everyone often knew each other fairly well. At scale, the same task became long and laborious. You'd have to figure out who you needed to talk to, whether their office was in your building, and who they reported to. Maybe you'd track them down yourself, but more often you'd have to ask your manager, who in turn would ask their managers or their peers—and every step took time. Success connected you with some person (or their manager) you'd ask to listen to your pitch and commit resources to your project. They would often be doing the same thing at the same time for their own projects. In any case, they might be reluctant to slow themselves down on your behalf. You often had to do this several times for a given project, and often without success.

If your team had the resources other people needed, such requests could also come your way—sometimes many in a single week. You had to balance each one against the priorities you already had, then decide which (if any) you could support based on your own best judgment about their merits. To get a sense of how much drag these escalating organizational dependencies were adding to the average Amazon project, you had to multiply that effort as much as five or ten times. Just like our software, many of our org structures had become tightly coupled and were holding us back.

Too much of any kind of dependency not only slows down the pace of innovation but also creates a dispiriting second-order effect: disempowered teams. When a team is tasked with solving a particular problem and is judged by their solution, they should expect to have the tools and authority to complete the job. Their success should be a source of team pride. But Amazon's tightly coupled software architecture and org structure too often made owners heavily dependent on outside teams, over whom they had little influence. Few teams were fully in control of their own destiny, and many were frustrated by the slow pace of delivery that was beyond their control. Disempowered workers increasingly became discouraged, unable to pursue innovative ideas in the face of so much structural resistance.

Better Coordination Was the Wrong Answer

Resolving a dependency usually requires coordination and communication. And when your dependencies keep growing, requiring more and more coordination, it's only natural to try speeding things up by improving your communication. There are countless approaches to managing cross-team coordination, ranging from formalized practices to hiring dedicated coordinators—and it seemed as though we looked at them all.

At last we realized that all this cross-team communication didn't really need refinement at all—it needed elimination. Where was it written in stone that every project had to involve so many separate entities? It wasn't just that we had had the wrong solution in mind; rather, we'd been trying to solve the wrong problem altogether. We didn't yet have the new solution, but we finally grasped the true identity of our problem: the ever-expanding cost of coordination among teams. This change in our thinking was of course nudged along by Jeff. In my tenure at Amazon I heard him say many times that if we wanted Amazon to be a place where builders can build, we needed to eliminate communication, not encourage it. When you view effective communication across groups as a "defect," the solutions to your problems start to look quite different from traditional ones. He suggested that each software team should build and clearly document a set of application program interfaces (APIs) for all their systems/services. An API is a set of routines, protocols, and tools for building software applications and defining how software components should interact. In other words, Jeff's vision was that we needed to focus on loosely coupled interaction via machines through well-defined APIs rather than via humans through emails and meetings. This would free each team to act autonomously and move faster.

NPI—An Early Response to Organizational Dependencies

Meanwhile, we faced no shortage of good business ideas. Indeed, we had many more ideas than we could support or execute—we could only take on a few big projects each quarter. Trying to prioritize which ones to pursue drove us crazy. We needed a way to ensure that our scarce resources, which mostly meant the software engineering teams, were working on the initiatives that would make the biggest impact to the business.

This gave rise to a process called New Project Initiatives (NPI), whose job was global prioritization. Not global in the sense of geographic expansion, but rather in comparing every project under consideration to decide which ones were worthy of doing immediately and which ones could wait. Such global prioritization proved to be very hard indeed. Which is more important, launching a cost-saving project for fulfillment centers, adding a feature that might boost sales in the apparel category, or cleaning up old code we cannot do without to extend its practical life? There were so many unknowns and so many long-term projections to compare. Could we be sure of the extent of the cost savings? Did we know how much sales might rise with this new feature in the expected case? How could we estimate the financial payback of the restructured code, or the cost of an unknown number of outages if the old code began to fail? Every project carried risks, and most competed for the same set of scarce resources.

Force-Ranking Our Options

NPI was our best solution at the time for ranking our global options intelligently and picking the winners. No one liked it, but it was a necessary evil given our organization then.

Here's how NPI worked: Once every quarter, teams submitted projects they thought were worth doing that would require resources from outside their own team—which basically meant almost every project of reasonable size. It took quite a bit of work to prepare and submit an NPI request. You needed a "one-pager"; a written summary of the idea; an initial rough estimate of which teams would be impacted; a consumer adoption model, if applicable; a P&L; and an explanation of why it was strategically important for Amazon to embark on the initiative immediately. Just proposing the idea represented a resource-intensive undertaking.

A small group would screen all the NPI submissions. A project could be cut in the first round if it wasn't thoroughly explained, didn't address a core company goal, didn't represent an acceptable cost/benefit ratio, or obviously wouldn't make the cut. The more promising ideas would move to the next round for a more detailed technical and financial scoping exercise. This step typically happened in real time in a conference room where a leader from each major area could review the project submission, ask any clarifying questions, and provide an estimate on how many resources from their area would be required to complete the project as stated. Usually 30 or 40 attendees were on hand to review a full list of projects, which made for long, long meetings—yuck.

Afterward, the smaller NPI core group would true up the resource and payback estimates, then decide which projects would actually go forward. After that group met, every project team leader would receive an email about their submission that came in one of three forms. From best to worst they were:

> "Congratulations, your project has been approved! The other teams you need to help complete your project are ready to get started too."

> "The bad news is that your project was not chosen, but the good news is that none of the approved NPI projects require work from you."

> "We're sorry that none of your projects were approved and you were probably counting on them to hit your team goals. There are, however, approved NPI projects for other teams that require resources from you. You must fully staff those NPI projects before staffing any of your other internal projects. Best of luck."

Choosing Our Priorities

A lot of NPI projects were presented with large error bars—that is, an unhelpfully broad range of the potential costs and of the predicted return. "We anticipate this feature will generate between $4 million on the low side and $20 million on the high side and expect it will take 20 to 40 person-months to develop." It's not easy to compare projects with estimates like that.

The toughest job for many project teams was to accurately predict consumer behavior. Time and time again, we learned that consumers would behave in ways we hadn't imagined during the development phase—especially for brand-new features or products. Even the most rigorous models we used to predict consumer adoption could be well off the mark, leading to long, vigorous debates that never quite felt conclusive. (See, for example, our story of the Fire Phone in the introduction to part two. It's not like we thought, "Here's a dud, but we're going to launch it anyway." We had high expectations for this product in which we had invested a great deal of time and money!)

In an effort to improve our assumptions, we established a feedback loop to measure how well a team's estimates matched its eventual results, adding another layer of accountability. Jeff Wilke stashed away paper copies of approved NPI proposals so he could check the predictions against actual results later. The added transparency and accountability helped bring team estimates closer to reality, but ultimately not close enough. A year or more could pass between the first presentation and measurable results, which is a long time to wait in order to learn what adjustments are needed.

All in all, the NPI process was not beloved. If you mention NPI to any Amazonian who went through it, you're likely to get a grimace and maybe a horror story or two. Sometimes you got lucky, your project was approved, and you could move forward smoothly enough. Too often, however, your plans were thwarted. Instead of doing vital work on something you owned, you'd be assigned to support another team's project while still taking care of everything that was left on your plate. "Getting NPI'd," as we called it, meant that your team was literally getting nothing for something.

The NPI process was deflating for morale. But figuring out how to "boost morale" is not Amazonian. Other companies have morale-boosting projects and groups with names like "Fun Club" and "Culture Committee." They view morale as a problem to be solved by company-sponsored entertainment and social interaction. Amazon's approach to morale was to attract world-class talent and create an environment in which they had maximum latitude to invent and build things to delight customers—and you can't do that if every quarter some faceless process like NPI smites your best ideas.

In chapter six, we discuss Amazon's belief that focusing on controllable input metrics instead of output metrics drives meaningful growth. Morale is, in a sense, an output metric, whereas freedom to invent and build is an input metric. If you clear the impediment to building, morale takes care of itself.

Our question was, "How do we do that?" It's not that the participants in the NPI arena—or the DB Cabal for that matter—fell short or had nefarious motives. They were all top-notch, talented, hardworking people who were swimming against a riptide of dependencies. If you're faced with a challenge that's growing exponentially, meeting it head-on with equal but opposing force just locks you into exponentially growing cost—a dead-end strategy. We needed to find some way to stem the tide of challenges, and we finally realized that the most effective way to do that was to recognize the assumption we'd been operating under was incorrect. Amazon ultimately invented its way around the problem by cutting off dependencies at the source.

First Proposed Solution: Two-Pizza Team

Seeing that our best short-term solutions would not be enough, Jeff proposed that instead of finding new and better ways to manage our dependencies, we figure out how to remove them. We could do this, he said, by reorganizing software engineers into smaller teams that would be essentially autonomous, connected to other teams only loosely, and only when unavoidable. These largely independent teams could do their work in parallel. Instead of coordinating better, they could coordinate less and build more.

Now came the hard part—how exactly could we implement such a tectonic shift? Jeff assigned CIO Rick Dalzell to figure it out. Rick solicited ideas from people throughout the company and synthesized them, then came back with a clearly defined model that people would talk about for years to come: the *two-pizza team*, so named because the teams would be no larger than the number of people that could be adequately fed by two large pizzas. With hundreds of these two-pizza teams eventually in place,

Rick believed that we would innovate at a dazzling pace. The experiment would begin in the product development organization and, if it worked, would spread throughout the rest of the company. He laid out the defining characteristics, workflow, and management as follows.

A two-pizza team will:

- **Be small.** No more than ten people.
- **Be autonomous.** They should have no need to coordinate with other teams to get their work done. With the new service-based software architecture in place, any team could simply refer to the published application programming interfaces (APIs) for other teams. (More on this new software architecture to follow.)
- **Be evaluated by a well-defined "fitness function."** This is the sum of a weighted series of metrics. Example: a team that is in charge of adding selection in a product category might be evaluated on:
    a) how many new distinct items were added for the period (50 percent weighting)
    b) how many units of those new distinct items were sold (30 percent weighting)
    c) how many page views those distinct items received (20 percent weighting)
- **Be monitored in real time.** A team's real-time score on its fitness function would be displayed on a dashboard next to all the other two-pizza teams' scores.
- **Be the business owner.** The team will own and be responsible for all aspects of its area of focus, including design, technology, and business results. This paradigm shift eliminates the all-too-often heard excuses such as, "We built what the business folks asked us to, they just asked for the wrong product," or "If the tech team had actually delivered what we asked for and did it on time, we would have hit our numbers."
- **Be led by a multidisciplined top-flight leader.** The leader must have deep technical expertise, know how to hire world-class

software engineers and product managers, and possess excellent business judgment.

- **Be self-funding.** The team's work will pay for itself.
- **Be approved in advance by the S-Team.** The S-Team must approve the formation of every two-pizza team.

As with any major innovation at Amazon, this plan was merely the beginning. Some of its tenets endured, some evolved, and some perished over the course of several years. The most important of these adaptations are worth exploring here in more detail.

Tearing Down Monoliths

"Be autonomous." Sounds simple, doesn't it? In fact, it would be hard to overstate the effort we expended to free these teams from the constraints that bound them so tightly at the beginning. The effort would necessitate major changes to the way we wrote, built, tested, and deployed our software, how we stored our data, and how we monitored our systems to keep them running twenty-four hours a day, seven days a week. The details are numerous and interesting in their own right, but most fall well beyond the scope of this book. One major effort is worth recounting in some detail, however, because it was both vital and extremely difficult for us to achieve.

Just as two-pizza teams replaced a single large organization with something faster and more flexible, a comparable reorganization was overdue for much of the Amazon software architecture to enable us to achieve Rick's "be autonomous" vision. In a 2006 interview by Jim Gray, Amazon CTO Werner Vogels recalled another watershed moment:

> We went through a period of serious introspection and concluded that a service-oriented architecture would give us the level of isolation that would allow us to build many software components rapidly and independently. By the way, this was way before service-oriented was a buzzword. For us service orientation means

encapsulating the data with the business logic that operates on the data, with the only access through a published service interface. No direct database access is allowed from outside the service, and there's no data sharing among the services.[3]

That's a lot to unpack for non–software engineers, but the basic idea is this: If multiple teams have direct access to a shared block of software code or some part of a database, they slow each other down. Whether they're allowed to change the way the code works, change how the data are organized, or merely build something that uses the shared code or data, everybody is at risk if anybody makes a change. Managing that risk requires a lot of time spent in coordination. The solution is to encapsulate, that is, assign ownership of a given block of code or part of a database to one team. Anyone else who wants something from that walled-off area must make a well-documented service request via an API.[4]

Think of it like a restaurant. If you are hungry, you don't walk into the kitchen and fix what you want. You ask for a menu, then choose an item from it. If you want something that is not on that menu, you can ask the waiter, who will send a request to the cook. But there is no guarantee you'll get it. What happens inside the walled-off area in question is completely up to the single team that owns it, so long as they don't change how information can be exchanged. If change becomes necessary, the owners publish a revised set of rules—a new menu, if you will—and all those who rely on them are notified.

This new system greatly improved upon the free-for-all it replaced. For the purposes of this book, suffice it to say that implementing this improvement meant replacing Obidos, acb, and many other key pieces of our software infrastructure piece by piece while it was still running our business nonstop. This required a major investment in development resources, systems architecture planning, and great care to ensure that the monolith continued to stand until its last surviving function had been replaced by a service. The rolling regeneration of the way we built and deployed technology was a bold move, an expensive investment that stretched over several years of intensive and delicate work.

Today the advantages of a microservices-based architecture are well understood, and the approach has been adopted by many tech companies. The benefits include improved agility, developer productivity, scalability, and a better ability to resolve and recover from outages and failures. In addition, with microservices, it becomes possible to establish small, autonomous teams that can assume a level of ownership of their code that isn't possible with a monolithic approach. The switch to microservices removed the shackles that had prevented the Amazon software teams from moving fast, and enabled the transition to small, autonomous teams.

The First Autonomous Teams

Autonomous teams are built for speed. When they are aligned toward a common destination, they can go a long way in a short time. But when they are poorly aligned, the team can veer far off course just as quickly. So they need to be pointed in the right direction and have the tools to quickly course-correct when warranted. That's why, before any proposed two-pizza team was approved, they had to meet with Jeff and their S-Team manager—often more than once—to discuss the team's composition, charter, and fitness function.

For instance, the Inventory Planning team would convene with Jeff, Jeff Wilke, and me to ensure that they were meeting the following criteria:

1. The team had a well-defined purpose. For example, the team intends to answer the question, "How much inventory should Amazon buy of a given product and when should we buy it?"
2. The boundaries of ownership were well understood. For example, the team asks the Forecasting team what the demand will be for a particular product at a given time,

and then uses their answer as an input to make a buying decision.

3. The metrics used to measure progress were agreed upon. For example, In-stock Product Pages Displayed divided by Total Product Pages Displayed, weighted at 60 percent; and Inventory Holding Cost, weighted at 40 percent.

Importantly, the specifics of how the proposed team would go about achieving its goal were not discussed at the meeting. That was the team's role to figure out for themselves.

These meetings were a classic example of the Dive Deep leadership principle. I participated in every one of the Fitness Function alignment meetings for the first set of two-pizza teams, which owned things like Forecasting, Customer Reviews, and Customer Service Tools. We questioned every metric from every angle, probing how those data would be collected and how the results would be used to drive the team accurately toward its goals. These meetings clearly established expectations and confirmed the team's readiness. Just as importantly, they also built up trust between Jeff and the new team, reinforcing their autonomy—and therefore their velocity.

We started with a small number of two-pizza teams so that we could learn what worked and refine the model before widespread adoption. One significant lesson became clear fairly early: each team started out with its own share of dependencies that would hold them back until eliminated, and eliminating the dependencies was hard work with little to no immediate payback. The most successful teams invested much of their early time in removing dependencies and building "instrumentation"—our term for infrastructure used to measure every important action—before they began to innovate, meaning, add new features.

For example, the Picking team owned software that directed workers in the fulfillment centers where to find items on the shelves. They spent much of their first nine months systematically identifying and removing dependencies from upstream areas, like receiving inventory from vendors, and downstream areas, like packing and shipping. They also built systems to track every important event that happened in their area at a detailed, real-time level. Their business results didn't improve much while they did so, but once they had removed dependencies, built their fitness function, and instrumented their systems, they became a strong example of how fast a two-pizza team could innovate and deliver results. They became advocates of this new way of working.

Other teams, however, put off doing the unglamorous work of removing their dependencies and instrumenting their systems. Instead, they focused too soon on the flashier work of developing new features, which enabled them to make some satisfying early progress. Their dependencies remained, however, and the continuing drag soon became apparent as the teams lost momentum.

A well-instrumented two-pizza team had another powerful benefit. They were better at course correcting—detecting and fixing mistakes as they arose. In the 2016 shareholder letter, even though he wasn't explicitly talking about two-pizza teams, Jeff suggested that "most decisions should probably be made with somewhere around 70% of the information you wish you had. If you wait for 90%, in most cases, you're probably being slow. Plus, either way, you need to be good at quickly recognizing and correcting bad decisions. If you're good at course correcting, being wrong may be less costly than you think, whereas being slow is going to be expensive for sure."[5]

Good examples like the Picking team demonstrated how long-term thinking, in the form of their up-front investments, generated compound returns over time. Later teams followed their lead. Sometimes it's best to start slow in order to move fast.

While it would be nice to trust that a swarm of loosely coupled, autonomous teams will always make the best tactical choices to deliver the company's larger strategic objectives, that's sometimes wishful thinking—even with the best of teams. The OP1 process we described in chapter one still framed the autonomy of these teams by aligning them with company strategy, giving them their initial bearing toward upcoming yearly targets.

And we came to realize that other limits to autonomy would also need to remain, with each team still tied to others by varying levels of dependency. While each two-pizza team crafted its own product vision and development roadmap, unavoidable dependencies could arise in the form of cross-functional projects or top-down initiatives that spanned multiple teams. For example, a two-pizza team working on picking algorithms for the fulfillment centers might also be called upon to add support for robotics being implemented to move products around the warehouse.

We found it helpful to think of such cross-functional projects as a kind of tax, a payment one team had to make in support of the overall forward progress of the company. We tried to minimize such intrusions but could not avoid them altogether. Some teams, through no fault of their own, found themselves in a higher tax bracket than others. The Order Pipeline and Payments teams, for example, had to be involved in almost every new initiative, even though it wasn't in their original charters.

Some Challenges Still Remained

Two-pizza teams were a much-talked-about topic at Amazon, but as originally defined, they didn't spread throughout the company as completely as some other new ideas had. While they showed great potential to improve the way Amazon worked, they also exhibited some shortcomings that limited their success and broader applicability.

Two-Pizza Teams Worked Best in Product Development

We weren't sure how far to take the two-pizza team concept, and at the beginning it was planned solely as a reorganization of product development. Seeing its early success in speeding up innovation, we wondered whether it might also work in retail, legal, HR, and other areas. The answer turned out to be no, because those areas did not suffer from the tangled dependencies that had hampered Amazon product development. Therefore, implementing two-pizza teams in those orgs would not increase speed.

Fitness Functions Were Actually Worse Than Their Component Metrics

Two-pizza teams had been meant to increase the velocity of product development, with custom-tailored fitness functions serving as the directional component of each team's velocity. By pointing each team in the right direction and alerting them early if they drifted off course, fitness functions were supposed to align the team uniquely to its goals. We tried them out for more than a year, but fitness functions never really delivered on their promise for a couple of important reasons.

First, teams spent an inordinate amount of time struggling with how to construct the most meaningful fitness function. Should the formula be 50 percent for Metric A plus 30 percent for Metric B plus 20 percent for Metric C? Or should it be 45 percent for Metric A plus 40 percent for Metric B plus 15 percent for Metric C? You can imagine how easy it was to get lost in those debates. The discussions became less useful and ultimately distracting—just another argument that people needed to win.

Second, some of these overly complicated functions combined seven or more metrics, a few of which were composite numbers built from their own submetrics. When graphed over time, they might describe a trend line that went up and to the right, but what did that mean? It was often impossible to discern what the team was doing right (or wrong) and how they should respond to the trend. Also, the relative weightings could change over time as business conditions changed, obscuring historic trends altogether.

We eventually reverted to relying directly on the underlying metrics instead of the fitness function. After experimenting over many months across many teams, we realized that as long as we did the up-front work to agree on the specific metrics for a team, and we agreed on specific goals for each input metric, that was sufficient to ensure the team would move in the right direction. Combining them into a single, unifying indicator was a very clever idea that simply didn't work.

Great Two-Pizza Team Leaders Proved to Be Rarities

The original idea was to create a large number of small teams, each under a solid, multidisciplined, frontline manager and arranged collectively into a traditional, hierarchical org chart. The manager would be comfortable mentoring and diving deep in areas ranging from technical challenges to financial modeling and business performance. Although we did identify a few such brilliant managers, they turned out to be notoriously difficult to find in sufficient numbers, even at Amazon. This greatly limited the number of two-pizza teams we could effectively deploy, unless we relaxed the constraint of forcing teams to have direct-line reporting to such rare leaders.

We found instead that two-pizza teams could also operate successfully in a matrix organization model, where each team member would have a solid-line reporting relationship to a functional manager who matched their job description—for example, director of software development or director of product management—and a dotted-line reporting relationship to their two-pizza manager. This meant that individual two-pizza team managers could lead successfully even without expertise in every single discipline required on their team. This functional matrix ultimately became the most common structure, though each two-pizza team still devised its own strategies for choosing and prioritizing its projects.

Sometimes You Need More Than Two Pizzas

We all agreed at the outset that a smaller team would work better than a larger one. But we later came to realize that the biggest predictor of a team's success was not whether it was small but whether it had a leader with the appropriate skills, authority, and experience to staff and manage a team whose sole focus was to get the job done.

Now free of its initial size limits, the two-pizza team clearly needed a new name. Nothing catchy came to mind, so we leaned into our geekdom and chose the computer science term "single-threaded," meaning you only work on one thing at a time. Thus, "single-threaded leaders" and "separable, single-threaded teams" were born.

Bigger and Better Still—The Single-Threaded Leader

Even though the two-pizza model hadn't taken root as quickly as we'd planned, nor had it spread across the organization as far as we'd hoped, the experiment showed enough promise that Jeff and the S-Team had the patience and discipline to stick with it. We learned as we went, adapting and refining the idea of two-pizza teams until, in the end, we had something far more capable.

What was originally known as a two-pizza team leader (2PTL) evolved into what is now known as a single-threaded leader (STL). The STL extends the basic model of separable teams to deliver their key benefits at any scale the project demands. Today, despite their initial success, few people at Amazon still talk about two-pizza teams.

We say that the STL is bigger and better, but better than what? Certainly it's an improvement on the two-pizza team it evolved from, but is it better than other alternatives too? To answer that question, let's look at a more common approach to developing something new.

Typically an executive, assigned to drive some innovation or initiative, would turn to one of his reports—possibly a director or senior manager—who might have responsibility for five of the executive's 26 total initiatives. The executive would ask the director to identify one of those direct reports—let's say a project manager—who would add the project to their to-do list. The PM, in turn, would prevail upon an engineering director to see if one of their dev teams could squeeze the work into their dev schedule. Amazon's SVP of Devices, Dave Limp, summed up nicely what might happen next: "The best way to fail at inventing something is by making it somebody's part-time job."[6]

Amazon learned the hard way how this lack of a single-threaded leader could hinder them in getting new initiatives off the ground. One example is Fulfillment by Amazon (FBA). Initially known as Self-Service Order Fulfillment (SSOF), its purpose was to offer Amazon's warehouse and shipping services to merchants. Rather than handling the storing, picking, packing, and shipping themselves, the merchants would send products to Amazon, and we would handle the logistics from there. The executives in the retail and operations teams thought this was a big, interesting idea, but for well over a year it did not gain significant traction. It was always "coming soon," but it never actually arrived.

Finally, in 2005, Jeff Wilke asked Tom Taylor, then a VP, to drop his other responsibilities and gave him approval to hire and staff a team. Only then did SSOF take off, eventually morphing into Fulfillment by Amazon. FBA launched in September 2006 and became a huge success. Third-party sellers loved it because, by offering them warehouse space for their products, Amazon turned warehousing into a variable cost for them instead of a fixed cost. FBA also enabled third-party sellers to reap the benefits of participating in Prime, which in turn improved the customer experience for buyers. As Jeff said in a letter to shareholders, "In just the last quarter of 2011, Fulfillment by Amazon shipped tens of millions of items on behalf of sellers."[7]

The leaders who had been trying to get this service off the ground before Tom Taylor took it over were exceptionally capable people, but while they were tending to all their other responsibilities, they just didn't have the bandwidth to manage the myriad details FBA entailed. FBA would have been, at best, much slower and more difficult to launch if Jeff Wilke hadn't freed up Tom to focus on nothing but this one project. The single-threaded leader concept hadn't yet been formalized at Amazon, but Tom became an important forerunner.

The other crucial component of the STL model is a *separable, single-threaded team* being run by a single-threaded leader like Tom. As Jeff Wilke explains, "Separable means almost as separable organizationally as APIs are for software. Single-threaded means they don't work on anything else."[8]

Such teams have clear, unambiguous ownership of specific features or functionality and can drive innovations with a minimum of reliance or impact upon others. Appointing a single-threaded leader is necessary but not sufficient. It's much more than a simple org chart change. Separable, single-threaded teams have fewer organizational dependencies than conventional teams. They clearly demarcate the boundaries of what they own and where the interests of other teams begin and end. As former Amazon VP Tom Killalea aptly observed, a good rule of thumb to see if a team has sufficient autonomy is deployment—can the team build and roll out their changes without coupling, coordination, and approvals from other teams? If the answer is no, then one solution is to carve out a small piece of functionality that can be autonomous and repeat.

A single-threaded leader can head up a small team, but they can also lead the development of something as large as Amazon Echo or Digital Music. For example, with Amazon Echo and Alexa, were it not for the fact that Amazon VP Greg Hart was assigned to be the single-threaded leader, there might have been one person in charge of hardware and another in charge of software for all of Amazon's devices—but no one whose job it was to create and launch Amazon Echo and Alexa as a whole. On the contrary, a single-threaded leader of Amazon Echo and Alexa had the freedom and autonomy to assess the novel product problems that needed to be solved, decide what and how many teams they needed, how the responsibilities should be divided up among the teams, and how big each team should be. And, crucially, since the technical dependencies problem had been solved, that leader no longer had to check with a prohibitively large number of people for each software change they needed to make.

The Payback

It took us a while to arrive at the approach of single-threaded leaders and separable, single-threaded teams, and we went through a number of solutions along the way that ultimately didn't last—like NPIs and two-pizza teams. But it was worth it, because where we landed was an approach to innovation that is so fundamentally sound and adaptable that it survives at Amazon to this day. This journey is also a great example of another phrase you'll hear at Amazon: be stubborn on the vision but flexible on the details.

The STL delivers high-velocity innovation, which in turn makes Amazon nimble and responsive even at its now-massive scale. Free of the hindrance of excess dependencies, innovators at every level can experiment and innovate faster, leading to more sharply defined products and a higher level of engagement for their creators. Ownership and accountability are much easier to establish under the STL model, keeping teams properly focused and accurately aligned with company strategies. While all these positive outcomes were possible before the first autonomous single-threaded team was created, now they have become the natural and expected consequence of this very Amazonian model for innovation.

4

Communicating

Narratives and the Six-Pager

The eerie silence at the beginning of Amazon meetings. The ban on Power-Point and the shift to narratives. How narratives produce clear thinking and stimulate valuable discussion. How to write an effective six-pager. The payoff: the "narrative information multiplier."

* * *

If you were to ask recently hired Amazon employees about what has surprised them most in their time at the company so far, one response would certainly top the list:

"The eerie silence in the first 20 minutes of many meetings."

At Amazon, after a brief exchange of greetings and chitchat, everyone sits at the table, and the room goes completely silent. Silent, as in not a word. The reason for the silence? A six-page document that everyone must read before discussion begins.

Amazon relies far more on the written word to develop and communicate ideas than most companies, and this difference makes for a huge competitive advantage. In this chapter we'll talk about how and why Amazon made the transition from the use of Power-Point (or any other presentation software) to written narratives, and how it has benefited the company—and can benefit yours too.

Amazon uses two main forms of narrative. The first is known as the "six-pager." It is used to describe, review, or propose just about any type of idea, process, or business. The second narrative form is the PR/FAQ. This one is specifically linked to the Working Backwards process for new product development. In this chapter, we'll focus on the six-pager and in the following chapter we'll look at the PR/FAQ.

The End of PowerPoint at S-Team Meetings

One of my (Colin's) roles as Jeff's shadow in the early days of the company was to manage the agenda of the weekly S-Team meeting, which took place every Tuesday and typically ran for four hours. Roughly 80 percent of the time was focused on execution, namely how the company was making progress toward achieving the S-Team goals. In the S-Team meeting, we would select between two and four S-Team goals and do a deep dive on their progress. The meeting was expensive: between preparation and attendance, it consumed at least half a day each week for the top leaders in the company. Given the types of decisions made in the meeting, the stakes were high.

In those early days, each deep dive would begin with a presentation by the relevant team on the status of their work toward the goal. Typically, this involved an oral presentation by one or more of the team members backed up by PowerPoint slides. Too often, we found, the presentations did not serve the purpose for which they were intended. The format often made it difficult to evaluate the actual progress and prevented the presentations from proceeding as planned. The deep dives were, in short, frustrating, inefficient, and error prone for both the presenter and the audience.

Jeff and I often discussed ways to improve the S-Team meetings. Shortly after a particularly difficult presentation in early 2004, we had some downtime on a business flight (no Wi-Fi yet on planes), so we read and discussed an essay called "The Cognitive Style of PowerPoint: Pitching Out Corrupts Within," by Edward Tufte, a Yale professor who is an authority on the visualization of information.[1] Tufte identified in one sentence the problem we'd been experiencing: "As analysis becomes more causal, multivariate, comparative, evidence based, and resolution-intense," he writes, "the more damaging the bullet list becomes." That description fit our discussions at the S-Team meetings: complex, interconnected, requiring plenty of information to explore, with greater and greater consequences connected to decisions. Such analysis is not well served by a linear progression of slides that makes it difficult to refer one idea to another, sparsely worded bits of text that don't fully express an idea, and visual effects that are more distracting than enlightening. Rather than making things clear and simple, PowerPoint can strip the discussion of important nuance. In our meetings, even when a presenter included supporting information in the notes or accompanying audio, the PowerPoint presentation was never enough.

Besides, the Amazon audience of tightly scheduled, experienced executives was eager to get to the heart of the matter as quickly as possible. They would pepper the presenter with questions and push to get to the punch line, regardless of the flow of slides. Sometimes the questions did not serve to clarify a point or move the presentation along but would instead lead the entire group away from the main argument. Or some questions might be premature and would be answered in a later slide, thus forcing the presenter to go over the same ground twice.

In his essay, Tufte proposed a solution. "For serious presentations," he wrote, "it will be useful to replace PowerPoint slides with paper handouts showing words, numbers, data graphics, images together. High-resolution handouts allow viewers to contextualize, compare, narrate, and recast evidence. In contrast, data-thin, forgetful displays tend to make audiences ignorant and passive, and also to diminish the credibility of the presenter."

Tufte offered wise advice on how to get started. "Making this transition in large organizations requires a straightforward executive order: *From now on your presentation software is Microsoft Word, not PowerPoint. Get used to it.*" That is essentially what we did.

While Tufte's essay wasn't the sole impetus behind the move to narratives, it crystallized our thinking. On June 9, 2004, the members of the S-Team received an email with the following subject line: "No PowerPoint presentations from now on at S-Team."[2] The message was simple, direct, and earthshaking: from that day forward, S-Team members would be required to write short narratives describing their ideas for presentation at S-Team meetings. PowerPoint was henceforth banned.

I (still Colin) was the one who sent the email—at Jeff's direction, of course, as he was the only person in the company who could mandate such a significant change. I felt great after sending it. We had finally found a way to meaningfully improve the effectiveness of the S-Team meetings, so I thought the email would be well received. Boy was I wrong. The email whipped through the Amazon management ranks, and the almost instantaneous and near-universal reaction was basically, "You must be kidding." That evening and for the next few days I fielded a flurry of phone calls and a deluge of emails asking about the change. The outcry was particularly intense from the S-Team members who were scheduled to present within the next two weeks. They had to quickly understand the new narrative process and learn to effectively use the tools at their disposal. And the fate of a new idea that may have been months in development was riding on the outcome of the meeting.

We probably should not have been surprised by that reaction. Until that June day in 2004, PowerPoint had been the default tool for communication of ideas in many meetings at Amazon, just as it was and still is at many companies. Everybody knew its delights and perils. What could be more exhilarating than listening to a charismatic executive deliver a rousing presentation backed up by snappy phrases, dancing clip art, and cool slide transitions? So what if you couldn't remember the details a few days later? And what could be worse than suffering through a badly organized presentation using a drab template and tons of text in a font too small to read? Or, worse still, squirming as a nervous presenter stumbled and faltered through slide after slide?

The real risk with using PowerPoint in the manner we did, however, was the effect it could have on decision-making. A dynamic presenter could lead a group to approve a dismal idea. A poorly organized presentation could confuse people, produce discussion that was rambling and unfocused, and rob good ideas of the serious consideration they deserved. A boring presentation could numb the brain so completely that people tuned out or started checking their email, thereby missing the good idea lurking beneath the droning voice and uninspiring visuals.

It would take time for people to get the hang of the narrative form. First, there were no codified rules about what the narrative should be, and Jeff offered a short explanation of the reason behind the change.

> The reason writing a good 4 page memo is harder than "writing" a 20 page powerpoint is because the narrative structure of a good memo forces better thought and better understanding of what's more important than what, and how things are related.
>
> Powerpoint-style presentations somehow give permission to gloss over ideas, flatten out any sense of relative importance, and ignore the interconnectedness of ideas.[3]

The first few narratives were laughably poor when evaluated by today's standards. Some teams ignored the length limit, which was meant to keep the narratives brief enough so they could be read in the meeting itself. Enthusiastic teams, who felt their idea could not be adequately expressed in such a limited space, came in with 30 or 40 pages of prose. When authors learned that we were serious about a page limit, some squeezed as much as text onto a page as possible, using tiny fonts, reducing the width of the margins, and single-spacing the text. We wanted to go back to the benefits of writing, but not to the look of a sixteenth-century document.

Gradually, we settled on a standard format. Maximum length: six pages, no desperate tricks in formatting please. Appendices with further information or supporting detail could be attached, but would not be required reading in the meeting itself.

How to Write an Effective Six-Pager

Six-pagers vary widely, so rather than attempting a complete style guide (impossible), we've written one in a style we might submit today, if we were recommending for the first time that we use narratives instead of PowerPoint at S-Team meetings—a six-pager about six-pagers. Some of this is a pared-down version of what you've just read, which may help you see how we squeeze big ideas into the format of a true six-pager. (Note: this example would fit easily onto six pages of 8.5 x 11–inch paper, single-spaced in 11-point type, but reproduction in this book may run longer due to formatting differences.)

Dear PowerPoint: It's Not You, It's Us

Our decision-making process simply has not kept up with the rapid growth in the size and complexity of our business. We therefore advocate that, effective immediately, we stop using PowerPoint at S-Team meetings and start using six-page narratives instead.

What's Wrong with Using PowerPoint?

S-Team meetings typically begin with a PowerPoint (PP) presentation that describes some proposal or business analysis for consideration. The style of the deck varies from team to team, but all share the constraints imposed by the PowerPoint format. No matter how complex or nuanced the underlying concepts, they are presented as a series of small blocks of text, short bullet-pointed lists, or graphics.

Even the most ardent PP fans acknowledge that too much information actually spoils the deck. Amazon's bestselling book on PowerPoint describes three categories of slides:

1. 75 words or more: A dense discussion document or white paper that is not suitable for a presentation—it's better distributed in advance and read before the meeting.
2. 50 words or so: A crutch for the presenter who uses it as a teleprompter, often turning away from an audience while reading aloud.
3. Even fewer words: A proper presentation slide, used to visually reinforce primarily spoken content. The presenter must invest time to develop and rehearse this type of content.*

---

* Nancy Duarte, *Slide:ology: The Art and Science of Creating Great Presentations* (Sebastopol, CA: O'Reilly Media, 2008), 7.

One widely accepted rule of thumb, the so-called 6x6 Rule, sets a maximum of six bullet points, each with no more than six words. Other guidelines suggest limiting text to no more than 40 words per slide, and presentations to no more than 20 slides. The specific numbers vary, but the theme—limiting information density—is a constant. Taken as a whole, these practices point to a consensus: there's only so much information one can fit into a PP deck without confusing, or losing, one's audience. The format forces presenters to condense their ideas so far that important information is omitted.

Pressed against this functional ceiling, yet needing to convey the depth and breadth of their team's underlying work, a presenter—having spent considerable time pruning away content until it fits the PP format—*fills it back in, verbally*. As a result, the public speaking skills of the presenter, and the graphics arts expertise behind their slide deck, have an undue—and highly variable—effect on how well their ideas are understood. No matter how much work a team invests in developing a proposal or business analysis, its ultimate success can therefore hinge upon factors irrelevant to the issue at hand.

We've all seen presenters interrupted and questioned mid-presentation, then struggle to regain their balance by saying things like, "We'll address that in a few slides." The flow becomes turbulent, the audience frustrated, the presenter flustered. We all want to deep dive on important points but have to wait through the whole presentation before being satisfied that our questions won't be answered somewhere later on. In virtually every PP presentation, we have to take handwritten notes throughout in order to record the verbal give-and-take that actually supplies the bulk of the information we need. The slide deck alone is usually insufficient to convey or serve as a record of the complete argument at hand.

Our Inspiration

Most of us are familiar with Edward Tufte, author of the seminal (and Amazon bestselling) book *The Visual Display of Quantitative Information*. In an essay titled "The Cognitive Style of PowerPoint:

Pitching Out Corrupts Within," Tufte encapsulates our difficulties precisely:

> As analysis becomes more causal, multivariate, comparative, evidence based, and resolution-intense, the more damaging the bullet list becomes.

This certainly describes S-Team meetings: complex, interconnected, requiring plenty of information to explore, with greater and greater consequences connected to decisions. Such analysis is not well served by a linear progression of slides, a presentation style that makes it difficult to refer one idea to another, to fully express an idea in sparsely worded bits of text, and to enlighten instead of distract with visual effects. Rather than making things clear and simple, PowerPoint is stripping our discussions of important nuance.

Tufte's essay proposes a solution. "For serious presentations," he writes, "it will be useful to replace PowerPoint slides with paper handouts showing words, numbers, data graphics, images together. High-resolution handouts allow viewers to contextualize, compare, narrate, and recast evidence. In contrast, data-thin, forgetful displays tend to make audiences ignorant and passive, and also to diminish the credibility of the presenter."

He goes on: "For serious presentations, replace PP with word-processing or page-layout software. Making this transition in large organizations requires a straightforward executive order: From now on your presentation software is Microsoft Word, not PowerPoint. Get used to it." We've taken this recommendation to heart, and we now propose to follow his advice.

Our Proposal:
Banish PP in Favor of Narratives

We propose that we stop using PowerPoint in S-Team meetings immediately and replace it with a single narrative document. These narratives may sometimes include graphs and bulleted lists, which are essential to brevity and clarity, but it must be emphasized: merely reproducing a PP deck in written form will NOT be acceptable. The goal is to introduce the kind of complete and self-contained presentation that only the narrative form makes possible. **Embrace it**.

Our Tenet: Ideas, Not Presenters, Matter Most

A switch to narratives places the team's ideas and reasoning center stage, leveling the playing field by removing the natural variance in speaking skills and graphic design expertise that today plays too great a role in the success of presentations. The entire team can contribute to the crafting of a strong narrative, reviewing and revising it until it's at its very best. It should go without saying—sound decisions draw from ideas, not individual performance skills.

The time now spent upon crafting gorgeous, graphically elegant slide presentations can be recaptured and used for more important things. We can give back the time and energy now wasted on rehearsing one's time at the podium and relieve a major, unnecessary stressor for many team leaders. It won't matter whether the presenter is a great salesperson, a complete introvert, a new hire out of college, or a VP with 20 years of experience; what matters will be found on the page.

Last, the narrative document is infinitely portable and scalable. It is easy to circulate. Anyone can read it at any time. You don't need handwritten notes or a vocal track recorded during the big presentation to understand its contents. Anyone can edit or make comments on the document, and they are easily shared in the cloud. The document serves as its own record.

The Readers' Advantage:
Information Density and Interconnection of Ideas

One useful metric for comparison is what we call the *Narrative Information Multiplier* (tip of the hat to former Amazon VP Jim Freeman for coining this term). A typical Word document, with text in Arial 11-point font, contains 3,000–4,000 characters per page. For comparison, we analyzed the last 50 S-Team PowerPoint slide presentations and found that they contained an average of just 440 characters per page. This means a written narrative would contain *seven to nine times the information density* of our typical PowerPoint presentation. If you take into account some of the other PowerPoint limitations discussed above, this multiplier only increases.

Tufte estimates that people read three times faster than the typical presenter can talk, meaning that they can absorb that much more information in a given time while reading a narrative than while listening to a PP presentation. A narrative therefore delivers much more information in a much shorter time.

The Narrative Information Multiplier is itself multiplied when one considers how many such meetings S-Team members attend in a single day. A switch to this denser format will allow key decision-makers to consume much more information in a given period of time than with the PowerPoint approach.

Narratives also allow for nonlinear, interconnected arguments to unfold naturally—something that the rigid linearity of PP does not permit. Such interconnectedness defines many of our most important business opportunities. Moreover, better-informed people make higher-quality decisions, and can deliver better, more detailed feedback on the presenting teams' tactical and strategic plans. If our executives are better informed, at a deeper level, on a wider array of important company initiatives, we will gain a substantial competitive advantage over executives elsewhere who rely on traditional low-bandwidth methods of communication (e.g., PP).

The Presenters' Advantage:
Forces Greater Clarity of Thought

We know that writing narratives will likely prove to be harder work than creating the PP presentations that they will replace; this is actually positive. The act of writing will force the writer to think and synthesize more deeply than they would in the act of crafting a PP deck; the idea on paper will be better thought out, especially after the author's entire team has reviewed it and offered feedback. It's a daunting task to get all the relevant facts and all one's salient arguments into a coherent, understandable document—**and it should be.**

Our goal as presenters is not to merely introduce an idea but to demonstrate that it's been carefully weighed and thoroughly analyzed.

Unlike a PP deck, a solid narrative can—and must—demonstrate how its many, often disparate, facts and analyses are interconnected. While an ideal PP presentation can do this, experience has shown that they rarely do in practice.

A complete narrative should also anticipate the likely objections, concerns, and alternate points of view that we expect our team to deliver. Writers will be forced to anticipate smart questions, reasonable objections, even common misunderstandings—and to address them proactively in their narrative document. You simply cannot gloss over an important topic in a narrative presentation, especially when you know it's going to be dissected by an audience full of critical thinkers. While this may seem a bit intimidating at first, it merely reflects our long-standing commitment to thinking deeply and correctly about our opportunities.

The old essay-writing adage "State, support, conclude" forms the basis for putting a convincing argument forward. Successful narratives will connect the dots for the reader and thus create a persuasive argument, rather than presenting a disconnected stream of bullet points and graphics that leave the audience to do all the work. Writing persuasively requires and enforces clarity of thought that's even more vital when multiple teams collaborate on an idea. The narrative form demands that teams be in sync or, if they are not, that they clearly state in the document where they are not yet aligned.

Edward Tufte sums up the benefits of narratives over PP with his own blunt clarity: "PowerPoint becomes ugly and inaccurate because our thoughts are foolish, but the slovenliness of PowerPoint makes it easier for us to have foolish thoughts."

How to Conduct a Meeting in This New Format

Narratives would be distributed at the start of each meeting and read by all in attendance during the time normally taken up by the slide deck—approximately the first 20 minutes. Many will want to take notes, or annotate their copy, during this time. Once everybody signals their readiness, conversation about the document begins.

We know that people read complex information at the rough

average of three minutes per page, which in turn defines the functional length of a written narrative as about six pages for a 60-minute meeting. Our recommendation is therefore that teams respect the six-page maximum. There will no doubt be times when it feels difficult to condense a complete presentation into this size, but the same limitation— which is really one of meeting lengths—faces PP presenters as well. We believe that six pages should be enough, but we will review over time and revise if necessary.

Conclusion

PowerPoint could only carry us so far, and we're thankful for its service, but the time has come to move on. Written narratives will convey our ideas in a deeper, stronger, more capable fashion while adding a key additional benefit: they will act as a forcing function that shapes sharper, more complete analysis. Six-page narratives are also incredibly inclusive communication, precisely because the interaction between the presenter and audience is zero during reading. No biases matter other than the clarity of reasoning. This change will strengthen not just the pitch, but the product—and the company—as well.

FAQ

Q: Most other companies of our size use PowerPoint. Why do we need to be different, and what if this switch turns out to be the wrong move?

A: In simplest terms, we see a better way. Amazon differs from other major companies in ways that help us stand out, including our willingness to go where the data lead and seek better ways of doing familiar things. If this move doesn't work out, we'll do what we always do—iterate and refine, or roll it back entirely if that's what the results show us is best.

Q: Why not distribute the narrative ahead of the meeting so we're ready?

A: The short time between distribution and the meeting might not give all attendees sufficient time for that task. Also, since the document replaces the deck, no time is lost by dedicating this phase of the meeting to a silent reading that brings everybody up to speed before Q&A begins. Last but certainly not least, this gives each presenting team the most possible time to complete and refine their presentation.

Q: My team has proven to be very good at PP presentations—do we HAVE to switch?

A: YES. One danger of an unusually strong PP presentation is that the stage presence or charm of the presenter can sometimes unintentionally blind the audience to key questions or concerns. Slick graphics can distract equally well. Most importantly, we've shown that even the best use of PP simply cannot deliver the completeness and sophistication that narratives can.

Q: What if we put our PP deck into printed form and add some extended comments to strengthen and extend the information content?

A: NO. Reproducing PP on paper also reproduces its weaknesses. There's nothing one can do in PP that cannot be done more thoroughly, though sometimes less attractively, in a narrative.

Q: Can we still use graphs or charts in our narratives?

A: YES. Most complex issues derive key insights from data and we expect that some of that data may be best represented in the form of a chart or graph. However, we do not expect that graphics alone can make the compelling and complete case we expect from a true written narrative. Include them if you must, but don't let graphics predominate.

Q: Six pages feels short. How much can we fit onto a page?

A: The six-page limit acts as a valuable forcing function that ensures we only discuss the most important issues. We also set aside 20 minutes for reading and expect that every attendee can read the entire thing during that time. Please don't fall prey to the temptation to fiddle with margins or font size to squeeze more into the document. Adding density to stay under the six-page limit works against this goal and tempts writers to stray into less important areas of consideration.

Q: How will we measure the success of this change?

A: Great question. We have not been able to identify a quantitative way to measure the quality of a series of S-Team decisions today, nor are we proposing a metric at this time. Comparing the two approaches will be a qualitative exercise. We propose implementing narratives for the next three months and then polling the S-Team to ask if they're making better-informed decisions.

Six-Pagers Vary in Structure and Content

In the mock-up six-pager above, we've included two optional sections that many presenters at Amazon have found helpful. The first is to call out one or more key tenets that our proposal relies upon—a foundational element of the reasoning that led us to make this recommendation. Tenets give the reader an anchor point from which to evaluate the rest. If the tenet itself is in dispute, it's easier to address that directly rather than take on all the logical steps that derive from that position.

The second optional section, perhaps more commonly used, is the inclusion of an FAQ. Strong six-pagers don't just make their case, they anticipate counterarguments, points of contention, or statements that might be easily misinterpreted. Adding the FAQ to address these saves time and gives the reader a useful focal point for checking the thoroughness of the authors' thinking. (See appendix B for additional FAQ and tenet examples.)

We should also note that some six-pagers are longer than six pages, because they include supporting data or documentation in appendices—data that's not usually read during the meeting.

Six-page narratives can take many forms. Our mock-up provides one example, laid out specifically for our topic. We wouldn't typically expect to see a section titled "Our Inspiration," for instance, even though it serves a useful purpose in this narrative. Headings and subheadings, graphs or data tables, and other design elements will be specific to the individual narrative.

An Amazon quarterly business review, for instance, might be broken down like this instead:

Introduction
Tenets

Accomplishments

Misses

Proposals for Next Period

Headcount

P&L

FAQ

Appendices (includes things like supporting data in the form
of spreadsheets, tables and charts, mock-ups)

The six-pager can be used to explore any argument or idea you want to present to a group of people—an investment, a potential acquisition, a new product or feature, a monthly or quarterly business update, an operating plan, or even an idea on how to improve the food at the company cafeteria. It takes practice to master the discipline of writing these narratives. First-time writers will do well to review and learn from successful examples.

The New Meeting Format

When the meeting topic is covered by a narrative, it works best if the entire audience reads the narrative, in the room, at the beginning of the meeting. The silence can be unsettling at first, but after you've been through the process a few times, it becomes routine. Even though you cannot hear it, with a well-written narrative there is a massive amount of useful information that is being transferred in those 20 minutes.

We mentioned earlier the estimated reading speed of three minutes per page, which led to the six-page limit. If yours is a 30-minute meeting, a three-page narrative would therefore be more appropriate. Our goal has been to leave two-thirds of the meeting time for discussing what we've read.

Still, people read at different speeds. Some will review the appendices, some won't. Some attendees will make comments in a shared online document, like Bill does, so that all meeting participants can see everyone's comments. I (Colin) prefer the old-fashioned way, making comments on paper so I can lose myself in the document. This also helps me avoid the confirmation bias that might arise were I to read the real-time comments others were adding to the shared document. Besides, I know I'll hear everybody's view soon enough.

When everyone has read the document, the presenter takes the floor. First-time presenters often start by saying, "Let me orally walk you through the document." **Resist that temptation**; it will likely be a waste of time. The whole point of the written document is to clearly present the reasoning and to avoid the hazards of live presentation. The attendees have already walked themselves through the argument.

Some groups at Amazon go around the room, ask for high-level feedback, then pore over the document line by line. Other groups ask a single individual to give all their feedback on the entire document, then ask the next person in the audience to do the same. Just pick a method that works for you—there's no single correct approach.

Then the discussion begins, which essentially means that the audience members ask questions of the presenting team. They seek clarification, probe intentions, offer insights, and suggest refinements or alternatives. The presenting team has put great care and thought into the narrative, and the audience members have a responsibility to take it seriously. The key goal of the meeting, after all, is to seek the truth about the proposed idea or topic. We want that idea to become the best it can possibly be as a result of any adjustments we make along with the presenting team.

During the discussion stage, it's also important that notes be taken on behalf of the entire audience, preferably by someone knowledgeable about the subject who is not the primary presenter. The presenter is generally too involved in answering questions to capture effective notes at the same time. If I don't see anyone taking notes at the discussion stage, I will politely pause the meeting and ask who is going to do so. It's vital that we capture and record the salient points of the ensuing discussion, as those comments become part of the output of the narrative process.

Feedback as Collaboration

Providing valuable feedback and insight can prove to be as difficult as writing the narrative itself. Two of the most cherished gifts I (Colin) received in my career are pens, given to me by people whose narratives I had read and commented on. (I would typically give a printout of the narrative with my handwritten notes on it to the presenters after the meeting.) Both people told me that my comments had played a key role in making their businesses successful. I say this not to boast but to provide evidence that when the reader takes the narrative process just as seriously as the writer does, the comments can have real, significant, and long-lasting impact. You are not just commenting on a document, you're helping to shape an idea, and thereby becoming a key team member for that business.

Because examples of excellent six-page narratives are disseminated throughout the company, and because expectations about their nature and quality are so well understood by employees, it rarely happens that a team presents a substandard narrative at a meeting. I did once receive a six-pager that was not up to snuff. The team who wrote it was glossing over hard problems with platitudes. I politely handed it back to them, said it wasn't ready to be discussed, adjourned the meeting, and suggested they use the time to work on improving the narrative. But, as I said, those scenarios are extremely rare. Mostly it's about supporting the team by giving robust feedback. Jeff has an uncanny ability to read a narrative and consistently arrive at insights that no one else did, even though we were all reading the same narrative. After one meeting, I asked him how he was able to do that. He responded with a simple and useful tip that I have not forgotten: he assumes each sentence he reads is wrong until he can prove otherwise. He's challenging the content of the sentence, not the motive of the writer. Jeff, by the way, was usually among the last to finish reading.

This approach to critical thinking challenges the team to question whether the current narrative has it right or if there are additional fundamental truths to uncover, and if they are aligned with the Amazon Leadership Principles. For example, say a narrative reads, "Our customer-friendly returns policy allows returns up to 60 days from the time of purchase compared to the 30 days typically offered by our competitors." A busy executive doing a cursory read and already thinking about their next meeting may be content with that statement and move on. However, a critical reader would challenge the implicit assumption being made, namely, that the longer allowable return duration makes the policy customer friendly. The policy may be better than a competitor's, but is it *actually* customer friendly? Then during the discussion, the critical reader may ask, "If Amazon is really customer obsessed, why do we penalize the 99 percent of customers who are honest and want to return an item by making them wait until our returns department receives the item to make sure it's the right item and that it's not damaged?" This type of thinking—in which you assume there is something wrong with the sentence—led Amazon to create the no-hassle return policy, which specifies that the customer should get a refund even before Amazon receives the returned goods. (The refund is reversed for the small percentage of people who do not send back the item.) Here is another instance where you don't need to "have a Jeff" in order to apply this exacting style of critical thinking to ideas at your company.

Final Thoughts About Narratives

Narratives are designed to increase the quantity and quality of effective communication in your organization—by an order of magnitude over traditional methods. Creating such solid narratives requires hard work and some risk-taking. Good ones take many days to write. The team writing the narrative toils over the topic, writes its first draft, circulates and reviews and iterates and repeats, then finally takes the vulnerable step of saying to their management and their peers, "Here's our best effort. Tell us where we fell short." At first this openness can prove intimidating.

But as we've seen, this model imposes duties and expectations upon the audience as well. They must objectively and thoroughly evaluate the idea, not the team or the pitch, and suggest ways to improve it. The work product of the meeting is ultimately a joint effort of the presenter and their audience—thinking that they can all stand behind. Silence in the discussion stage is the equivalent of agreement with what is presented, but it carries the same weight as a full-blown critique.

In this way, the presenter and audience become integrally linked to the subsequent success or failure of the initiative, or the correctness or incorrectness of a team's business analysis. When looking at any of Amazon's big wins, remember that every major success has gone through multiple narrative reviews; it's likely there were meaningful contributions from the audience as well as the team. On the other hand, for every failed initiative or analysis that fell short, there were senior leaders who looked at it and thought, "This makes sense," or, "Yes, this should work." Either way, if the narrative process works to its fullest potential, you're all in it together.

5

Working Backwards

Start with the Desired Customer Experience

Start with the customer and work backwards—harder than it sounds, but a clear path to innovating and delighting customers. A useful Working Backwards tool: writing the press release and FAQ before you build the product.

* * *

Most of Amazon's major products and initiatives since 2004 have one very Amazonian thing in common—they were created through a process called Working Backwards. It is so central to the company's success that we used it as the title for our book. Working Backwards is a systematic way to vet ideas and create new products. Its key tenet is to start by defining the customer experience, then iteratively work backwards from that point until the team achieves clarity of thought around what to build. Its principal tool is a second form of written narrative called the PR/FAQ, short for press release/frequently asked questions.

We both witnessed its birth. Colin was in his tenure as Jeff's shadow when the Working Backwards process was launched and he participated in every Working Backwards review presented to Jeff in the twelve months thereafter. And Bill's experience was forged by applying and refining the Working Backwards concept in the early stages of the process that led to the development of every digital media product.

Trial and Error, Then Success

Working as Jeff's shadow was a bit like drinking from a fire hose. One surprising challenge of the job I (Colin) noticed early on was just how much context switching went on each day. Every week Jeff—and therefore I—had three recurring meetings: the four-hour S-Team meeting discussed in the previous chapter, a Weekly Business Review (chapter six), and an informal Monday-morning S-Team breakfast near the office. In addition to those, on any given day we'd usually meet with two to four product teams, where we'd spend between one and two hours doing a deep dive on new products and features. Throw in the occasional retail, finance, and operations updates, plus a fire drill or two requiring immediate attention, and you have a typical week.

The product team meetings usually took up a plurality of the available hours in the week. Jeff and I would need to get up to speed on where we left off with any given team, so the first part of each product meeting could be viewed as setup cost. Then we'd discuss the progress made since our last meeting, ask and answer questions, discuss new issues or problems, and agree on next steps that needed to be addressed before we met with the team again. Despite everyone's best intentions, the meetings were often error prone and inefficient. Sometimes the "setup time" would consume too much of the meeting: teams, rightfully proud of their recent accomplishments, wanted to talk about them at the expense of the important decisions we needed to know about, so by the time the team recapped their progress, there was not enough time left for what actually needed to get done. Other times we'd discover, too late, that the team was not aligned with Jeff and had veered off path from the previous meeting. When that happened, it was extremely frustrating for everyone, not to mention a waste of valuable time.

As I mentioned earlier, part of my role as Jeff's shadow was to help him be as effective as possible. We needed to improve each stage of these product meetings. We needed to begin by quickly and accurately caching the right information during the setup portion of the meeting. Then we had to focus on the most important issues moving forward. Finally, we had to map out a clear trajectory for the teams to follow between the current meeting and the next one. If we could do all that, it would be a huge win for everyone. We'd be more efficient in addressing the hard problems, which would help us make higher-quality decisions more quickly. With that increase in the speed of good decision-making, Jeff would be able to connect deeply with a greater number of teams.

While I was trying to help sort all this out, Jeff was spending a disproportionate amount of his time on Amazon's digital transformation, and on what would eventually become the first set of Amazon's cloud computing services.

So my goal was not easy to reach. It required trial and error over the course of many months. Jeff tried many different ideas, some of them seemingly crazy, like starting a project proposal by writing a user manual or a technical API guide, relying solely on mock-ups, and other approaches to visualizing the outcome of a project. I remember getting frantic calls from nontechnical product managers saying, "Colin, I'm supposed to meet with Jeff next week. Can you send me a good example of a user manual? Also, I'm supposed to write something called an API guide but have no idea what that is!" We were not committed to any of these experimental formats and stopped using them when we realized they were counterproductive.

In the end, what turned out to work best was relying on the core Amazon principle of customer obsession and a simple yet flexible way of writing narrative documents. These two elements form the Working Backwards process—starting from the customer experience and working backwards from that by writing a press release that literally announces the product as if it were ready to launch and an FAQ anticipating the tough questions. While this next section describes the evolution of Working Backwards as seen through the experience of the digital team, a handful of other teams went through a similar process. Bringing together the experience of these teams enabled us to hone and refine Working Backwards into its final form.

Where Are the Mock-Ups? Bill and the Launch of Digital

In 2004, I (Bill) was one of the leaders selected to create and lead Amazon's digital media organization. I was itching to launch new stores for digital music, movies, and TV shows. I also needed to revamp our e-book store, which had gone online in 2000 and was then a tiny business because books could only be read on a PC and were more expensive than the print edition.

I assumed that the launch process for digital media would essentially be the same as it was for other new Amazon businesses—toys, electronics, and tools, for example—which were known as "category expansions." For those launches, the process had been straightforward. The team would gather the data to build a catalog of items, establish relationships with vendors to source them, set prices, build content for category pages, and then launch. It wasn't easy, but we weren't inventing a new store or customer experience from scratch.

As I was to learn, the process for creating the digital media business would be quite different because there was so much more to creating a great digital media customer experience than simply adding the next retail category to the Amazon website.

The first part of the process went as normal. Our team of three or four people developed plans using the tried-and-true MBA-style methods of the time. We gathered data about the size of the market opportunity. We constructed financial models projecting our annual sales in each category, assuming, of course, an ever-increasing share of digital sales. We calculated gross margin assuming a certain cost of goods from our suppliers. We projected an operating margin based on the size of the team we would need to support the business. We outlined the deals we would make with media companies. We sketched out pricing parameters. We described how the service would work for customers. We put it all together in crisp-looking

PowerPoint slides (this was still several months before the switch to narratives) and comprehensive Excel spreadsheets.

We had several meetings with Jeff to present our ideas. At each one, he would listen carefully to what we had to say. He would ask probing questions and study the financials. But he never seemed satisfied or convinced. He found our proposals light on the details as to how the service would work for customers. Finally, inevitably, he would ask, "Where are the mock-ups?"

Jeff was referring to the visual representations that would show exactly how the new service would look on the Amazon website. Mock-ups should be detailed, showing the entire customer experience from landing page to purchase—screen design, buttons, text, the sequence of clicks, everything. To create a meaningful and informative mock-up you have to think through every element of what the service will offer, what the experience will be for the customer, how all the features will work on the page. It requires a ton of work to think through the whole business and a ton more work to create and refine the visuals.

We didn't have any mock-ups. We just wanted to sell Jeff on the opportunity, show him that these digital media businesses could be large, set a budget, and get the green light to start building the team. We would deal with the customer experience and other details once we got his go-ahead.

But if Jeff wants to see mock-ups, you had better make mock-ups.

A few weeks later we were back with rough mock-ups in hand. Jeff listened carefully to our presentation and then began asking detailed questions about every button, word, link, and color. For music, he asked how our service would be better than iTunes. For e-books, he wanted to know how much the e-books would cost. He asked if people would be able to read their e-books on a tablet or a phone as well as their PC.

We answered as we had before. We hadn't figured out all that stuff! We just needed his basic approval so we could hire the team, start negotiating deals with media companies, and get something launched. That answer did not go over well. At all. Jeff wanted to know exactly what we were going to build and how it would be better for customers than the competition. He wanted us to agree on those details before we started hiring a team or establishing vendor relationships or building anything.

It was clear that half-baked mock-ups were no better, perhaps worse, than no mock-ups at all. To Jeff, a half-baked mock-up was evidence of half-baked thinking. And he was quick to say so, often using strong language to make his point inescapably clear. Jeff wanted us to know that we couldn't just charge down the first available and most convenient path to chase after this opportunity. We needed to think through our plan in detail.

We went back to work. The deeper we dug, the clearer it became that digital media was going to be unlike any other Amazon business. The obvious difference was that we would not be shipping brown boxes to customers but rather delivering digital bits over wires. That was the least complicated part. There also had to be a great way for the customer to manage, read, listen to, or watch those bits once they had them. This would require custom apps and hardware.

As we continued to meet with Jeff, we tried various kinds of spreadsheets and PowerPoint slides to present and explore our ideas, none of which seemed to be particularly effective. At some point, I don't remember exactly when, Jeff suggested a different approach for the next meeting. Forget the spreadsheets and slides, he said. Instead, each team member would write a narrative document. In it, they would describe their best idea for a device or service for the digital media business.

The next meeting arrived, and we all showed up with our narratives. (As mentioned, ours was one of several teams involved in the early experimentation with narratives at the company. They were not yet official Amazon policy.) We distributed them and read them to ourselves and then discussed them, one after another. One proposed an e-book reader that would use new E Ink screen technology. Another described a new take on the MP3 player. Jeff wrote his own narrative about a device he called the Amazon Puck. It would sit on your countertop and could respond to voice commands like, "Puck.

Please order a gallon of milk." Puck would then place the order with Amazon.

The great revelation of this process was not any one of the product ideas. As we've described in chapter four, the break-through was the document itself. We had freed ourselves of the quantitative demands of Excel, the visual seduction of PowerPoint, and the distracting effect of personal performance. The idea had to be in the writing.

Writing up our ideas was hard work. It required us to be thorough and precise. We had to describe features, pricing, how the service would work, why consumers would want it. Half-baked thinking was harder to disguise on the written page than in Power-Point slides. It could not be glossed over through personal charm in the presentation.

After we started using the documents, our meetings changed. There was more meat and more detail to discuss, so the sessions were livelier and longer. We weren't so focused on the pro forma P&L and projected market segment share. We talked at length about the service itself, the experience, and which products and services we thought would appeal most to the customer.

After a lot of trial and error, and incremental moves in this direction among many teams involved in the narrative experiment, Jeff then pushed the idea further. What if we thought of the product concept narrative as a press release? Usually, in a conventional organization, a press release is written at the end of the product development process. The engineers and product managers finish their work, then "throw it over the wall" to the marketing and sales people, who look at the product from the customer point of view, often for the first time. They're the ones who write the press release, which describes the killer features and fantastic benefits and is designed to create buzz, capture attention, and, above all, get customers to leap out of their chairs to buy.

In this standard process, the company works forward. The leaders come up with a product or business that is great for the company, and then they try to shoehorn it into meeting previously unmet customer needs.

That approach can lead to some undesirable results, Jeff believed. To make his point, he used Sony as a hypothetical example. Suppose Sony decides to introduce a new TV. The sales and marketing group has done its research into customer preferences and market trends (but not necessarily the customer experience) and has determined that Sony should offer a 44-inch TV at a price point of $1,999. The engineering team, however, has been working on the new TV for quite some time, and their focus has been on picture quality, which means higher resolution, and they have not been especially concerned about price point. The TV they come up with will cost $2,000 just to manufacture. So there is no way that the retail price can be $1,999.

If the two organizations had started the process by writing a press release, they would have had to agree on the features, cost, customer experience, and price. Then they could have worked backwards to figure out what to build, thereby surfacing the challenges they would face in product development and manufacturing.

The Kindle Press Release

Kindle was the first product offered by the digital media group, and it, along with several AWS products, was among the first at Amazon to be created using the press release approach.

Kindle was a breakthrough in multiple dimensions. It used an E Ink display. The customer could shop for, buy, and download books directly from the device—no need to connect to a PC or to Wi-Fi. Kindle offered more e-books than any other device or service available at the time and the price was lower. Today, that set of features sounds absolutely standard. In 2007, it was pioneering.

But Kindle had not started out that way. In the early stages of its development—before we got started on the press release approach and when we were still using PowerPoint and Excel—we had not described a device that could do all these things from the customer perspective. We had focused on the technology challenges, business constraints, sales and financial projections, and marketing opportunities. We were working forward, trying to invent a product that would be good for Amazon, the company, not the customer.

When we wrote a Kindle press release and started working backwards, everything changed. We focused instead on what would be great for customers. An excellent screen for a great reading experience. An ordering process that would make buying and downloading books easy. A huge selection of titles. Low prices. We would never have had the breakthroughs necessary to achieve that customer experience were it not for the press release process, which forced the team to invent multiple solutions to customer problems. (We tell the whole Kindle story in chapter seven.)

As we got more adept at using the Working Backwards process, we refined the press release document and added a second element: the FAQ, frequently asked questions, with, of course, answers.

The FAQ section, as it developed, included both external and internal questions. External FAQs are the ones you would expect to hear from the press or customers. "Where can I purchase a new Amazon Echo?" or "How does Alexa work?"

Internal FAQs are the questions that your team and the executive leadership will ask. "How can we make a 44-inch TV with an HD display that can retail for $1,999 at a 25 percent gross margin?" or "How will we make a Kindle reader that connects to carrier networks to download books without customers having to sign a contract with a carrier?" or "How many new software engineers and data scientists do we need to hire for this new initiative?"

In other words, the FAQ section is where the writer shares the details of the plan from a consumer point of view and addresses the various risks and challenges from internal operations, technical, product, marketing, legal, business development, and financial points of view.

The Working Backwards document became known as the PR/FAQ.

The Features and Benefits of the PR/FAQ

The primary point of the process is to shift from an internal/company perspective to a customer perspective. Customers are pitched new products constantly. Why will this new product be compelling enough for customers to take action and buy it? A common question asked by executives when reviewing the product features in the PR is "so what?" If the press release doesn't describe a product that is meaningfully better (faster, easier, cheaper) than what is already out there, or results in some stepwise change in customer experience, then it isn't worth building.

The PR gives the reader the highlights of the customer experience. The FAQ provides all the salient details of the customer experience as well as a clear-eyed and thorough assessment of how expensive and challenging it will be for the company to build the product or create the service. That's why it's not unusual for an Amazon team to write ten drafts of the PR/FAQ or more, and to meet with their senior leaders five times or more to iterate, debate, and refine the idea.

The PR/FAQ process creates a framework for rapidly iterating and incorporating feedback and reinforces a detailed, data-oriented, and fact-based method of decision-making. We found that it can be used to develop ideas and initiatives—a new compensation policy, for example—as well as products and services. Once your organization learns how to use this valuable tool, it is addicting. People start to use it for everything.

Over time, we refined and normalized the specifications for the PR/FAQ. The press release (PR) portion is a few paragraphs, always less than one page. The frequently asked questions (FAQ) should be five pages or less. There are no awards for extra pages or more words. The goal isn't to explain all the excellent work you have done but rather to share the distilled thinking that has come from that work.

People who write press releases for a living, or indeed anyone who has been professionally edited, knows the importance of boiling things down as much as possible, but the people in product development don't always understand this. In the early days of the PR/FAQ, a common mistake people made was to assume that more means better. They'd produce long documents, attach page after page of narrative, insert charts and tables in an appendix. The virtue of this approach, at least from the perspective of the writer, is that it shows all their work and allows them to avoid hard decisions about what's important and what's not—leaving those for the group. However, restricting the length of the document is, to use a term that came up when describing the narratives, a forcing function—we have seen that it develops better thinkers and communicators.

The creation of the PR/FAQ starts with the person who originated either the idea or the project writing a draft. When it's in shareable condition, that person sets up a one-hour meeting with stakeholders to review the document and get feedback. At the meeting, they distribute the PR/FAQ in either soft or hard copy, and everyone reads it to themselves. When they have finished, the writer asks for general feedback. The most senior attendees tend to speak last, to avoid influencing others.

Once everyone has given their high-level responses, the writer asks for specific comments, line by line, paragraph by paragraph. This discussion of the details is the critical part of the meeting. People ask hard questions. They engage in intense debate and discussion of the key ideas and the way they are expressed. They point out things that should be omitted or things that are missing.

After the meeting, the writer distributes meeting minutes to all the attendees, including notes on the feedback. Then they get to work on the revision, incorporating responses to the feedback. When it is polished, they present it to the executive leaders in the company. There will be more feedback and discussion. More revision and more meetings may be required.

The PR/FAQ review process can be stressful, no matter how constructive and unbiased the feedback. Gaps will be found! A PR/FAQ under serious consideration for implementation will typically require multiple drafts and meetings with the leadership. Senior managers, directors, and executive leaders who oversee the authors of PR/FAQs become skilled evaluators and contributors to the process. The more PR/FAQs they read, and the more products they build and launch using the PR/FAQ process, the more capable they become at identifying the omissions and flaws in the author's thinking. And so the process itself creates a tier of master evaluators as it vets and strengthens the idea and aligns everyone involved in the project, from individual contributor to CEO. It also increases the likelihood that a project will be approved and funded. You should plan on making many revisions to the PR/FAQ document, even after the project has formally started, to reflect changes and new elements.

Example: Blue Corp. Announces the Launch of Melinda, the Smart Mailbox

Melinda is the physical mailbox designed to securely receive and keep safe all your e-commerce and grocery deliveries.

PR Newswire, Atlanta, GA, November 5, 2019

Today Blue Corp. announced the launch of Melinda, a smart mailbox that ensures secure and properly chilled delivery and storage for your online purchases and groceries. With Melinda, you no longer need to worry about getting your deliveries stolen from your doorstep or spoiled groceries. Plus, you're notified as soon as your packages are delivered. Packed with smart technology, Melinda costs just $299.

Today, 23 percent of online shoppers report having packages stolen from their front porch, and 19 percent complain of grocery deliveries being spoiled. With no easy solution to these problems, customers give up and stop ordering online.

Melinda, with its smart technology and insulation, makes stolen packages and spoiled groceries a thing of the past. Each Melinda includes a camera and a speaker. When a delivery courier arrives at your home, Melinda tells the courier to scan the package barcode by holding it up to the camera. If the code is valid, the front door opens and Melinda instructs the courier to place the package inside and close the door securely. The built-in scale in the base of each Melinda verifies that the weight of the delivery matches the weight of the item(s) you ordered. The courier receives a voice confirmation, and your purchase is safe and secure. Melinda sends you a text letting you know that your item arrived along with a video of the courier making the delivery.

When you return home and are ready to retrieve your delivery, just use the built-in fingerprint reader to unlock the door. Melinda can store and recognize up to ten saved fingerprints so that all members of your family can access Melinda.

Do you use Instacart, Amazon, or Walmart for online grocery delivery? If so, are you tired of spoiled groceries in the hot sun? Melinda keeps your chilled and frozen food cold. The walls of Melinda are two inches thick and made with the same pressure-injected foam used in the best coolers, keeping your groceries cool for up to twelve hours.

Melinda fits easily on your porch or stoop, taking up just a few feet of space, and you can choose from a variety of colors and finishes to make Melinda an attractive addition to the appearance of your home.

"Melinda is a breakthrough in safety and convenience for online shoppers," says Lisa Morris, CEO of Blue Corp. "In creating Melinda we combined a number of the latest technologies at the low price of just $299."

"Melinda is a lifesaver," said Janet Thomas, a frequent online shopper and customer of Instacart. "It is so frustrating when one of my packages is stolen from my front porch, and it can be time-consuming to work with customer support to get a refund. I use Instacart every week for grocery delivery, and many times I am not home when my groceries arrive. I love knowing that they are kept cool and secure in my Melinda. I selected the natural teak finish for my Melinda—it looks great on my front porch."

To order your Melinda, simply visit keepitcoolmelinda.com, or visit amazon.com, walmart.com, Walmart stores, and other leading retailers.

Internal FAQs

Q: How large is the estimated consumer demand for Melinda?

A: Based on our research, we estimate that ten million households in the United States, Europe, and Asia would want to buy Melinda at a $299 price point.

Q: Why is $299 the right price point?

A: There are no directly comparable products in the marketplace today. One similar product is Amazon Key, which allows couriers access to your home, garage, or car using smart lock technology. Another similar product is Ring Doorbell, which ranges in price from $99 to $499. We based our price on customer surveys and focus groups combined with the price needed to ensure profitability.

Q: How does Melinda recognize barcodes on packages?

A: We will license barcode-scanning technology from Green Corp. at a cost of $100K per year. In addition, we need to develop an API that will allow us to link a Melinda customer account with any e-commerce provider (Amazon, Walmart, eBay, OfferUp, etc.), which provides us with the item tracking number from the e-commerce or delivery merchant. This way we can recognize the barcode with the package tracking number and know either the exact or an estimated weight for each item.

Q: What if a customer receives an order from an e-commerce provider and they haven't linked their account yet?

A: We make it easy for customers to link their orders because we will offer a browser plug-in for Melinda customers that detects when they place an order with an e-commerce provider, which then links their account and the order details to their Melinda.

Q: Why will e-commerce providers like Amazon and Walmart be willing to share these package delivery details with us? What is in it for them?

A: We believe we can convince them that the customer experience benefits will enable them to increase their sales. In addition, we will work closely with their business and legal groups to ensure that we handle their customer data in ways that meet their stringent requirements. Alternatively, we will offer a simple UI for customers to copy and paste each tracking number from their e-commerce provider to the Melinda app.

Q: What happens if a customer gets more than one delivery in a day?

A: Melinda can accept multiple deliveries each day until the unit is full.

Q: What if the package is too big for Melinda?

A: Packages exceeding 2'x2'x4' won't fit in Melinda. Melinda can still record the delivery person and scan the barcode, but the item is stored outside Melinda.

Q: How does Melinda prevent a courier from stealing items that are already in Melinda from a prior order?

A: There are several ways. The first is that the forward-facing camera records any activity or access to Melinda. The second is that there is a scale at the base of the unit that detects the weight of the shipment and verifies that this matches the item(s) ordered. If a second delivery is made in one day, Melinda knows the weight of the first delivery and the estimated weight of the second delivery, so if the net weight is lower, Melinda knows that the courier has removed something and will sound an alarm.

Q: What is the estimated bill of materials (BOM) or cost to manufacture each Melinda, and how much profit will we make per unit?

A: The estimated BOM is $250 for each Melinda, meaning that our gross profit per unit is $49. The most expensive parts in Melinda are the shell and insulation ($115), the fingerprint reader ($49), and the scale.

Q: What is the power source for Melinda?

A: Melinda requires a standard AC outlet.

Q: What size team is required to build Melinda?

A: We estimate that we need a team of 77 at an annualized cost of $15 million. There are several teams required to build Melinda, but these can be broken down into hardware and software teams. On the hardware side, we need a team for each of the following:

- The physical shell, color choices, and finishes (6)
- Integration of the various smart and mechanical components, including the fingerprint reader, the camera, the automatic (open/close) door, the speaker, and the camera (12)

On the software side, we will need a team for each of the new services. Below is our current assessment of what teams will be required and how many people should be on each team, including product managers, engineers, designers, and so on:

- Voice commands to couriers (10)
- Fingerprint capture and storing (8)
- Package tracking and item weight details (11)
- Barcode reader (7)
- API to link e-commerce accounts to Melinda (12)
- Browser plug-in/web interface for account linking (5)
- Melinda app for iOS and Android (6)

***

This fictitious PR/FAQ is designed to illustrate the kinds of thinking and problems that the author and readers of a PR/FAQ should consider.

The product itself is both realistic and unrealistic. The customer problem of stolen packages and melting groceries is very real (although the research/stats here are phony), and the various components and technologies all exist. The Melinda, as described, is not realistic in that the costs are almost certainly underestimated (the product is overly complex), and the total addressable market for the product is probably very small.

However, the example enables us to illustrate the ways in which the PR/FAQ process helps authors assess the viability of any new product by forcing them to consider and document all elements and constraints, including (but not limited to) the consumer needs and total addressable market, the per-unit economics and P&L, key dependencies, and the feasibility (how challenging it is to build the product). A good PR/FAQ is one in which the author has clearly considered and grappled with each of these issues, seeking truth and clarity on each.

Press Release Components

These are the key elements of the press release:

Heading: Name the product in a way the reader (i.e., your target customers) will understand. One sentence under the title.

"Blue Corp. announces the launch of Melinda, the smart mailbox."

Subheading: Describe the customer for the product and what benefits they will gain from using it. One sentence only underneath the heading.

"Melinda is the physical mailbox designed to securely receive and keep safe all your e-commerce and grocery deliveries."

Summary Paragraph: Begin with the city, media outlet, and your proposed launch date. Give a summary of the product and the benefit.

"PR Newswire, Atlanta, GA, November 5, 2019. Today Blue Corp. announced the launch of Melinda, a smart mailbox that ensures secure and properly chilled delivery and storage for your online purchases and groceries."

Problem Paragraph: This is where you describe the problem that your product is designed to solve. Make sure that you write this paragraph from the customer's point of view.

"Today, 23 percent of online shoppers report having packages stolen from their front porch, and 19 percent complain of grocery deliveries being spoiled."

Solution Paragraph(s): Describe your product in some detail and how it simply and easily solves the customer's problem. For more complex products, you may need more than one paragraph.

"With Melinda, you no longer need to worry about getting your online purchases and deliveries stolen . . ."

Quotes and Getting Started: Add one quote from you or your company's spokesperson and a second quote from a hypothetical customer in which they describe the benefit they are getting from using your new product. Describe how easy it is to get started, and provide a link to your website where customers can get more information and purchase the product.

"Melinda is a breakthrough in safety and convenience for online shoppers . . ."

FAQ Components

Unlike the PR, the FAQ section has a more free-form feel to it—there are no mandatory FAQs. The PR section does not typically include visuals, but it is more than appropriate to include tables, graphs, and charts in the FAQ. You must include things like your pro forma P&L for a new business or product. If you have high-quality mock-ups or wireframes, they can be included as an appendix.

Often FAQs are divided into external (customer focused) and internal (focused on your company). The external FAQs are those that customers and/or the press will ask you about the product. These will include more detailed questions about how the product works, how much it costs, and how/where to buy it. Because these questions are product specific, they are unique to an individual PR/FAQ. For internal FAQs, there is a more standardized list of topics you will need to cover. Here are some of the typical areas to address.

Consumer Needs and Total Addressable Market (TAM)

- How many consumers have this need or problem?
- How big is the need?
- For how many consumers is this problem big enough that they are willing to spend money to do something about it?
- If so, how much money would they be willing to spend?
- How many of these consumers have the characteristics/capabilities/constraints necessary to make use of the product?

These consumer questions will enable you to identify the core customers by filtering out those who don't meet the product constraints. In the case of Melinda, for example, you would eliminate people who:

- don't have enough space on their front porch for this product
- don't have a front porch or similar outdoor area with access to the street at all (e.g., most apartment dwellers)
- don't have a suitable source of electricity
- wouldn't be pleased to have a large storage/mailbox on their front porch
- don't receive many deliveries or deliveries that need refrigeration

- don't live in areas where package theft is a problem
- don't have interest or ability to pay $299 to answer the need

Only a discrete number of people will pass through all these filters and be identified as belonging to the total addressable market.

Research into these questions (e.g., how many detached homes are there in a given area?) can help you estimate the total address-able market (TAM), but like any research, there will be a wide error bar. The author and readers of the PR/FAQ will ultimately have to decide on the size of the TAM based on the data gathered and their judgment about its relevance. With Melinda, this process would likely lead to the conclusion that the TAM is in fact pretty small.

Economics and P&L

- What are the per-unit economics of the device? That is, what is the expected gross profit and contribution profit per unit?
- What is the rationale for the price point you have chosen for the product?
- How much will we have to invest up front to build this prod-uct in terms of people, technology, inventory, warehouse space, and so on?

For this section of the PR/FAQ, ideally one or more members of your finance team will work with you to understand and cap-ture these costs so you can include a simplified table of the per-unit economics and a mini P&L in the document. A resourceful entrepreneur or product manager can do this work themselves if they do not have a finance manager or team.

For new products, the up-front investment is a major consider-ation. In the case of Melinda, there is a requirement for 77 people to work on the hardware and software, for an annualized cost of roughly $15 million. This means that the product idea needs to have the potential to earn well in excess of $15 million per year in gross profit to be worth building.

The consumer questions and economic analysis both have an effect on the product price point, and that price point, in turn, has an effect on the size of the total addressable market.

Price is a key variable in the authoring of your PR/FAQ. There may be special assumptions or considerations that have informed your calculation of the price point—perhaps making it relatively low or unexpectedly high—that need to be called out and explained. Some of the best new product proposals set a not-to-exceed price point because it forces the team to innovate within that constraint and face the tough trade-offs early on. The problem(s) associated with achieving that price point should be fully explained and explored in the FAQ. Suppose your research into Melinda leads you to conclude that to realize the largest possible TAM, you need to offer the product at no more than $99. The bill of materials (BOM), however, comes to $250. Now you have two choices to suggest. First, alter the specs, strip out features, or take other actions that will reduce the BOM to below $99. Second, construct a financial plan that shows heavy losses in the early days of release, but also shows that the losses can eventually be mitigated with BOM reductions as the product achieves scale or can be enhanced with some additional source of revenue (e.g., an associated service or subscription).

Dependencies

- How will we convince couriers (USPS, UPS, FedEx, Amazon Fulfillment, Instacart, etc.) to actually use this device instead of their current/standard delivery methods?
- How will we ensure that couriers (who don't work for you and over whom you have no control) will use the Melinda UI properly and bother to actually put packages in it instead of just leaving the package by the front door like they typically do?
- Won't it take more time (which is precious) for them to make a delivery than it does today?
- What third-party technologies are we dependent on for Melinda to function as promised?

A common mistake among less-seasoned product managers is to not fully consider how third parties who have their own agendas and incentives will interact with their product idea, or what potential regulatory or legal issues might arise.

The role of third parties is a major issue with Melinda, whose success largely depends on their involvement and proper execution. Without the correct package tracking data or the cooperation of the companies that own that data and the couriers who deliver the packages, Melinda (as described) would be useless. The only alternative would be for customers to manually enter their tracking information for every single delivery into the Melinda app, which they are unlikely to do—and even if they did, it would still require couriers to be willing and able to use it. A good PR/FAQ honestly and accurately assesses these dependencies and describes the specific concepts or plans for the product to solve them.

Feasibility

- What are the challenging product engineering problems we will need to solve?
- What are the challenging customer UI problems we will need to solve?
- What are the third-party dependencies we will need to solve?
- How will we manage the risk of the up-front investment required?

These questions are intended to help the author clarify to the reader what level of invention is required and what kind of challenges are involved in building this new product. These criteria vary from product to product, and there are different types of challenges ranging from technical to legal to financial to third-party partnerships and customer UI or acceptance.

With Melinda, the engineering challenges are probably quite manageable, since no new technologies need to be developed or employed. The user interface is also familiar. The third-party dependencies present the greatest challenge to making Melinda work.

Go Ahead?

It is important to note that, during our time with Amazon, most PR/FAQs never made it to a stage where they were launched as actual products. What this means is that a product manager will put in a lot of time exploring product ideas that never get to market. This may be because of the intense competition for resources and capital among the hundreds of PR/FAQs that are authored and presented each year within the company. Only the very best will rise to the top of the stack and get prioritized and resourced, whether the pool of capital comes from within a large company like Amazon or from a startup investor. The fact that most PR/FAQs don't get approved is a feature, not a bug. Spending time up front to think through all the details of a product, and to determine—without committing precious software development resources—which products not to build, preserves your company's resources to build products that will yield the highest impact for customers and your business.

Another one of the biggest benefits of a written PR/FAQ is that it enables the team to truly understand the specific constraints and problems that would prevent a new product idea from being viable and aligning on them. At that point, the product or leadership team must decide if they will keep working on the product, addressing the problems and constraints surfaced by the PR/FAQ and developing solutions that will potentially make the product viable, or if they will set it aside.

In the case of Melinda, the author and team would certainly come to the conclusion that this isn't a viable product for many reasons. The TAM may be just too small, no matter what the product price point. The product might be too bothersome to use, even if the functionality itself is familiar to most customers. It may be unrealistic that Amazon and Walmart would provide a data feed or that couriers would bother to use the product. The device may simply be too expensive to build and profitably sell for $299, no matter how big the TAM might grow to be.

This process enables a product team and the company leadership to gain a thorough understanding of the opportunity and the constraints. Leadership and management are often about deciding what *not* to do rather than what *to* do. Bringing clarity to why you aren't doing something is often as important as having clarity about what you are doing.

If, after the PR/FAQ process, the leadership team still believes in the product and wants it to become a reality, the process will have given them a thorough understanding of the problems that would need to be solved in order to move forward with it. Perhaps a problem can be solved through an acquisition or a partnership. Perhaps it can be solved with the passage of time—new technologies may become available, or the costs of the technology might come down. Perhaps the company decides that the problem or constraint is solvable, that the solution will require risk and cost, and that they are willing to assume that risk and cost because the TAM is large and therefore the potential rewards are great.

This last consideration came up frequently in reviews with Jeff, as we would wrestle with product ideas using the PR/FAQ process. A team might identify a hard problem during a review that we did not know how to solve, and didn't know if we *could* solve. Jeff would say something to the effect of, "We shouldn't be afraid of taking on hard problems if solving them would unlock substantial value."

Above all, keep in mind that the PR/FAQ is a living document. Once it is approved by the leadership team, it will almost certainly still be edited and changed (a process that should be directed by or reviewed with the leadership team). There is no guarantee that an idea expressed in an excellent PR/FAQ will move forward and become a product. As we've said, only a small percentage will get the green light. But this is not a drawback. It is, in fact, a huge benefit of the process—a considered, thorough, data-driven method for deciding when and how to invest development resources. Generating and evaluating great ideas is the real benefit of the Working Backwards process.

6

Metrics

Manage Your Inputs, Not Your Outputs

Why metrics become more important as a company grows. The metrics life cycle. The difference between input metrics and output metrics. Making sure your metrics are unbiased. Using metrics at business reviews. The key pitfalls of the review meeting.

* * *

Jeff and I (Colin) once visited a Fortune 500 company to meet privately with the CEO in his office. During our meeting, an assistant dashed in and handed the boss a sheet of paper. The CEO glanced at it, waved it at us, and proudly said, "Our stock is up 30 cents this morning!" His mood brightened, as if he had personally caused the rise.

As we drove to our next meeting, Jeff said, "There's nothing that CEO did to cause that 30-cent blip in the stock price." I agreed, and added that I wouldn't be surprised if the assistant had thrown multiple printouts in the recycle bin that morning when the blip wasn't so big. Would the same scene have played out if the share price had dropped 30 cents? The deeper lesson, one that we'll explore in this chapter, is this: share price is what Amazon calls an "output metric." The CEO, and companies in general, have very little ability to directly control output metrics. What's really important is to focus on the "controllable input metrics," the activities you directly control, which ultimately affect output metrics such as share price.

All too often, companies pay attention to the wrong signals, or lack the ability to see into key business trends, even while they feel positively awash in data. In this chapter, we'll show you how to select and measure metrics that will enable you to focus on which activities will drive your business in a meaningful and positive direction. We'll look at how Amazon chooses its metrics by focusing on controllable input metrics, which are the drivers that, when managed well, can lead to profitable growth. We'll talk about how we present and interpret data, and how rigorous metrics ownership drives accountability. We'll also share some hard lessons we learned when optimizing the wrong metrics, and why we struggled at times to put even the best of our data to good use. We'll show what can happen if your company focuses its attention on the wrong kind of data trends, and we'll describe some common pitfalls.

Unlike the topics covered in previous chapters, there is no single playbook or written set of rules for how Amazon uses metrics to run its businesses. The material we'll discuss is based on our own Amazon experiences as well as discussions we've had with other current and past senior Amazon leaders.

Staying Close to the Business

We've alluded to Amazon's growing pains. Not long into the company's trajectory, there reached a point when Jeff could no longer see each part of the process with his own eyes. Firsthand experience and direct observation were replaced by the proxies of management layers and canned reports. Some business-critical information, such as number of new customers and sales by category, was simply there for the taking and easy to collect. But there were other kinds of information that we could only produce with a series of bespoke ad hoc reports. It was difficult to reliably and quickly answer the question, "How is the business trending?"

This early history is fascinating, and the development of every metric has its own story, but let's skip ahead to 2000 when Amazon recognized $2.76 billion in annual revenue and its famously data-driven culture was prevalent throughout the company. During the fourth quarter—in which our net sales ended up increasing by 44 percent over Q4 of the previous year—there was a daily "war room" meeting where the senior Amazon leaders would analyze a three-page metrics deck and figure out what actions we'd have to take to successfully respond to the demands of what was shaping up to be a record-breaking holiday season. A key component of the deck was the backlog, which was a tally of the orders we had taken minus the shipments we had made. The backlog indicated the amount of work we'd need to do to make sure our customers received their gifts before the holidays. It would take a massive, concentrated effort. Many corporate employees were conscripted for work in the fulfillment centers and customer service. Colin worked the night shift from 7 p.m. to 5:30 a.m. in the Campbellsville, Kentucky, fulfillment center and telecommuted from the Best Western hotel to stay on top of his day job. Bill stayed in Seattle to keep the Video store running smoothly during the day and traveled south 2.5 miles each night to work in the Seattle fulfillment center.

It was touch and go for a while. If we overpromised, we'd ruin a customer's holiday. If we underpromised and stopped accepting orders, we were basically telling our customers to go elsewhere for their holiday needs.

It was close, but we made it. Shortly after that holiday season we held a postmortem, out of which was born the Weekly Business Review (WBR). The purpose of the WBR was to provide a more comprehensive lens through which to see the business.

The WBR has proved very useful over the years and is widely adopted throughout the company. We'll show how the WBR is constructed and implemented so the company can improve each and every week. It has a fractal nature that allows us to easily adapt to different situations, from small groups to billion-dollar businesses. Small teams, business category lines, and the entire online retail business all have their own WBRs. In addition to our discussion of the benefits of the WBR, we'll point out some common mistakes in their design and execution, including a few big ones we made ourselves. Though we focus on the WBR in this chapter, the same principles and techniques can be applied wherever you need to look at data to help make informed decisions.

The Metrics Life Cycle

When the retail, operations, and finance teams began to construct the initial Amazon WBR, they turned to a well-known Six Sigma process improvement method called DMAIC, an acronym for Define-Measure-Analyze-Improve-Control.[1] Should you decide to implement a Weekly Business Review for your business, we recommend following the DMAIC steps as well. The order of the steps matters. Progressing through this metrics life cycle in this order can prevent a lot of frustration and rework, allowing you to achieve your goals faster.

Define

First, you need to select and define the metrics you want to measure. The right choice of metrics will deliver clear, actionable guidance. A poor choice will result in a statement of the obvious, a nonspecific presentation of everything your company is doing. Donald Wheeler, in his book *Understanding Variation*, explains:

> Before you can improve any system . . . you must understand how the inputs affect the outputs of the system. You must be able to change the inputs (and possibly the system) in order to achieve the desired results. This will require a sustained effort, constancy of purpose, and an environment where continual improvement is the operating philosophy.[2]

Amazon takes this philosophy to heart, focusing most of its effort on leading indicators (we call these "controllable input metrics") rather than lagging indicators ("output metrics"). Input metrics track things like selection, price, or convenience—factors that Amazon can control through actions such as adding items to the catalog, lowering cost so prices can be lowered, or positioning inventory to facilitate faster delivery to customers. Output metrics—things like orders, revenue, and profit—are important, but they generally can't be directly manipulated in a sustainable manner over the long term. Input metrics measure things that, done right, bring about the desired results in your output metrics.

We can't tell you how many times we've heard people say, when talking about a recently launched Amazon initiative, "You can do that at Amazon because you don't care about profits." That simply isn't true. Profits are just as important to Amazon as to any other major company. Other output metrics like weekly revenue, total customers, Prime subscribers, and (over the long term) stock price—or more accurately, free cash flow per share—matter very much to Amazon. Early detractors mistook Amazon's emphasis on input metrics for a lack of interest in profits and pronounced the company doomed, only to be stunned by its growth over the ensuing years.

1. The Flywheel: Input Metrics Lead to Output Metrics and Back Again

In 2001 Jeff drew the simple diagram below on a napkin to illustrate Amazon's virtuous cycle, also called the "Amazon flywheel." This sketch, inspired by the flywheel concept in Jim Collins's book *Good to Great*, is a model of how a set of controllable input metrics drives a single key output metric—in this case, growth. In this closed-loop system, as you inject energy into any one element, or all of them, the flywheel spins faster:

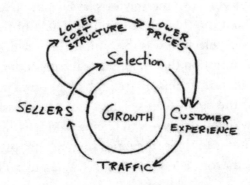

Since it's a cycle, you can start at any input. The metrics for Customer Experience, for example, could include speed of shipping, breadth of selection, richness of product information, ease of use, and so forth. Watch what happens when we improve customer experience:

- Better customer experience leads to *more traffic.*
- More traffic attracts *more sellers* seeking those buyers.
- More sellers lead to *wider selection.*
- Wider selection enhances *customer experience*, completing the circle.
- The cycle drives *growth*, which in turn *lowers cost structure.*
- Lower costs lead to *lower prices*, improving *customer experience*, and the flywheel spins faster.

The Amazon flywheel captures the major aspect of what makes Amazon's retail business successful. Therefore, it should be no surprise that almost all the metrics discussed in the WBR can be categorized into one of the flywheel elements. In fact, the first page of the WBR deck has a picture of the very same flywheel above.

2. Identify the Correct, Controllable Input Metrics

This step sounds easy but can be deceptively tricky, and the details matter. One mistake we made at Amazon as we started expanding from books into other categories was choosing input metrics focused around selection, that is, how many items Amazon offered for sale. Each item is described on a "detail page" that includes a description of the item, images, customer reviews, availability (e.g., ships in 24 hours), price, and the "buy" box or button. One of the metrics we initially chose for selection was the number of new detail pages created, on the assumption that more pages meant better selection.

Once we identified this metric, it had an immediate effect on the actions of the retail teams. They became excessively focused on adding new detail pages—each team added tens, hundreds, even thousands of items to their categories that had not previously been available on Amazon. For some items, the teams had to establish relationships with new manufacturers and would often buy inventory that had to be housed in the fulfillment centers.

We soon saw that an increase in the number of detail pages, while seeming to improve selection, did not produce a rise in sales, the output metric. Analysis showed that the teams, while chasing an increase in the number of items, had sometimes purchased products that were not in high demand. This activity did cause a bump in a different output metric—the cost of holding inventory—and the low-demand items took up valuable space in fulfillment centers that should have been reserved for items that were in high demand.

When we realized that the teams had chosen the wrong input metric—which was revealed via the WBR process—we changed the metric to reflect consumer demand instead. Over multiple WBR meetings, we asked ourselves, "If we work to change this selection metric, as currently defined, will it result in the desired output?" As we gathered more data and observed the business, this particular selection metric evolved over time from

- number of detail pages, which we refined to
- number of detail page views (you don't get credit for a new detail page if customers don't view it), which then became
- the percentage of detail page views where the products were in stock (you don't get credit if you add items but can't keep them in stock), which was ultimately finalized as
- the percentage of detail page views where the products were in stock and immediately ready for two-day shipping, which ended up being called Fast Track In Stock.

You'll notice a pattern of trial and error with metrics in the points above, and this is an essential part of the process. The key is to persistently test and debate as you go. For example, Jeff was concerned that the Fast Track In Stock metric was too narrow. Jeff Wilke argued that the metric would yield broad systematic improvements across the retail business. They agreed to stick with it for a while, and it worked out just as Jeff Wilke had anticipated.

Fast Track In Stock, combined with inventory holding cost,

provided the teams with an actionable and correct set of input metrics to add selection in a way that would profitably drive sales. Once you have metrics solidified, you can then set a standard and measure teams against that standard. For instance, we decided that in each category, we wanted 95 percent of detail page views to display a product that was in stock and ready for immediate shipping.

These new input metrics created a substantial change in the work and behavior of the category teams. Their focus shifted to reviewing other websites and retail stores and combing through Amazon search logs to determine what items people were searching for in each category but weren't finding on Amazon. From this they could develop a "stack-ranked" or prioritized list of manufacturers to approach and items to acquire that mattered most to consumers. Rather than focusing on the sheer number of items added, they could instead add the items that would make the biggest impact on sales. Sounds simple, but with the wrong input metrics or an input metric that is too crude, your efforts may not be rewarded with an improvement in your output metrics. The right input metrics get the entire organization focused on the things that matter most. Finding exactly the right one is an iterative process that needs to happen with every input metric.

Note: Most of the examples we give in this chapter are of large companies with substantial resources. But DMAIC and the WBR process is eminently scalable. Your level of investment should be on par with the resources you have.

If you are a nonprofit, figure out a modest number of key metrics that reliably show how well you are doing. For example, how often do you contact your donor base, and how does that frequency affect your funding?

A big mistake people make is not getting started. Most WBRs have humble beginnings and undergo substantial changes and improvement over time.

Measure

Building tools to collect the metrics data you need may sound rather simple, but—like choosing the metrics themselves—we've found that it takes time and concerted effort to get the collection tools right. In chapter two, we discussed how important it is to understand and remove bias in the interview process. Removing bias is just as important in metrics. Each of Jeff's direct reports who ran a business unit had an inherent bias to choose metrics and collect data that would show that their units were trending positive. It's just human nature to want to succeed.

In the early 2000s, Jeff and CFO Warren Jenson—who was succeeded in 2002 by Tom Szkutak—stated explicitly how critical it was for the finance team to uncover and report the unbiased truth. Jeff, Warren, and Tom all insisted that, regardless of whether the business was going well or poorly, the finance team should "have no skin in the game other than to call it like they see it," based on what the data revealed. This truth-seeking mentality permeated the entire finance team and was critical because it ensured that company leaders would have unvarnished, unbiased information available to them as they made important decisions. Having an independent person or team involved with measurement can help you seek out and eliminate biases in your data.

The next step after determining which tools to use is to collect the data and present it in a usable format. Often the data you want will be scattered across different systems and may take some serious software resources to compile, aggregate, and display correctly. Do not compromise here. Make the investment. If you don't, you may find that you are flying blind with respect to some important aspect of the business.

As you develop the collection tools, make sure they are measuring what you think they are measuring. Diving deep to understand exactly how the data is collected helps spot potential problems. Consider the metric "in stock," which attempts to answer the question, "What percentage of my products are immediately available to purchase and ship?" There are many ways to define and collect data about in-stock items—for example:

- We take a snapshot of our catalog each night at 11 p.m., determine which items are in stock, and weight each item by trailing 30-day product sales. That is, if product A has sold 30 units in the past month and product B has sold 10 units in the past month, and they are both out of stock at the time the in-stock measurement is recorded, product A will impact the in-stock metric three times more than product B will.

- We add software to the product pages that performs the following actions. Every time a product page is displayed, we add one to the metric "Total Number of Product Pages Displayed." If that product is in stock when it is displayed, we add one to the metric "Total Number of In-Stock Product Pages Displayed." At the end of the day, we divide the "Total Number of In-Stock Product Pages Displayed" by the "Total Number of Product Pages Displayed," to get our overall in-stock metric for the day. For example, suppose you displayed one million detail pages total across every product in your catalog, and 850,000 of those product pages displayed a product that was in stock. Then your demand-weighted in-stock percentage for that day would be 85 percent. Products that customers view more have a greater impact on this metric than products that are viewed rarely.

Each of these metrics measures in-stock in a different way and can yield quite a different result for the same business on the same day. The first metric may skew the data depending on the time of day the company receives the bulk of its inventory. If most of the inventory comes in at night, the item could have been out of stock for most of the day but replenished just before the in-stock data is collected. The result will be that the in-stock performance will look better to the company than what the bulk of the customers actually experienced that day. And if a popular item is out of stock for a long period of time, it will have less of an impact on the metric each day since the metric is weighted by trailing 30-day sales of that item.

The second metric, while more expensive to collect (at least in the short run), is a more accurate representation of what customers experienced that day. It captures, from a customer point of view, what percent of the time they experienced that Amazon was in-stock on the item(s) they viewed. The first metric is inward-facing and operations-centric, while the second metric is outward-facing and customer-centric. Start with the customer and work backwards by aligning your metrics with the customer experience.

One often-overlooked piece of the puzzle is determining how to audit metrics. Unless you have a regular process to inde-pendently validate the metric, assume that over time something will cause it to drift and skew the numbers. If the metric is im-portant, find out a way to do a separate measurement or gather customer anecdotes and see if the information trues up with the metric you're looking at. So, a recent example would be testing for COVID-19 by region. It is not enough to look at the number of positive tests in your region as compared to another region with a population of a similar size. You must also look at the number of tests per capita performed in each region. Since both the number of positive tests and the number of tests per capita in each location will keep changing, you will need to keep updating your audit of the measurements.*

Analyze

This stage has been given many different labels by different teams—reducing variance, making the process predictable, getting the pro-cess under control, to name a few. But the Analyze stage is all about developing a comprehensive understanding of what drives your metrics. Until you know all the external factors that impact the process, it will be difficult to implement positive changes.

The objective in this stage is separating signals from noise in

---

* If you, like the CEO mentioned at the beginning of the chapter, still insist that the company stock price be hand-delivered to you each morning, you should require that the paper be printed at exactly the same time each day, insist that the paper have a time stamp on it, and once in a while look at the price at the stated collection time yourself to see if it trues up with what's on the paper you've been handed. We don't recommend this process, but it's better than what was there before!

data and then identifying and addressing root causes. Why is it we can pick 100 items per hour in a fulfillment center on one shift and 30 items per hour on another? Why are we able to display pages in under 100 milliseconds most of the time yet some pages take 10 seconds to display? Why are customer service contacts per order always higher on Mondays than on other days of the week?

When Amazon teams come across a surprise or a perplexing problem with the data, they are relentless until they discover the root cause. Perhaps the most widely used technique at Amazon for these situations is the Correction of Errors (COE) process, based upon the "Five Whys" method developed at Toyota and used by many companies worldwide. When you see an anomaly, ask why it happened and iterate with another "Why?" until you get to the underlying factor that was the real culprit. This COE process requires the team who had a significant error or problem to write a document describing the problem or error, and to drill down on what caused it by asking and answering "Why?" five times in order to get to the true root cause.

Charlie Bell, an SVP in AWS and a great operational guru at Amazon, put it aptly when he said, "When you encounter a problem, the probability you're actually looking at the actual root cause of the problem in the initial 24 hours is pretty close to zero, because it turns out that behind every issue there's a very interesting story."

In the end, if you stick with identifying the true root causes of variation and eliminating them, you'll have a predictable, in-control process that you can optimize.

Improve

Once you have developed a solid understanding of how your process works along with a robust set of metrics, you can devote energy to improving the process. For instance, if you reach the point where you can reliably achieve a weekly 95 percent in-stock rate, you can then ask, "What changes do we need to make to get to 98 percent?"

If you have progressed through the prior three steps (Define, Measure, and Analyze), then your actions to improve the metric will have a higher chance of succeeding because you'll be responding to signals instead of noise. If you immediately jump to the Improve stage, you'll be working with imperfect information on a process you likely don't fully understand yet, and the actions you take will be much less likely to generate desired results. In the forthcoming example, we'll show how a large Amazon department neglected to complete the first three steps, which caused lots of thrash and yielded no meaningful results.

After you have been operating a WBR for a while, you may notice that a metric is no longer yielding useful information. In that case, it's okay to prune it from the deck.

Control

This final stage is all about ensuring that your processes are operating normally and performance is not degrading over time. As your fundamental understanding of what drives the business improves, it's common for the WBR to become an exception-based meeting rather than a regular one for discussing each and every metric.

Another thing that can happen in this stage is that you'll identify processes that can be automated. Once a process is well understood and the decision-making logic can be encoded in software or hardware, it's a potential candidate for automation. Forecasting and purchasing are two examples of processes that were eventually automated at Amazon. It took years of collaborative effort among category buyers and software engineers—and involving plenty of trial and error—to automate the forecasting and purchasing decisions across the hundreds of millions of products in Amazon's catalog. But it's now done with greater accuracy than even a large team of buyers could do manually.

The WBR: Metrics at Work

At Amazon, the Weekly Business Review (WBR) is the place where metrics are put into action. We'll talk first about how data presentation (mostly graphic) is designed to draw attention where it's most needed. Second, we'll describe the meeting itself, how it's structured to maximize results, and some cautionary notes about how it can fail.

The Deck

Each meeting begins with the virtual or printed distribution of the data package, which contains the weekly snapshot of graphs, tables, and occasional explanatory notes for all your metrics. In this book, we use the term "the deck" to refer to this overall data package. Data visualization software has advanced greatly since the advent of the WBR deck. There are many excellent choices ranging in price from free to modest for smaller organizations, while more advanced tools are available for large enterprises. In practice, many of today's organizations do not assemble a single WBR deck. Instead, separate departments rely on a virtual deck where they can access these data visualization tools to generate the information for their own area. We'll show you a few example graphs in the pages that follow, but first let's review some of the Amazon deck's distinctive features:

> *The deck represents a data-driven, end-to-end view of the business.* While departments shown on org charts are simple and separate, business activities usually are not. The deck presents a consistent, end-to-end review of the business each week that is designed to follow the customer experience with Amazon. This flow from topic to topic can reveal the interconnectedness of seemingly independent activities.
>
> *It's mostly charts, graphs, and data tables.* With so many metrics to review, written narrative or explanatory notes would undercut the efficiency of the read-through. One notable exception we'll discuss below is how to deal with anecdotes.
>
> *How many metrics should you review?* There is no magic number or formula. Coming up with the right metrics takes time, and you should seek to improve them continuously. Over time you and your team should modify, add, and remove metrics based on the strength and quality of the signal each emits.

Emerging patterns are a key point of focus. Individual data points can tell useful stories, especially when compared to other time periods. In the WBR, Amazon analyzes trend lines to highlight challenges as they emerge rather than waiting for them to be summed up in quarterly or yearly results.

Graphs plot results against comparable prior periods. Metrics are intended to trend better over time. Care is taken to ensure that prior periods are structured to provide apples-to-apples comparisons so as not to highlight false variances due to predictable things like holidays or weekends.

Graphs show two or more timelines, for example, trailing 6-week and trailing 12-month. Trend lines for the short term can magnify small but important issues that are hard to spot when averaged out over longer periods.

Anecdotes and exception reporting are woven into the deck. One trait of an Amazon WBR deck that people often remark upon is the liberal use of two tools: anecdotes and exception reporting—that is, the description of an element that falls outside some standard or usual situation. Both tools enable you to dive into examples that contain something that doesn't follow the natural or accustomed patterns and that can sometimes, but not always, reveal a defect, a broken process, or a problem with system logic. The use of anecdotes and exception reporting has enabled leaders to audit at scale in a very detailed way. This ability to flag, evaluate, examine, dig deep, and seek specific solutions for a wide range of issues in a very large organization is something we've noticed is uniquely Amazonian, and it's helpful for small and large businesses alike. We'll provide some examples.

The Meeting

What happens inside the WBR is critical execution not normally visible outside the company. A well-run WBR meeting is defined by intense customer focus, deep dives into complex challenges, and insistence on high standards and operational excellence. One may wonder, at what level is it appropriate for executives to shift focus to output metrics? After all, companies and their senior executives are routinely judged by output metrics like revenue and profit. Jeff knows this well, in part based on his time spent working at a Wall Street investment firm. The simple answer is that the focus does not shift at any level of management. Yes, executives know their output metrics backward and forward. But if they don't continue to focus on inputs, they lose control over and visibility into the tools that generate output results. Therefore, at Amazon, everyone from the individual contributor to the CEO must have detailed knowledge of input metrics to know whether the organization is maximizing outputs.

The deck is usually owned by someone in finance. Or more accurately, the data in the deck are certified as accurate by finance. However, because multiple people in the room are responsible for each section of the deck, no one "runs" the meeting per se. For most companies, excluding large companies with tens of billions in revenue and multiple big divisions, the audience for the WBR is the CEO and CFO. The meeting attendees should include the executive team and their direct reports as well as anyone who owns or is speaking to any specific section in the deck. Because technology now enables virtual meetings, it is possible to include many more people in the meeting. Adding more junior members of the company to the WBR can increase their engagement in the business and further their growth and development—by allowing them to observe the discussions and thinking of more seasoned leaders.

It is worth noting here that, at Amazon, even the most senior executives review the full WBR deck of metrics, including all the inputs and outputs. Metrics—as well as anecdotes about the customer experience—are the area where the leadership principle Dive Deep is most clearly demonstrated by senior leaders. They carefully examine the trends and changes in the metrics; audit incidents, failures, and customer anecdotes; and consider whether the input metrics should be updated in some way to improve the outputs.

The WBR is an important embodiment of how metrics are put into action at Amazon, but it isn't the only one. Metrics dashboards and reports are established by every engineering, operations, and business unit at the company. In many cases metrics are monitored in real time, and each critical technical and operational service receives an "alarm" to ensure that failures and outages are identified instantly. In other cases, teams rely on dashboards that are updated hourly or daily for their metrics. The WBR meeting and process is distinctive in how it has enabled Amazon to drive the flywheel faster every year, which in turn has yielded exceptional results.

We use consistent and familiar formatting to speed interpretation

A good deck uses a consistent format throughout—the graph design, time periods covered, color palette, symbol set (for current year/prior year/goal), and the same number of charts on every page wherever possible. Some data naturally lend themselves to different presentations, but the default is to display in the standard format.

Amazon thereby looks at the same set of data every week, in the same order, and gets a holistic view of the business. The team builds up expertise in spotting trends and picks up the rhythm of the review; anomalies stand out more distinctly, and the meeting runs more efficiently.

We focus on variances and don't waste time on the expected

People like talking about their area, especially when they're delivering as expected, and even more so when they exceed expectations, but WBR time is precious. If things are operating normally, say "Nothing to see here" and move along. The goal of the meeting is to discuss exceptions and what is being done about them. The status quo needs no elaboration.

Our business owners own metrics and are prepared to explain variances

Amazon business owners are responsible for tracking the success of their area as defined by their metrics. In the weekly review, the owners, not the finance team, are expected to provide a crisp explanation for variances against expectations. As a result, business owners quickly become adept at spotting trends. Every week they review the deck before the WBR and respond by discussing what action they plan to take to address the variances.

This is a hard-earned lesson; we've seen a metric owner display their metrics in front of a group where it's obviously the first time that person has seen the data. That's a big mistake, a waste of everyone else's time, and will most definitely result in a kerfuffle with the senior leader in the room. By the time the WBR meeting occurs, each metric owner should have thoroughly analyzed the metrics they own.

Sometimes even the well prepared are hit with a question to which the right answer isn't immediately apparent. In that case, the owner is expected to say something like, "I don't know. We are still analyzing the data and will get back to you." This is preferable to guessing, or worse, making something up on the fly.

We keep operational and strategic discussions separate

The WBR is a tactical operational meeting to analyze performance trends of the prior week. At Amazon, it was not the time to discuss new strategies, project updates, or upcoming product releases.

We try not to browbeat (it's not the Inquisition)

It's okay to dig into a meaningful variation that needs more attention, and to point out when high standards have not been met. Still, success demands an environment where people don't feel intimidated when talking about something that went wrong in their area. Some Amazon teams were better at exemplifying this than others were, and, quite honestly, it's an area where the company could improve. Sometimes WBRs can devolve into downright hostile environments, especially at times when a major slip-up caused the comments to focus more on the presenter than on the issue. While fear may be a good short-term motivator, it will ultimately cause more problems than it solves.

Mistakes should be a learning experience for all. If people become afraid of pointing out their own mistakes because they will feel humiliated in front of their peers, it's human nature for them to do whatever they can to hide those mistakes in future meetings. Variances that get glossed over are lost learning opportunities for everybody. To prevent this, mistakes should be acknowledged as a chance to take ownership, understand the root cause, and learn from the experience. Some tension is unavoidable and appropriate, but we think it's better to establish a culture where it's not just okay, it's actually encouraged to openly discuss mistakes.

We make transitions easy

We've attended many executive meetings where the most expensive team in the company wastes valuable time, for example, fumbling the handoff of the presentation from one person to the next because the second person's dashboard doesn't load easily, or what have you. To make these transitions quick and seamless, you have to put in the up-front work. The WBR is Amazon's most expensive and impactful weekly meeting, and every second counts—plan ahead and run the meeting efficiently.

Anatomy of a Metrics Chart

A WBR can easily include charts that number in the hundreds, and that much data benefits enormously from consistency of presentation. In our sample charts below, we've included different types of metrics from different functional business areas to illustrate the flexibility of this approach.

Zooming In: Weekly and Monthly Metrics on a Single Graph

As we noted above, at Amazon we routinely place our trailing 6 weeks and trailing 12 months side by side on the same x-axis. The effect is like adding a "zoom" function to a static graph that gives you a snapshot of a shorter time period, with the added bonus that you're seeing both the monthly graph and the "zoomed-in" version of it simultaneously. Here we provide an example of what that dual view looks like in practice. (The following charts do not contain actual data; they are for illustration purposes only.)

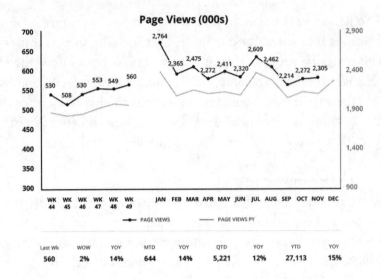

This graphic measures page views for a business, and conveys a lot of data in a small space:

- The gray line is prior year, the black line is current year
- The left graph, those first 6 data points, shows the trailing 6 weeks
- The right graph, with 12 data points, shows the entire trailing year month by month
- This built-in "zoom" adds clarity by magnifying the most recent data, which the 12-month graph puts into context.

At the bottom of the chart, we call out additional key data points, most of which compare one period to another.

Why We Watch Year-over-Year (YOY) Trends

This example graph, similar to ones you may see in a typical monthly business review (the monthly version of the WBR), compares actual monthly revenue against both planned revenue and prior year revenue. As you can see below, it looks like we are beating plan and growing at a decent clip year over year:

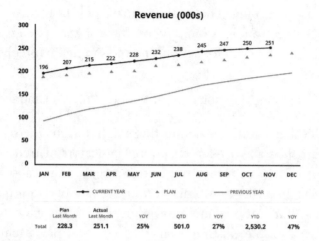

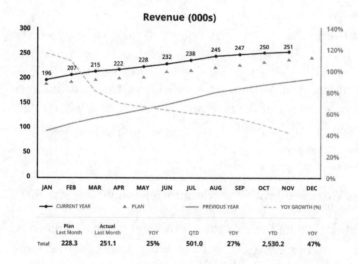

There's nothing to see here, so let's move on—right? Maybe not. Here's the same graph with one additional trend line: YOY growth rates plotted with a dotted line against a secondary y-axis:

Without the dotted line, you might not have noticed the rate at which the current and projected year trends are slowly converging. Adding YOY *growth rates* in addition to the underlying metric you are measuring is a great way to spot trends. In this example, YOY growth has actually decelerated 67 percent since January with no signs of plateauing. The business may look healthy at a cursory glance, but trouble is looming on the horizon. The enhanced graphic reveals the need for action that the simpler graph obscures.

Output Metrics Show Results. Input Metrics Provide Guidance.

There's another familiar lesson in this graph: output metrics—the data we graphed above—are far poorer indicators of trend causes than input metrics. It turned out in this case that the cause of our decelerating growth was a reduction in the rate of acquiring new customers—but nothing in these graphs gives any clue to that cause. With a sizable existing business, if you only pay attention to the output metric "revenue," you typically won't see the effects of new customer deceleration for quite some time. However, if you look at input metrics instead—things like "new customers," "new customer revenue," and "existing customer revenue"—you will detect the signal much earlier, and with a much clearer call to action.

Not Every Chart Compares Against Goals

Some WBR charts don't include goals, but that's often appropriate. If the goal of the metric is to spot trends or highlight when a process is out of control, or if we don't have a target at all (e.g., percentage of Android vs iOS mobile users), plotting against a goal is not necessary.

Data Combined with Anecdote to Tell the Whole Story

Numerical data become more powerful when combined with real-life customer stories. The Dive Deep leadership principle states, "Leaders operate at all levels, stay connected to the details, audit frequently, and are skeptical when metrics and anecdotes differ. No task is beneath them."

Amazon employs many techniques to ensure that anecdotes reach the teams that own and operate a service. One example is a program called the Voice of the Customer. The customer service department routinely collects and summarizes customer feedback and presents it during the WBR, though not necessarily every week. The chosen feedback does not always reflect the most commonly received complaint, and the CS department has wide latitude on what to present. When the stories are read at the WBR, they are often painful to hear because they highlight just how much we let customers down. But they always provide a learning experience and an opportunity for us to improve.

One Voice of the Customer story was about an incident when our software barraged a few credit cards with repeated $1.00 pre-authorizations that normally happen only once per order. The customers weren't charged, and such pre-authorizations expire after a few days, but while they were pending, they counted against credit limits. Usually, this would not have much of an effect on the customer. But one customer wrote to say that just after buying an item on Amazon, she went to buy medicine for her child, and her card was declined. She asked that we help resolve the issue so she could purchase the medicine her child needed. At first, an investigation into her complaint revealed that an edge-case bug—another way of saying a rare occurrence—had bumped her card balance over the limit. Many companies would dismiss such cases as outliers, and thus not worthy of attention, on the assumption that they rarely happen and are too expensive to fix. At Amazon, such cases were regularly attended to because they *would* happen again and because the investigation often revealed adjacent problems that needed to be solved. What at first looked to be just an edge case turned out to be more significant. The bug had caused problems in other areas that we did not initially notice. We quickly fixed the problem for her and for all other impacted customers.

These stories remind us that the work we do has direct impact on customers' lives. There are comparable programs that capture similar anecdotes for Amazon's third-party sellers and corporate AWS customers.

Exception reports come in many flavors, but the following Contribution Profit (CP) example should illustrate the basic concept and its usefulness. CP is defined as the incremental money generated after selling an item and deducting the variable costs associated with that item. It's essentially the money the company has left over after the sale of the item, which goes to pay for the fixed costs of the business and, ideally after that, contributes a profit. There is a CP Exception report that lists the top ten CP negative products (ones that did not generate a profit) within a category for the previous week. Doing a deep dive into these ten products, which often vary from week to week, can reveal very useful information about problems that require action. Here are a few findings that could result from reviewing a top-ten CP negative report:

- CP was negative due to price markdowns that were necessary because we had purchased too many of a certain item, which took up valuable fulfillment center space and capital. The purchase was initiated by the automated purchasing system that had been fed faulty input data. Action: investigate the source of the faulty input data to correct the system.
- CP was negative due to price markdowns originating from a manual purchase order error. The order quantity the buyer entered on the purchase order was too large, and they did not follow the correct process due to a lack of training. Action: use the incident as a teaching moment.
- CP was negative due to faulty cost allocation. The finance system was not allocating costs correctly for a certain class of item. Action: fix the cost allocation system.
- CP was negative because the logistics provider charged more than double the appropriate fee for shipping a particular item. The provider charged the higher fee based on incorrect size and weight information listed for the item in the catalog. Action: fix the catalog data and come up with a plan to put a mechanism in place to prevent the same error from happening for other items in the catalog.
- CP was negative because the item is sold at a low price but is expensive to ship. Whiteboards and yard rakes are examples of products that can fall into this category. Action: evaluate whether these items should be stocked and sold or some

other change should be made, such as changing suppliers or changing the default shipping method.

Data and anecdotes make a powerful combination when they're in sync, and they are a valuable check on one another when they are not.

Perhaps the most powerful anecdote in this regard features Jeff himself. Though it happened outside the WBR, it's worth mentioning here. Amazon has a program called Customer Connection, which is mandatory for corporate employees above a certain level. While the details have changed over the years, the premise has remained the same. Every two years the corporate employee is required to become a customer service agent for a few days. The employee gets some basic refresher training from a CS agent, listens in on calls, watches email/chat interactions, and then handles some customer contacts directly. Once they learn the tools and policies, they perform some or all of those tasks under the supervision of a CS agent. (One of my own calls was from a customer whose neighbor's dog had eaten his Amazon package. He offered to send us the uneaten bits to prove his case.)

Jeff is not exempted from this program. While I was working as his shadow, it came time for his Customer Connection recertification, and we dutifully traveled an hour each day to the customer service center in Tacoma, Washington. Jeff was particularly good with customers over the phone, though he was sometimes overly generous. He gave one customer a full product refund when the policy was to refund the shipping cost only.

On the first day of training, we listened to the CS agent handle a few calls. On one call, the customer complained that her lawn furniture had arrived damaged. The CS agent asked for the product number. As the customer was looking for it, the CS agent muted the call, and said to us, "I bet she's referring to this lawn chair," and pointed to the product on the Amazon site. Sure enough, when the customer read out the number from the packing slip it was the one that the CS had predicted it would be. Jeff and I raised our eyebrows in surprise but didn't want to interrupt the call.

After the issue had been resolved and the call ended, Jeff asked, "How did you know the customer was going to say this?" The CS agent responded that it happened quite often with this newly listed product. The packaging was inadequate, and the furniture often got banged or bruised in transit.

Jeff had recently been learning about how Toyota approached quality control and continuous improvement. One technique they used in their automobile assembly line was the Andon Cord. The car-in-progress moves along the line, and each employee adds a part or performs a task. When any worker notices a quality problem, they are authorized to pull a cord that stops the entire assembly line. A team of specialists swarms to the cord-puller's station, troubleshoots the issue, and develops a fix so the error never happens again.

Here was a similar situation at Amazon, except without the Andon Cord. The CS agent knew of a problem but had no way to improve the process. All the agent could do was offer a concession, make an apology, and ship a new product. We did have a process where each category manager looked at their monthly performance, including products with higher return rates and customer service inquiries. So this issue would have eventually been detected and fixed. But it likely would have taken several weeks and too many additional dissatisfied customers before that would happen.

As we considered the problem of the damaged lawn furniture before the next call arrived, Jeff blurted out, "We need an Andon Cord for customer service." There was no assembly line to halt, but the CS agent would be given the authority to click on what we called "the big red button" on their control screen. Once that button was clicked, two things happened: the "Add to Cart" and "1-Click" buttons would disappear from the product page so no customers could buy that product, and the category manager would immediately be notified that purchasing for one of their products had been disabled until they could investigate and fix the issue.

It took some time to put Jeff's idea into operation. We had to build the tools that would remove the Buy Now or Add to Cart button and alert the appropriate internal teams, put together the necessary reporting infrastructure, and train the CS team on how and when to press the big red button. There was some concern that the big red button would be pressed too often. Selling products on a regular basis, after all, was quite important for the health of the company.

That concern proved to be unwarranted—the CS agents were not overly zealous in pressing that button. It turns out that the Amazon version of the Andon Cord empowered the right people, those on the front lines who were talking directly to customers. It surfaced serious issues as soon as they were noticed. It proved once again that giving employees the right tools to solve problems and relying on their good judgment is a powerful combination. It is used widely across Amazon.

That story has been told many times and proves the power of anecdote to illuminate data and make it memorable.

* * *

Now, as effective as the WBR process can be, it can also go astray in several ways, including poor meeting management, focusing on normal variations rather than signals, and looking at the right data but in the wrong way.

Pitfall 1: Disaster Meetings

One large software group, run by a senior leader who is no longer at Amazon, had memorably rough WBR meetings. Learning and taking ownership of problems and their solutions were two important goals of the WBR process, and on that front these meetings were a huge missed opportunity. They wasted a lot of everyone's time.

One issue was that the attendee list got more and more bloated, and we had to keep finding bigger conference rooms to fit everyone. Likewise, the number of metrics we were trying to track kept ballooning—sometimes for the better, but more often for the worse.

The meetings were also just really unpleasant. There was a lack of ground rules and decorum, with quite a bit of interruption and sniping. Any anomaly was blood in the water, with accusatory questions fired at the presenter. The conversation would quickly regress, as multiple people, usually with little to add, would chime in—seemingly to show off, or to curry favor. Worse yet, some of these lengthy asides seemed to be aimed at running out the clock—with the speaker extending unproductive conversations before their own area would come under fire.

Meetings like that were painful to attend. The Earn Trust leadership principle exists in part to prevent this behavior from occurring. It states, "Leaders listen attentively, speak candidly, and treat others respectfully. They are vocally self-critical, even when doing so is awkward or embarrassing. Leaders do not believe their or their team's body odor smells of perfume. They benchmark themselves and their teams against the best." But these meetings, in the early days, clearly exemplified where we failed to live up to that principle. The original, well-intentioned meeting was set up to improve the software systems from one week to the next. But it gained a life of its own, and sometimes turned a roomful of smart people with probing questions into an angry mob, devouring those who could make a difference and robbing them of their very will to succeed.

What should we have done? Even though, as we've mentioned, there is no one person running the meeting—different people take over for different slides—the most senior person should be responsible for setting the tone and ground rules every week. That person should also, in this case, have limited attendance to owners and key stakeholders, and also limited the metrics to be reviewed to a specific, essential set: irrelevant metrics should have been deleted from the deck. All of us leaders of that software group, not just that one individual, should have examined the meeting as relentlessly as the participants were examining one another. Collectively, we should have recognized that many of the areas being measured were not yet operationally under control and predictable. Many of the teams had skipped the first three DMAIC steps—define, measure, analyze—in an attempt to operate at the Improve stage.

They ended up chasing blips on a graph with not much to show for their effort. We should have—politely and constructively!—recommended they do the necessary legwork to convert their metrics from noise to signal.

Last, we should have recognized that implementing a WBR for this new group for the first time was bound to be messy, requiring trial and error. In the end, we should have ensured that attendees felt free to talk about their mistakes and were actively encouraged to do so, allowing others to learn from them. The key to these meetings is to create a balance between extremely high standards and an atmosphere where people feel comfortable talking about mistakes.

One Amazonian still recalls those disaster meetings even though they occurred more than 15 years ago. He said,

> You're really looking for teams to be willing to take themselves apart, to become naked in front of everyone, to say: "I screwed up. This wasn't right. Here's where it broke." But I remember one particular leader who said instead, "Who is the person with poor judgment who did that?"
>
> The problem with statements like that is that people are basically convicted and sentenced before they've even responded. The leader should have reserved judgment instead of attacking, then begun to understand what actually happened. People are only trying to do the right thing; they're not trying to sabotage the business, and they don't hate customers. They feel tremendous responsibility for what they build.
>
> Since then, we've gotten to be more mature, grounded in freedom from fear. Every time we do the awesome thing, of course we try to reward it. And the more a team eviscerates itself, being vocally self-critical, the more we try to reward that too. If a team is papering things over, and hasn't looked at the customer experience, *then* you might ask hard questions.

Two things are striking about this recollection. The first is how vivid it remains so many years after the fact—evidence that a punishing environment can leave indelible marks. The second is that this team learned from these early missteps, made adjustments, and eventually built a better process.

Pitfall 2: Noise Obscuring the Signal

Contradictory as this may sound, variation in data is normal. And unavoidable. It's therefore critical to differentiate normal variation (noise) from some fundamental change or defect in a process (signal). Trying to attach meaning to variations within normal bounds is at best a waste of effort and at worst dangerously misleading. It's bad enough when someone proudly explains how their herculean efforts moved their key metric up by 0.1 percent this week, taking precious time away from more important things. Worse, if that same metric went *down* by 0.1 percent, you could easily waste time chasing down the root cause and "fixing" an issue that's really nothing more than normal variation.

At Amazon, understanding what's normal is the responsibility of the metrics owner, whether that's an individual contributor or a manager of thousands. Many statistical methods, such as XMR control charts,[3] can highlight when a process is out of control. For us, however, experience and a deep understanding of the customer most often turned out to be the best way to filter out the signal from the background noise. For the most part, metrics are reviewed daily by their owners and weekly in the WBR, so that expected fluctuations become familiar and exceptions stand out.

* * *

Amazon's approach to metrics embodies the Customer Obsession leadership principle. The relevance of Customer Obsession becomes evident in the company's focus on input versus output metrics. If you look at the input metrics for Amazon, they often describe things customers care about, such as low prices, lots of available products, fast shipping, few customer service contacts, and a speedy website or app. A lot of the output metrics, such as revenue and free cash flow, are what you'd typically see in a company's financial report. Customers don't care about those. But as we stated at the beginning of this book, Amazon has an unshakable conviction that the long-term interests of shareowners are perfectly aligned with the interests of customers. Controllable input metrics are a quantitative (diving deep with data) and qualitative (anecdotes) way of measuring how well the organization is satisfying these customer interests so that the output metrics trend the way the company desires.

Properly evaluating your business and striving to improve each week requires a willingness to openly discuss failures, learn from them, and always look for inventions that will delight customers even more.

Part Two

The Invention
Machine at Work

Introduction to Part Two

Now we come to the application—the proof that the elements that go into *being Amazonian* produce results. In 2015 Jeff wrote, "We want to be a large company that's also an invention machine. We want to combine the extraordinary customer-serving capabilities that are enabled by size with the speed of movement, nimbleness, and risk-acceptance mentality normally associated with entrepreneurial start-ups."[1] And as we'll see, there is a direct link between careful observation of the practices enumerated in part one and the impressive successes and breakthroughs at Amazon, including services like Amazon Prime and Prime Video, hardware like Kindle and Alexa (Kindle is also a service), practices like Bar Raiser hiring and Working Backwards, and businesses like Amazon Web Services and Amazon Echo and Alexa.

Of course, Jeff also wrote in that same shareholder letter, "I believe we are the best place in the world to fail (we have plenty of practice!), and failure and invention are inseparable twins. To invent you have to experiment, and if you know in advance that it's going to work, it's not an experiment. Most large organizations embrace the idea of invention, but are not willing to suffer the string of failed experiments necessary to get there." Thus for Amazon, its less successful inventions, such as Fire Phone, are valuable. The same is true of the off-target early iterations of later successes, such as Amazon Unbox, which evolved into Prime Video, and Amazon Auctions and zShops, which developed into Amazon Marketplace. These "failures" are important parts of the company's story, both as precursors to later successes and as evidence that experimentation is happening.

Naturally, if you don't have the budget to invent, don't do it. But, even with a limited budget, you can be successful over time if your approach is patient and frugal. *Being Amazonian* means approaching invention with long-term thinking and customer obsession, ensuring that the Leadership Principles guide the way, and deploying the practices to drive execution. "Long-term thinking levers our existing abilities and lets us do new things we couldn't otherwise contemplate," Jeff wrote. "Long-term orientation interacts well with customer obsession. If we can identify a customer need and if we can further develop conviction that that need is meaningful and durable, our approach permits us to work patiently for multiple years to deliver a solution."[2] Key word: patiently. Many companies will give up on an initiative if it does not produce the kind of returns they are looking for within a handful of years. Amazon will stick with it for five, six, seven years—all the while keeping the investment manageable, constantly learning and improving—until it gains momentum and acceptance.

The other key is frugality. You can't afford to pursue inventions for very long if you spend your money on things that don't lead to a better customer experience, like trade show booths, big teams, and splashy marketing campaigns. Amazon Music and Prime Video are examples of how we kept our investment manageable for many years by being frugal: keeping the team small, staying focused on improving the customer experience, limiting our marketing spend, and managing the P&L carefully. Once we had a clear product plan and vision for how these products could become billion-dollar businesses that would delight tens, even hundreds of millions of consumers, we invested big. Patience and carefully managed investment over many years can pay off greatly.

Invention is not the solution to every problem. For instance, when Amazon started, the company did not create its own computer hardware. On the flip side, when we were planning our e-book business, we decided to get into the hardware game with Kindle. The reason: invention works well where differentiation matters. In the company's early days, the hardware that powered Amazon's data centers was not the point of differentiation with the customer—creating a compelling book-buying online experience was. Whereas with Kindle, as we will describe in chapter seven, others were selling e-books, so there was real value in owning and controlling the creation of an outstanding device for our customers to read them on. Differentiation with customers is often one of the key reasons to invent.

And what was true yesterday may not be true today. In fact, today Amazon does make some computer hardware to power its data centers. That's because this special-purpose hardware designed for AWS's data centers reduces costs and increases reliability in a nontrivial way. These benefits can be passed on to AWS customers in the form of meaningful price decreases and services that offer higher reliability.

When we have invented, our long-term, patient approach—driven by customer need—has been fundamentally different from the more conventional "skills-forward" approach to invention, in which a company looks for new business opportunities that neatly fit with its existing skills and competencies. While this approach can be rewarding, there is a fundamental problem with it: the company will never be driven to master new skills and develop new competencies, hire new kinds of leaders, or create different types of organizations. Amazon's Working Backwards process—starting with customer needs, not corporate needs or competencies—often demands that, in Jeff's words, we "exercise new muscles, never mind how uncomfortable and awkward-feeling those first steps might be."

In this part of the book, we look at four key examples of successful Amazonian invention—Kindle, Amazon Prime, Prime

Video, and Amazon Web Services (AWS)—but there are many others we could highlight and haven't mentioned, such as Fulfillment by Amazon, Amazon Echo and Alexa, and Kindle Direct Publishing.

We won't dedicate a full chapter to one of the failures, but it's worth mentioning one here in brief. The Amazon Fire Phone is an example of a well-executed process that produced, well, a dud. The launch of the Fire Phone was one of the largest new product initiatives the company had undertaken. The phone's primary differentiator was a feature called "dynamic perspective," a 3D effect produced by four cameras within the phone, along with a positioning gyroscope. More than a thousand people worked on the many elements required to create the phone's 3D capability and a number of smaller innovations, as well as the more standard features and functions that would affect the customer experience. Some 30 apps were involved, for one-touch customer service, free photo storage in the Amazon cloud, a clock, a calendar, a music player, Kindle, and on and on.

Fire Phone launched in June 2014. In August 2015, it was discontinued. What happened?

First, even with the PR/FAQ process, the Fire Phone did not solve a sufficiently important customer problem or create a notably wonderful customer experience. I (Bill) remember wondering, when I first learned about the project in 2012, why anybody would want a 3D effect on their phone, cool though it was. Here's a snippet from the press release the day it launched:

SEATTLE—(BUSINESS WIRE)—Jun. 18, 2014—(NASDAQ: AMZN)—Amazon today unveiled Fire, the first smartphone designed by Amazon. Fire is the only smartphone with Dynamic Perspective and Firefly, two new breakthrough technologies that allow you to see and interact with the world through a whole new lens. Dynamic Perspective uses a new sensor system to respond to the way you hold, view, and move Fire, enabling experiences not possible on other smartphones. Firefly quickly recognizes things in the real world—web and email addresses, phone numbers, QR and bar codes, movies, music, and millions of products, and lets you take action in seconds—all with the simple press of the Firefly button.[3]

Second, the phone sold at a premium price. One of Amazon's guiding principles is Frugality, and we had demonstrated to the world that we were the cost-effective, break-the-business-model company. To customers, the core principle simply meant low prices. Now we were offering a phone for $200, the same price as the iPhone, and it required a two-year commitment with a mobile carrier. ($200 sounds cheap now, but back then mobile phones were subsidized and prices were a lot lower.) We dropped the price to $99 and then offered it for free. It didn't matter. Nobody wanted it.

Finally, the Fire Phone came late to market and with only a single carrier, AT&T. By that time, iPhone service was available through four carriers that all offered a number of other brands as well. There was a lot of competition on the shelf and in the air.

If we had offered the Fire Phone at a lower price point than the iPhone, with most of the features and a commitment to Prime, would that have made the difference? Possibly.

The point of the story, however, is that the process improves your odds of success but by no means guarantees it. Jeff himself was deeply involved in the development of the Fire Phone. He was effectively one of the authors of the PR/FAQ, along with project leaders Ian Freed and Cameron Janes. He and the team either believed or convinced themselves that they were creating a phone customers would love, but they were wrong. Even the best process can only improve the quality of your decision-making; no process will make the decision for you.

Indeed, the failure of the Fire Phone did not cause Jeff to question the process that created it. "We all know that if you swing for the fences," he wrote, "you're going to strike out a lot, but you're also going to hit some home runs." Unlike baseball, where a home run can bring in no more than four runs, a big business hit can score an almost infinite number of runs. What's crucial to understand is that a small number of very big winners can pay for a large number of experiments that fail or succeed only modestly.

In an interview after the Fire Phone was withdrawn, Jeff was asked about its failure and answered, "If you think that's a big failure, we're working on much bigger failures right now—and I am not kidding."[4] The magnitude of your inventions, and therefore your mistakes, needs to grow in lockstep with the growth of your organization. If it doesn't, your inventions will likely not be big enough to move the needle.

As a company grows larger, it can become more difficult to keep the invention machine humming, and one impediment is "one-size-fits-all" decision-making. In the same 2015 shareholder letter, Jeff wrote, "Some decisions are consequential and irreversible or nearly irreversible—one-way doors—and these decisions must be made methodically, carefully, slowly, with great deliberation and consultation. If you walk through and don't like what you see on the other side, you can't get back to where you were before. We can call these Type 1 decisions. But most decisions aren't like that—they are changeable, reversible—they're two-way doors. If you've made a suboptimal Type 2 decision, you don't have to live with the consequences for that long. You can reopen the door and go back through. Type 2 decisions can and should be made quickly by high judgment individuals or small groups." Prime was a two-way door decision. If Prime's particular combination of subscription, free shipping, and quick delivery had not worked, we'd have kept tinkering with the formula until we got it right. In fact, Prime was not our first go at solving the problem—it was preceded by another two-way door decision, Super Saver Shipping, which eventually morphed into Prime. The Fire Phone, on the other hand, was more of a one-way door decision: upon withdrawing it from the market, Amazon did not turn around and say, "Okay, that happened, now let's try another phone."

Big companies tend to develop a decision-making process that is designed to manage one-way door decisions, precisely because poor decisions can lead to big problems, even disaster. The process is typically slow, cumbersome, and riddled with risk aversion. This process tends to become the dominant one in large companies, and it is routinely, almost thoughtlessly, applied to two-way door decisions. The result is reduced speed, impaired idea generation, stifled innovation, and longer development cycles.

That's why Amazon focuses on the speed of movement, nimbleness, and a risk-acceptance mentality associated with a Day One startup—all the while adhering to the highest standards. This approach has been part of *being Amazonian* since the early days of the company. In 1999 Jeff wrote, "We must be committed to constant improvement, experimentation, and innovation in every initiative. We love to be pioneers, it's in the DNA of the company, and it's a good thing, too, because we'll need that pioneering spirit to succeed."[5]

7

Kindle

Bill gets an unwelcome assignment. Amazon's move to digital as an example of Working Backwards. Can Amazon build hardware? To outsource, or not to outsource? Building a device that gets out of the reader's way. The launch and a boost from Oprah.

* * *

AMAZON SVP (*aggressively skeptical*): Exactly how much more money are you willing to invest in Kindle?

JEFF (*turns calmly to CFO, smiling, shrugging his shoulders*): How much money do we have?

In January 2004, my manager, Steve Kessel, invited me (Bill) to a meeting in his office, where he proceeded to drop the bombshell I described in the introduction. After rising through the ranks over the previous four years at Amazon to become VP of worldwide media (books, music, video) retail, Steve was being promoted to SVP, would now report directly to Jeff (joining the S-Team), and would be taking on the task of building a new digital media business. He wanted me to join him to become the leader of the digital media business team (H. B. Siegel would run the engineering org), a move Jeff had blessed.

Initially I was upset about being passed over to take the job Steve was leaving. After serving as a director in the U.S. books, music, and video unit—which accounted for 77 percent of Amazon's global revenue at that time[1]—and feeling my career was finally taking off, now my boss was asking me to help lead one of the company's smallest ventures, if not the smallest. At that time, the Amazon digital media business consisted of our newly launched Search Inside the Book feature plus the e-books team (roughly five people), all buried deep in Steve's organization and generating a few million dollars in annual revenue—and based on the e-book market at that time, there didn't seem to be any real prospects for growth. This small team would move, along with Steve, H. B., and me, out of the retail org and initiate the Amazon digital media org.

But as Steve explained Jeff's thinking, I began to feel differently. Jeff, Steve told me, had decided that Amazon was at an important crossroads, and now was the time to act. Though the physical media business was growing, we all understood that over time it would decline in popularity and importance as the media business shifted to digital. That year, fiscal 2004, Apple sold 4.4 million iPods—about four times more than the prior year—and the proliferation of shared digital music files online had already prompted a decline in sales of music CDs. It seemed only a matter of time before sales of physical books and DVDs would decline as well, replaced by digital downloads.

Jeff felt we had to act right away. And once Jeff made up his mind, he exercised the Bias for Action leadership principle.

For my career path, this could either mean getting one of the best seats on a rocket ship or working for years on a small business that never gets off the ground. As I was to discover, the path to success in digital would be long and riddled with setbacks, hard lessons, false starts, and painful failures. But as noted, we didn't expect anything different. There were times when we had heated debates about what products to build and how we should build them. Should we focus on books, music, or video? Should we build a subscription service, make it free with advertisements, let people buy à la carte, or all of the above? Should we build our own devices or partner with manufacturers? Should we acquire companies to accelerate our entry into digital? Throughout the organization, leaders, including some members of the board of directors, questioned why we should invest so much time, effort, and money on digital media. For as you'll see, the skills required to succeed in digital media are quite different from what's needed to excel at delivering physical goods sold online.

But we (the leaders and members of the digital media team) were persistent, always ready to reinvent our approach, change our tactics, and iterate on our strategy. We were guided by an unwavering long-term goal—to create a large digital media business that invested in new services (and devices) that consumers loved—and by Jeff's ever-present reminder that no matter what we did, we had to constantly push to figure out the right experience for our customers.

It would take several years for our digital effort to gain a foothold and become a meaningful business.

A few days after that first meeting with Steve, I accepted the digital media role. A few months later, I was promoted to vice president. After an org change or two, I settled into my role as the VP of Amazon's digital Music and Video groups until I left the company at the end of 2014. During that time, I either observed, participated in, or acted as the leader of the development of the Kindle e-book reader, Fire Tablet, Fire TV, Prime Video, Amazon Music, Amazon Studios, and our voice-activated Echo speaker and the underlying Alexa voice assistant technology.

Over our long march to building Amazon's digital business, we proved a powerful lesson: it takes exceptionally patient and unwavering leadership to persevere through the prolonged process of building a new business and navigating through transformative times in an established industry with entrenched interests. The fact that we entered as total beginners and emerged as industry leaders is in no small part a result of our adherence to *being Amazonian* in our principles and our way of thinking, including thinking big, thinking long-term, being obsessed with customers, being willing to be misunderstood for long periods of time, and being frugal—principles that few companies are capable of maintaining in the face of quarterly reporting requirements and the daily gyrations of the stock market. Many companies with a lot more capital than Amazon had at the time tried and failed to build a digital business. Even if your company is smaller than your competitors, adhering to these principles will enable you to punch above your weight.

Making the Turn to Digital

Amazon was not alone in recognizing the need to invest in digital media and acquire new capabilities. The popularity of the digital music file-sharing service Napster, which had taken off in June 1999, had been a signal to all of us that there was a shift in consumer demand away from physical media to digital media.

In fall 2003, Jeff, Colin, and Diego Piacentini—a former Apple VP who was at that time Amazon's SVP of Worldwide Retail—left the Amazon offices in Seattle late one afternoon and traveled to the Apple campus in Cupertino to meet with Steve Jobs, who had invited us down for a visit. Jobs and another Apple employee greeted us, then ushered us into a nondescript conference room with a Windows PC and two platters of takeout sushi. We had an informal discussion about the state of the music industry while doing some serious damage to the sushi platters, for it was already past dinnertime. After dabbing his mouth with a napkin, Jobs segued into the real purpose of the meeting and announced that Apple had just finished building their first Windows application. He calmly and confidently told us that even though it was Apple's first attempt to build for Windows, he thought it was the best Windows application anyone had ever built. He then personally gave us a demo of the soon-to-be launched iTunes for Windows.

During the demo, Jobs talked about how this move would transform the music industry. Up until this point, if you wanted to buy digital music from Apple, you needed a Mac, which comprised less than 10 percent of the home computer market. Apple's first foray into building software on the competing Windows platform showed how serious they were about the digital music market.

Now anyone with a computer would be able to purchase digital music from Apple.

Jobs said that CDs would go the way of other outdated music formats like the cassette tape, and their importance and portion of overall music sales would drop quickly. His next comment could reasonably be construed as either a matter-of-fact statement, an attempt to elicit an angry retort, or an attempt to goad Jeff into making a bad business decision by acting impulsively. He said, "Amazon has a decent chance of being the last place to buy CDs. The business will be high-margin but small. You'll be able to charge a premium for CDs, since they'll be hard to find." Jeff did not take the bait. We were their guests and the rest of the meeting was uneventful. But we all knew that being the exclusive seller of antique CDs did not sound like an appealing business model.

While it is tempting to suggest the meeting impacted Jeff's thinking, only Jeff can speak to that. What we can say is what Jeff did and did not do afterward. What he didn't do (and what many companies would have done) is to kick off an all-hands-on-deck project to combat this competitive threat, issue a press release claiming how Amazon's new service would win the day, and race to build a copycat digital music service. Instead, Jeff took time to process what he learned from the meeting and formed a plan. A few months later, he appointed a single-threaded leader—Steve Kessel—to run Digital, who would report directly to him so that they could work together to formulate a vision and a plan for digital media.

In other words, his first action was not a "what" decision, it was a "who" and "how" decision. This is an incredibly important difference. Jeff did not jump straight to focusing on what product to build, which seems like the straightest line from A to B. Instead, the choices he made suggest he believed that the scale of the opportunity was large and that the scope of the work required to achieve success was equally large and complex. He focused first on *how* to organize the team and *who* was the right leader to achieve the right result.

Though the shift to digital was already beginning to happen, no one could predict when the tide would really turn. No one wanted to get in too early, with a product that did not yet have a market. But no one wanted to miss the moment either and be unable to catch up. We knew that we'd need to invent our way out of this dilemma by obsessing over what the best customer experience would be in this new paradigm. Our inherent DNA of customer focus, long-term thinking, and invention were assets in this case.

Retailers like Walmart, Barnes & Noble, and even Amazon's online media business—as well as such media giants as Disney, Universal Music, Warner, and Random House—were all major players in either the creation or the distribution of physical media. Microsoft, Apple, Google, Netflix, Walmart, Disney, Samsung, Sony, Warner, and many more would pour billions of dollars into digital media in the coming years. It was plain for all these companies to see that the change was coming. Some of these companies were better positioned than Amazon was to capitalize on it, and others were ill equipped to take advantage of that change or to lead it. Some of their investments would produce successes (YouTube, Hulu, Spotify, almost everything Apple touched) while many others led to write-offs and failures (Microsoft Zune, Sony E-Reader, Nook, PressPlay, MusicNet). At that time Amazon decidedly did not have billions to spend on digital media or anything else, so we would need to lean heavily on the Frugality principle to stay in the game with the bigger players.

Jeff was a student of history and regularly reminded us that if a company didn't or couldn't change and adapt to meet shifting consumer needs, it was doomed. "You don't want to become Kodak," he would say, referring to the once-mighty photography giant that had missed the turn from film to digital. We weren't going to sit back and wait for this to happen to Amazon.

Conceptually, I understood and accepted this history lesson. What I didn't get was why Steve and I had to change jobs and build up a whole new organization. Why couldn't we manage digital media as part of what we were already doing? After all, we would be working with the same partners and suppliers. The media had to come from somewhere and that somewhere was media companies: book publishers, record companies, and motion picture studios. I already managed the co-op marketing relationships with those companies, so it made sense that we should do this within the same organization and build off the knowledge and success of our strong team. Otherwise, Amazon would have two different groups responsible for business relationships with partners and suppliers.

But Jeff felt that if we tried to manage digital media as a part of the physical media business, it would never be a priority. The bigger business carried the company after all, and it would always get the most attention. Steve told me that getting digital right was highly important to Jeff, and he wanted Steve to focus on nothing else. Steve wanted me to join him and help him create the new business.

This change would be one of the first major examples of the single-threaded leader org structure concept at Amazon. Before Steve moved over to head Digital, the most senior leader of the digital media business was a product manager, four levels below Steve. There was no way that someone at that level could lead and develop the kinds of new products and initiatives that we would launch in the coming years. For this to become one of Amazon's biggest and most important businesses, Jeff needed Steve, an experienced and proven vice president (now promoted to senior vice president), reporting to Jeff, single-threaded on digital. Steve would in turn need to build a team of senior leaders under him, each of whom would be single-threaded on one aspect of the business, such as device hardware, e-books, music, or video.

Eventually, I appreciated the importance of organizing this way. If we had tried to figure out how to deliver digital media while also managing our online physical-media business, we could not have moved quickly enough. We would not have thought big enough about how to reinvent the customer experience as we did when we built our own e-reader device and service. The customer experience would undoubtedly have been a subpar mishmash of the physical and digital business approaches. We had to start from scratch.

And this sudden job change, the one I'd been so disappointed by, would prove to be not only the right thing for the company but also one of the best things to ever happen for my career.

The Startup Phase for Amazon Digital Media and Devices

To work through the details of our approach to digital books, music, and video, we spent roughly six months researching the digital media landscape and meeting as a leadership team with Jeff on a weekly basis to review and brainstorm countless ideas and concepts.

We met with our partners at the media companies (book publishers, record companies, motion picture studios) to discuss the current state and future of e-books, digital music, and video. The e-book business already existed, but publishers were not investing in it, and they certainly weren't positioning it for growth; they produced a small catalog of books and applied the same high prices as hardcovers. With piracy rapidly killing the CD business and Apple selling millions of songs on iTunes to millions of iPod customers, the record companies were eager for us to jump in fast so they would have more retailers to deal with—not just Apple.

There was no digital movie and TV show business at the time. The content creators were, by nature, risk averse, skilled at maximizing the cash flow from their existing operations, but not at creating new ones. So they were not interested in licensing their shows or movies to digital service providers like Amazon hoped to be.

In December 2004, Steve, Jeff, and I attended Music 2.0, a digital music industry conference at the Hilton in Universal City. At the time, Jeff was already well known to the business and media world—*Time* had named him Man of the Year in 1999. It certainly wasn't common for such a high-profile CEO to show up at a conference like this one, so a palpable buzz surrounded us wherever we went. People kept approaching me, wanting me to help them get in front of Jeff.

We listened to a number of speakers, one of whom was Larry

Kenswil, a senior executive at Universal Music, who spoke about the current state of the digital music business. At the time, it was divided into two camps: in one were services like Napster that facilitated free file sharing; in the other, by itself, was Apple, selling songs to load onto the iPod for 99 cents each. Larry was eager for more big tech companies to enter the business, as that would mean more revenue for Universal Music. He obviously knew that we were in the audience, because he made a few comments pointed directly at Jeff, effectively dissing Amazon for not being in the digital music space and prodding us to jump in fast.

One of the decisions we had to make in that first year was whether to build a business or to buy a company already operating in that space. We had many meetings with Jeff where Steve and I would present our ideas for our music product or a company we might acquire. Each time we had these meetings, Jeff would reject what he saw as copycat thinking, emphasizing again and again that whatever music product we built, it had to offer a truly unique value proposition for the customer. He would frequently describe the two fundamental approaches that each company must choose between when developing new products and services. We could be a fast follower—that is, make a close copy of successful products that other companies had built—or we could invent a new product on behalf of our customers. He said that either approach is valid, but he wanted Amazon to be a company that invents.

Why? For digital in particular, part of the answer was that the industry was changing more rapidly than most. With a fast-follower strategy, by the time we could have built and deployed a reasonable replica of a competitor's service, they or someone else would have already created something better, and we wouldn't have had enough time to recoup returns on our existing service before we had to build a different one. The quick evolution of Apple's music service from a tethered iPod to a Mac to seamless discovery and playback on the iPhone and iPad makes its own case for why the fast-follower strategy would not have worked in the digital business. Jeff made clear that people like the exec who'd baited him at the digital music conference wouldn't drive our process. He recognized that building copycat versions of products like the iPod and the iTunes store was a nonstarter. And he had no interest in making a PR splash by announcing to the public that Amazon had arrived in the digital business. He chose the path of invention by looking beyond the music category, which led him to begin Amazon's foray into digital by focusing on e-books and an e-reader device. In so doing, Jeff demonstrated his belief that true invention leads to greater long-term value for customers and shareholders.

My team and I quickly learned that invention is a more challenging path than fast following. The roadmap for fast following is relatively clear—you study what your competitor has built and copy it. There is no roadmap for invention.

The invention approach required the endurance to evaluate and discard many options and ideas. So, as we were considering which path to take—build or buy—we took countless meetings with different companies in the digital media business. In addition to enabling us to understand our options for potential acquisition, it was a productive way for us to get up to speed quickly on different aspects of the digital media business, as the founders and leaders of these companies shared their experience and insights from working on a variety of product challenges. In parallel, we were writing some of our first PR/FAQs for digital media products, which we would review and discuss with Jeff. The two processes reinforced one another, and by the end of 2004, our thinking and vision had become clearer. As that vision came into focus, we began to design the organization and assemble a team.

When Jeff asked Steve to run Digital, he also changed the org structure at the top of the company. Previously, Steve had reported to Diego Piacentini, SVP of Worldwide Retail, who reported to Jeff. Now Steve reported directly to Jeff, a clear sign that Digital was a high priority.

There were two important benefits to this approach. First, this meant that Steve was not encumbered with the many responsibilities that went with managing any of Amazon's then-current businesses or operations; he was given the autonomy and authority to devote single-threaded focus to Digital. Second, it meant that Diego and his peers would not be required to spend any of their time on Digital. They were free to continue to devote their single-threaded focus to building our retail and marketplace businesses as well as our fulfillment network. Additionally, Jeff made an explicit choice at this juncture that he would devote a significant portion of his time to working directly with Steve and the leaders in Digital, to align with them on product direction, and to ensure they had the resources necessary to succeed. This necessarily meant that Jeff was reducing his time and oversight of retail and marketplace, ceding more autonomy to leaders like Diego and Jeff Wilke.

It was thanks to the combination of Amazon processes, which we discussed in part one of the book, that Jeff was able to make these changes. For example, the six-page document and S-Team goals allowed Jeff to stay aligned on all major retail and marketplace programs and give feedback in an efficient manner, even as he devoted less calendar time to those businesses. And for new initiatives in Digital (as well as AWS), the PR/FAQ process enabled him to spend weeks or months to gain alignment and clarity at a high level of detail on each project. Once he and the team had aligned on each detailed PR/FAQ, Digital and AWS leaders could then run as hard as possible to build their teams and launch new products, with the knowledge that they were in lockstep with the CEO. This enabled Jeff to direct and influence multiple projects simultaneously. This kind of alignment existed not because Jeff was CEO but because we had a process in place that enabled it. The same process could allow teams at any company to work autonomously and yet be in sync with the intentions of their leaders.

On the organizational side, we used the two-pizza team structure, which allowed our Digital teams to not be dependent on or a distraction to the engineering and business teams running the retail and marketplace business. Our people were autonomous with respect to their ability to achieve the goals that they had agreed to with Jeff. From Jeff's point of view, this meant he wouldn't be stymied by arbitrating resource conflicts and dependencies at the ground level. He could hold each two-pizza team leader account-able for staffing their team and achieving their goals. Furthermore, he could easily audit whether an important initiative was staffed to succeed. Because the teams were not dependent on other teams, Jeff could be sure that planned work would actually get done and wouldn't be pocket vetoed elsewhere in the org. Without these new processes, it would have been difficult or impossible for him to make these big changes in how he organized the company and allocated his time while achieving the right outcomes. These methods allow the CEO (or other leader) to achieve and maintain alignment with their org on what to build and whether they have the resources to build it or not.

Like other leaders at Amazon, I learned how to apply these processes as my organization grew to increase my span of control and achieve the right results across a variety of complex products and projects. Thanks to these tools, within a few years, I was able to dive deep, audit, and manage hundreds of annual S-Team goals and new product initiatives for which my many teams were re-sponsible.

We applied the new two-pizza structure to every part of the org chart below Steve and his direct reports. The two-pizza struc-ture became more complicated at the top of the org chart. For example, should product, engineering, and business functions all report to a single leader? Or should each one be run by its own leader, with those leaders in turn working as a team on the prod-uct, engineering, and business details?

We decided that there would be separate leaders for business and tech for each digital product category—books, music, and video. Each of these category leaders would hire leaders for each business function, such as product management, marketing/merchandising, and vendor/content management (licensing digital content from publishers, studios, and record companies). Each general manager (GM) category leader had a corresponding peer leader on the en-gineering side. Each engineering category had a two-pizza team for each major component of the software services (e.g., content in-gestion and transformation) and for client application software. This was mostly a pragmatic decision based on the skills of the leaders. For example, I had no experience at that time managing an engineering organization. The same was true of my peers on the engineering side with respect to business. This would change in the years to come.

Within months, it became clear that we would need to add more senior leaders (who would report directly to Steve) to run and manage each of the various component parts of the vision. In the beginning of 2004, Steve had just two direct reports: Bill, the business leader for Digital, and H. B. Siegel, the engineering leader. By mid-2005, Steve had hired leaders of the appropriate level and expertise to run each element of our product and business vision and had modified the org structure to accommodate them. With each modification, the scope of each leader's responsibilities would become narrower, but the intended scale of each role was greater. At most companies, reducing a leader's scope would be considered a demotion, and in fact there were many VPs and directors who saw each of these changes in that way. At Amazon, it was not a demotion. It was a signal that we were thinking big and investing in digital for the long term.

In my case, this meant that by 2005, instead of leading the business team for digital books, music, and video, I was focused on leading just music and video. In 2007, my scope grew when I took on leadership of the engineering organizations in addition to busi-ness. This process was continuous as each year changes were made where the scope of the work had become too broad to break up or divide teams into subteams. A simple example: in 2004, video client application development was handled by one two-pizza team. It then became three teams, one for web, one for mobile devices, one for TV devices. Then the mobile team became four teams (iPhone, Android phone, iPad, Android tablet) and the TV team became five-plus teams (Xbox, PlayStation, TiVo, Sony Bra-via, Samsung, etc.), such that by 2011 our original two two-pizza teams were now more than ten.

Some of the digital media leaders—including Neil Roseman and Dan Rose—came from inside the company. Others, like Erich Ringewald, had been with Amazon and left for other pursuits, but near the end of 2004, we persuaded him to return and lead the engineering team for digital music. We recruited other leaders, including Gregg Zehr and Ian Freed, to join us from companies including Palm and RealNetworks. By mid-2005, the core leadership team was in place.

In retrospect, the organizational structure we employed was not radical or different from those of other companies. The radical part was that these teams were established outside of the then-current retail and marketplace business and engineering organizations, and we were thinking big and long term by hiring and building a large organization to support three speculative, new businesses.

Amazon: A Device Maker?!

The reasons we needed not only a new team but also new capabilities like device hardware became evident through our product ideation sessions. Jeff zeroed in on the fundamental difference between the digital media retail business and our existing physical media retail business. Our competitive advantage in physical media was based on having the broadest selection of items available on a single website. But this could not be a competitive advantage in digital media, where the barrier to entry was low. Any company, whether a well-funded startup or an established enterprise, could match our offering. In those days, while it took time and effort, any company could build an e-book store or a 99-cent music download store where they offered the same breadth and depth of books and songs as every other digital venue. They just had to be willing to undertake the tedious work of aggregating all the digital music files or e-books into a single online catalog. So we knew we couldn't meet Jeff's requirement that our digital business have a distinct and differentiated offering just on selection and aggregation.

Another key element of our competitive advantage in the

physical retail business was our ability to offer consistently low prices. If you think back to the flywheel of growth, this was associated with our lower cost structure in comparison to other retailers, because we had no stores. But cost structure was not a factor in digital. The process and costs associated with hosting and serving digital files were basically the same whether you were Amazon, Google, Apple, or a startup. There was no known fundamental difference that would allow one company to gain a competitive advantage and win over the long term by having lower digital media operating costs and passing those savings on to the consumer in the form of lower digital media prices.

When Jeff first met with Steve and asked him to take on leadership of Digital and Devices, he drew a version of this picture on the whiteboard (without the now-current icons and graphics that we have added here to make it easier to understand):

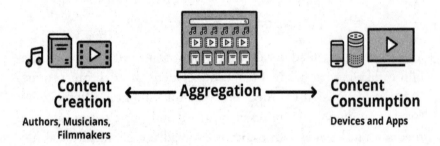

Content Creation ⟵ **Aggregation** ⟶ **Content Consumption**

Authors, Musicians, Filmmakers   Devices and Apps

He explained to Steve that there was an important difference in the digital media value chain as well. In physical retail, Amazon operated at the middle of the value chain. We added value by sourcing and aggregating a vast selection of goods, tens of millions of them, on a single website and delivering them quickly and cheaply to customers.

To win in digital, because those physical retail value adds were not advantages, we needed to identify other parts of the value chain where we could differentiate and serve customers well. Jeff told Steve that this meant moving out of the middle and venturing to either end of the value chain. On one end was content, where the value creators were book authors, filmmakers,

TV producers, publishers, musicians, record companies, and movie studios. On the other end was distribution and consumption of content. In digital, that meant focusing on applications and devices consumers used to read, watch, or listen to content, as Apple had already done with iTunes and the iPod. We all took note of what Apple had achieved in digital music in a short period of time and sought to apply those learnings to our long-term product vision.

Our core competencies did not extend to either end of the value chain.

Steve did not let this get in the way. In one of our meetings, he said that a typical company that wanted to grow would take stock of its existing capabilities and ask, "What can we do next with our skill set?" He emphasized that Amazon's approach was always to start from the customer and work backwards. We would figure out what the customers' needs were and then ask ourselves, "Do we have the skills necessary to build something that meets those needs? If not, how can we build or acquire them?" Once we determined what was necessary to create value for our customers and to differentiate ourselves from our competitors, we didn't let our lack of ability deter us from achieving this important end result—our own device.

So, although we knew nothing about building hardware, Jeff and Steve decided that the place to start was at the consumption end of the chain: hardware, specifically e-books. There were multiple reasons for this. One was that books were still the single largest category at Amazon and the one most associated with the company. Music was the first category to move to digital in the marketplace, but Apple had a big head start and our sessions did not produce a PR/FAQ for a music device or service idea that was sufficiently compelling. Video had not gone digital yet, which seemed like an opportunity, but it became apparent that there were a number of barriers to creating a great video experience at that time. These included getting the rights from the studios to offer their movies and TV shows digitally, the time it would take to download massive video files over the slow (at the time) internet, and uncertainty about how consumers would play these video files on their TVs.

Based on these factors, we decided to make a big investment of people and funds in e-books and a reading device and establish much smaller teams to work on music and video.

The other reason for starting with books was that the e-book business as a whole was tiny; there was no good way to read e-books on a device other than a PC, and reading on a PC was definitely not a good experience. We believed that customers would want the e-book equivalent of the iTunes/iPod experience: an app paired with a mobile device that offered consumers any book ever written, the content available at a low price that they could buy, download, and start reading in seconds. But we would need to invent the device ourselves, and the potential development time might take years.

The idea that Amazon, a pure e-commerce distributor of retail products made by others, would become a hardware company and make and sell its own reader device was controversial. Like nearly everyone at Amazon outside our Digital leadership team, I had a really hard time accepting that it was a good idea to make our own hardware when it seemed that nearly every leader in the company and on the board of directors was questioning it. Like everyone else, I thought it was super expensive (not adhering to the Frugality leadership principle!) and would fail. I now recognize that going through that process and seeing the outcome transformed my understanding of how innovation works.

I was a big believer in Steve, but I was vocal with my concerns when we would meet one-on-one to discuss it. "We're an e-commerce company, not a hardware company!" I would insist. I thought we should partner with third-party equipment companies that were good at designing and building hardware and stick to what we knew: e-commerce. I regularly pointed out to Steve that he knew nothing about hardware—he wasn't a gadget guy, and his ancient Volvo didn't even have a car stereo.

In our one-on-ones, Steve patiently explained why this was the right decision. We had worked through countless drafts of our PR/FAQ for an e-book store and device, and the end result was clear: we needed to build an e-book store that was deeply integrated with a reading device. This combination was the key to delivering a book-buying and reading experience that would delight customers. Through our research, we learned that relying on third parties, while operationally and financially less risky, was much riskier from the point of view of customer experience. If we start with the customer and work backwards, then the most logical conclusion is that we need to create our own devices.

The second point he made was that if you decide that the long-term success and survival of your company, like any company at a crossroads, is predicated on having a specific capability that you do not currently have, then the company must have a plan to build or buy it. We had to figure out how to build the capability to make hardware devices internally. If we wanted to ensure a great customer experience that was differentiated on the far end of the value chain, we couldn't outsource—and therefore cede—that important innovation to others. We had to do it ourselves.

Our decision to become a hardware device manufacturer would inform a number of decisions down the road. Many companies that decide to enter a business area in which they have little internal expertise or capability choose to outsource, as happened in the early days of e-commerce when brick-and-mortar retailers created their first online retail sites. They brought in third-party developers, consultants, and sometimes both. This approach enabled them to move much more quickly. But it deprived them of the flexibility to innovate and differentiate, and to continuously incorporate customer desire. Retailers who outsourced e-commerce lacked the ability to ideate and test new products like Super Saver Shipping, Prime, or Fulfillment by Amazon (FBA). They could only pick from a menu of options from their outsourced provider. At best, they would be fast followers of what the innovators built. At worst, in order to compete effectively they would have to implement an end-to-end experience for the product (like Prime), from their website, to their order management systems, to their fulfillment centers, to their delivery methods. You can't outsource a customized, integrated, end-to-end experience.

Furthermore, outsourcing in this context offers a classic example of short-term decisions with devastating long-term implications.

Practically every day, Amazon could tweak its offering to make things a little better. And so practically every day, the distance between itself and its competitors widened. Outsourcing turned out to be the more expensive path.

There was another reason we decided to build the device ourselves. If we had outsourced the work and succeeded in creating the first great reader device, much of the knowledge and know-how would accrue outside Amazon, in the minds and methods of the outsourcer. Since the kind of partner we would need was typically in the business of building custom spec hardware for a wide range of clients, not just us, the outsourcer might further develop the technology and eventually offer a comparable or even better reader to other companies, including our competitors. We wanted to be the keepers of the intellectual property.

The only way we had a chance at success was to put in place strong leaders, so Steve set out to find a subject matter expert with knowledge of the industry to lead our team in creating a great hardware device. In September 2004, Steve hired Gregg Zehr, a Silicon Valley veteran who had been a VP of hardware engineering at Palm Computing and Apple.

Gregg would set up a separate office in Silicon Valley, not Seattle, in order to tap into the Silicon Valley technical talent pool, which was much deeper than in Seattle, particularly for hardware developers. It would be an important step in our effort to hire outside leaders who could bring new capabilities to our company and to develop centers of excellence away from our home base. Unlike today, where the vast majority of Amazon's workforce is based outside the Seattle HQ, there were at the time only two or three other remote development centers, so it was still a relatively new concept for Amazon and felt risky. We saw a remote operation like this one as a means to an end, not an end in itself. We needed talent, and Silicon Valley was where the talent was.

There was considerable risk by putting so much on the shoulders of senior external hires like Gregg Zehr. How could we be sure that he would become Amazonian? The culture of Silicon Valley is markedly different from Amazon's culture. How would he learn and adapt to our peculiar processes like Bar Raiser, PR/FAQs, and six-pagers? These were issues that we addressed through the Bar Raiser process itself, which was the same whether you were a new college hire or a VP. I don't recall how many people we interviewed for Gregg's role, but there were quite a few, and most of them were more than qualified with respect to their device hardware development experience. Nevertheless, our interview process revealed the ways in which they didn't meet the bar for Amazon's Leadership Principles—it wasn't easy to find a senior leader who demonstrated them. In this case, the Bar Raiser interview process with Steve acting as hiring manager clearly delivered the right result. As of the writing of this book, Gregg remains with Amazon fifteen years after he was hired, and he has been responsible for the development and launch of many Amazon devices.

Steve tasked Gregg to build out a hardware organization, which he did with the code name Lab126 (the 1 and 26 stood for the letters A and Z), and earmarked a meaningful amount of capital to the effort. In parallel, Neil Roseman and Felix Anthony (both were experienced and trusted Amazon Engineering VPs) established and hired software engineering teams in Seattle to build the cloud and back-end systems that would power the Kindle experience and e-book store. Later, Ian Freed would become the leader of the product and business organization. The combination of Gregg (device hardware), Felix and Neil (cloud software), and Ian (product and business), and the respective teams that they built, were critical to the success of the Kindle. At a time when resources were scarce throughout the company and groups operated as leanly as possible, other teams were envious of the new Kindle venture and its leaders who got to hire a big (about 150 people) team of engineers and product managers.

In April 2005, we also acquired Mobipocket, a small company based in France that had built a software application for viewing and reading books on PCs and mobile devices. We used the Mobipocket software as the basis for the software on the first Kindle. Had we not acquired the company, we would have needed to hire a team and build the same software ourselves. We were impressed by their founder, Thierry Brethes, and the team he had assembled, so we believed that they would be great additions to the Amazon digital media team. Since the Mobipocket team consisted of about ten people, they remained in place as an Amazon two-pizza team with a single-threaded focus on Kindle reader client-application development.

With the Mobipocket team and their software on board, Gregg, Neil, Felix, and Ian started working in partnership with Jeff to map out the details of the first device. Jeff told the team that they had the audacious goal of improving on an invention that had withstood the test of time, over five hundred years, without much change: the book. The overarching theme in the design stage was that our electronic book reader should "get out of the way" so the reader could make a direct connection with the content. Once the person started reading, they should not notice they were using a device.

At some point early in the process, a name for the device emerged: Kindle.

Between 2004 and 2007, the vast majority of the people, money, and resources earmarked for digital media was poured into the Kindle effort. The organization grew by dozens of people, most of them new to Amazon—including Ian Freed, who was a veteran of Real Networks. Jeff stayed so deeply involved in the project that he was unofficially known as the chief product manager for Kindle.

We'd known the Kindle would take time and money to develop, but by the middle of 2005, it became clear that it was taking much longer and consuming more funds than we had anticipated. Sometime in 2005, a subset of the S-Team met with members of the finance team to review the company's consolidated OP1. There was a heated discussion about the surprising ramp-up in expenses across many areas, particularly with Kindle. At some point in the debate, someone asked Jeff point blank: "How much more money are you willing to invest in Kindle?" Jeff calmly turned to our CFO, Tom Szkutak, smiled, shrugged his shoulders, and asked the rhetorical question, "How much money do we have?" That was his way of signaling the strategic importance of Kindle and assuring the team that he was not putting the company at risk with the size of the investment. In Jeff's view, it was way too early to give up on the project.

Development continued.

Kindle Takes Shape

The idea of "getting out of the way" of the reading experience drove several key decisions in the Kindle design process, and we drew inspiration from devices that others had built, particularly the BlackBerry. In those days Jeff and the other senior executives at Amazon, including me, were addicted to the Canadian wireless email device that had transformed itself into the world's first commercially successful smartphone. Jeff went through many Black-Berry devices, not a few of which had been fried by sweat dripping on them during his workouts.

The feature that really attracted us was BlackBerry's constant connectivity. Like everyone, Jeff loved that his phone was always connected and automatically refreshed itself to display new email. In those early days of digital media, this was a first. At the time, the only way to load content onto an MP3 player or other portable device was to connect it to your PC with a wire and sync the content between the two machines. This process was known as "sideloading." While it was convenient to be able to take your music with you on your portable device, the sideloading process was a pain for consumers, and we learned from studies that the average consumer would only bother to connect their iPod to their PC once a year. That meant most people walked around without the latest music on their devices. It was known as the "stale iPod" syndrome.

Jeff saw this as an opportunity. He wanted the Kindle to be like the BlackBerry—no wires, never a need to connect to your PC. Not only did he want us to eliminate sideloading altogether, he wanted to build the bookstore right into the device so you could shop and read on the go. For this to work, he pushed hard for the Kindle to have a 3G modem so that it could connect to a wireless carrier network (Sprint was our first partner) and automatically download new e-books as soon as they were available. The feature was named Whispernet.

Whispernet was another incredibly controversial part of the Kindle project. It had never been done before. Wireless carriers jealously protected their relationships with cellular customers. Here we were, proposing to create a direct wireless relationship that eliminated the need for Kindle customers to set up an account with a carrier, and we didn't plan to charge customers for the network access. Amazon would cover the cost. Jeff, who insisted that Kindle have this capability, instructed the team to find a way to absorb the expense within the overall Kindle product design. Luckily, that requirement wasn't quite as onerous as it might sound, because e-book files are quite small and the connection cost was therefore modest.

This essential feature, Whispernet, was not easy to develop. Establishing relationships with the wireless carriers was a big hurdle. Adding a 3G modem would make the Kindle a much more expensive device. Achieving the breakthrough required a ton of invention by the team, but it would add a great deal to the customer experience. With the ability to download any book almost instantly and never have to link up to a PC, the customer could become engrossed in their reading much faster and with less friction.

The other key feature we debated was the use of E Ink, a nascent technology. It had been developed in the MIT Media Lab and spun out as a company in 1997, but there were no major commercial applications in 2005. Although Jeff and the team were unified in their desire to use the new E Ink technology,[2] we recognized there would be some trade-offs. E Ink screens were black-and-white only, so the Kindle could not support color graphics or video. The transition from one page to the next was slow. But the E Ink screen was much easier on the eyes than the traditional backlit computer screen and was readable in direct sunlight. It would also allow for a much longer battery life, enabling the device to stay on for up to one week without needing a charge. Both of these features were ways for the Kindle to "get out of the way" so customers would forget they were reading on a machine.

We also constantly evaluated the "form factor" of the Kindle—the size, shape, and ease of use—during the iterative design review process. The first prototypes were nothing more than Styrofoam cutouts with mocked-up screens and keyboards. As the form took shape, we evaluated models made of plastic that were weighted so the shape and feel would be as close as possible to the real thing. At every review, Jeff would spend several minutes holding each prototype in one hand, then the other, then in both. When he rejected a prototype it was typically not because the design wasn't sleek or hip enough but rather because something about it would "get in the way" of the customer's reading.

These two features—wireless delivery and the E Ink screen—proved to be two of the keys to making the Kindle great. Wireless delivery meant that customers could search, browse, buy, download, and start reading a new book in under 60 seconds. The E Ink screen's paper-like display meant that, unlike with an iPad, you could read by the pool, and its low power consumption meant you could read throughout a 12-hour plane flight without worrying about the device dying on you. We take these features for granted today, but in those days they were unheard of.

Another issue we had to manage was the availability of titles: selection did matter. As we prepared for launch, we decided it would be necessary to push publishers to digitize many more of their books—only a fraction of their lists was available in e-book form at the time. We knew that to have a successful e-book business, we would need to have a library of millions of e-book titles—ideally, we would eventually offer a digital copy of every book that had ever been in print.

We knew that building such a vast library would be a monumental undertaking, largely because publishers' systems were so antiquated. Once they sent the digital file of a new book to the printer, they often didn't bother to retain it. This meant that for thousands and thousands of books, a digital version would have to be created. Fortunately, we had an advantage in this area. We had already developed the capability for customers to preview several pages of a book they were interested in—first called Look Inside the Book and then improved to Search Inside the Book. We had worked with publishers to manually digitize their books, so we understood the process. And so we launched Kindle, with its connected e-bookstore, with a selection of 90,000 e-books. The Sony e-reader store, by contrast, offered only about 20,000 e-books.

Then it was time to think about pricing. The goal was to find a price point that would compel consumers to start buying and reading e-books. We wanted to make e-books a growth segment of the book business for authors, publishers, and us—prior to the launch of Kindle, it was a tiny business (a few million in annual sales) that wasn't growing. We offered selected bestsellers and new releases at $9.99, which was roughly equal to Amazon's wholesale cost for those e-books. The price for the Kindle device itself was also very close to our cost. And we were absorbing the cost of Whispernet. While we made money on most of the books we sold and our overall margins on e-book sales were positive (even after the publishers raised their wholesale prices in an unsuccessful attempt to force us to raise our $9.99 price on bestsellers and new releases), the early P&L for this business projected little returns in the near term. We were making a big up-front investment in the customer experience, investing some near-term profit in order to get the e-book business and our digital media and devices business off the ground.

We didn't know if or when the cost per e-book would come down and make this a more profitable and sustainable business. We didn't look at it through the short-term lens that the publishers did. We focused on what would make sense to customers and what it would take to get customers excited to buy a Kindle and load it up with their favorite books. We took a leap of faith, hoping that, over time, we would be able to reduce the cost of the device and the books themselves.

The Kindle went on sale for the first time on November 19, 2007. It retailed for $399 and featured a six-inch screen, a keyboard, and 250 MB of memory, enough to hold about two hundred non-illustrated books.[3] It sold out so astonishingly quickly—in less than six hours—that the team had to scramble to find parts so they could manufacture more. While the market seemed to like us, early reviews were mixed. Some critics[4] called Kindle inferior to the rival Sony Reader, which sold for $100 less. Yet, when the team was finally able to build more and get the device back in stock in February 2008, sales continued to be strong.

And then came Oprah.

On October 24, 2008, she devoted an entire episode of her show to Kindle, gushing, "It's absolutely my new favorite favorite thing in the world."[5] Because millions of viewers looked to Oprah, the "Queen of Reading," for book recommendations, sales exploded.

After the huge boost we got from Oprah, all the doubters and naysayers and questioners jumped on the bandwagon—Kindle was a hit! While Oprah was an important accelerant, long-term sales of the Kindle were ensured by the excellence of the product itself. Steve Kessel, who had devoted the vast majority of his time to the Kindle effort, was asked to focus solely on creating new versions of the Kindle and developing other hardware devices as well.

Our first big initiative in our shift to digital media—books— was a success. But at that time, 2008, our digital music and video businesses, which I'd been single-threaded focused on since 2005, were a tiny effort struggling to find a path to growth. With limited resources, no other breakthrough ideas, and daunting competition from Apple (who had a big head start), we had a lot more work to do before we could claim digital as our future.

8
Prime

Amazon's need for top-line growth. Get it done in 11 weeks. Early iterations achieve success. Controlling the "click-to-ship" part of the delivery process. The effect on Amazon's fulfillment process and organization. Jeff walks the store. The launch of Amazon Prime.

* * *

In mid-October 2004, several senior Amazon executives received an email from Jeff Bezos that read roughly as follows:

> We should not be satisfied with the growth of our retail business. This is a house-on-fire issue and we need to dramatically improve the customer experience around shipping. We need a shipping membership program. Let's build and launch it by the end of the year.

We were on the cusp of the always-frantic holiday retail season. Jeff's directive had all the earmarks of what corporate denizens groaningly refer to as a "fire drill" or a "pet CEO project"—an urgent, all-hands-on-deck order to deliver on what seems like a rash decision. A pet project can blow the company off the course of its longer-term strategy and create even larger issues in its wake.

Crisis-driven, out-of-the-blue initiatives are antithetical to Amazon's culture and Leadership Principles. This email from Jeff superficially appeared to be such an initiative, but, as we will show in this chapter, the history behind it and the innovation it gave rise to were quintessentially Amazonian.

Amazon Prime provided a compelling, game-changing customer experience, and as a result it became the greatest driver of growth for the retail business. But Prime's journey from idea to launch was an unusual one for Amazon. It did not have a single-threaded leader or team until very late in the process. There was no clear mission statement, and it did not follow the then-nascent Working Backwards process until well after the project was underway. Few Amazonians thought it was a good idea even when it launched.

But make no mistake about it: we still adhered to many of the Amazonian principles, without which Amazon Prime would not have launched. You'll see that what really drove the launch of Prime was our realization, after a monthslong deep dive into the data, that our customers' needs and the capabilities of the fulfillment network we had spent the better part of nine years and $600 million building were not aligned. There were two options:

1) Stay the course. The company is still growing. Let's maximize our return on this multiyear investment we just made to build our fulfillment centers and tweak them to improve along the way. The next batch of quarterly results will reflect that we're moving in the right direction.
2) Two-day shipping and eventually one-day and same-day shipping will become the norm. Therefore, while what we've built is good, it is not good enough. Buoyed by our "unshakeable conviction that the long-term interests of shareowners are perfectly aligned with the interests of customers," we should embark on this new journey right now.

Option one would be the skills-forward path—that is, using the existing skills and assets of the company to drive business opportunities. Leaders at most companies would likely be praised for choosing this path. The danger is that while they stand atop this local optimum, someone else will figure out how to scale a higher peak they couldn't see at the time due to risk aversion.

In the case of Prime we chose the second path. This realization caused us to take some bold steps that we knew would likely be misunderstood by Wall Street investors and analysts and take years to pay off. But if it worked, we'd earn even more customer trust and set a new standard for e-commerce. Jeff insisted on this path, which resulted in Amazon Prime. Now, this may be one of those moments when you're thinking, "But we don't have a Jeff." The good news is that you don't need a Jeff to make this type of decision. You only need to ruthlessly stick to the simple-to-understand (but sometimes hard-to-follow) principles and process that insist on customer obsession, encourage thinking long term, value innovation, and stay connected to the details. None of us, including Jeff, knew exactly what we would end up building; it's more like we stuck with the process and surrendered to where it was taking us. Prime was a perfect example of the multicausal, nonlinear way in which business initiatives both major and minor got decided on and executed at Amazon. Correspondingly, we can't tell a linear story of how we came up with Prime because there isn't one. Instead, this chapter will reflect that there were a lot of little tributaries that emptied into the river of Prime.

Back to that day in mid-October 2004: we got the answer in the form of Jeff's email directing us to get it done. *In 11 weeks. During the busy holiday season.*

To say that Jeff's proclamation came as a complete surprise to many team members, particularly to those asked to drop what they were doing and shift immediately to this new, undefined program, would be an understatement. But they had not been part of the conversation and formulation and calculation that had been going on for several months. Jeff's decision to launch a free shipping program was bold, but hardly sudden or rash. It was informed by the most basic Amazonian drive: customer obsession.

Amazon Prime—launched in February 2005—would prove to be one of the best decisions Amazon ever made. Not only did it secure Amazon's survival, it became a key driver of its explosive growth over the following decade. Customers loved the ability to get things in mere days, and later hours, after placing their order. And it would shift many of their purchases away from offline, brick-and-mortar stores to online shopping, ensuring also that Amazon was the primary beneficiary of this shift.

The Need for Growth

To understand Amazon's decision to place such a big bet on Prime, you have to understand why we'd come to seek radical ideas to fuel growth. Our third-quarter financial results released on October 21, 2004, showed that sales had grown by 29 percent year over year. Free cash flow had increased by 76 percent. Many corporations would look at such growth figures with envy, but a closer look at our financials at the time revealed a more concerning picture.

Throughout 2004, Amazon sales had continued to grow, but the rate of growth decreased from the prior year, across all lines of business. The output metric of sales revenue was not growing as fast as we wanted. One example can be found embedded in the Supplemental Net Sales Information section of Amazon's earnings results.[1] Amazon's largest product segment at the time, the U.S. Media business, comprised retail sales of books, music, and video, and had grown 12 percent year over year. One year earlier, that same business had been growing by 15 percent year over year. From 15 to 12 is a 20 percent drop in growth rate. Every other product segment was experiencing the same slow decline—growing more slowly than before.

Amazon's Product Segment	Three Months Ended September 30 Y/Y Net Sales Growth	
	2003	2004
US Media	15%	12%
US Electronics & other General Merchandise	35%	27%
Non-US Media	50%	41%
Non-US Electronics & other General Merchandise	259%	132%

That trend of decelerating growth was not good news for a relatively new company seeking to participate in a market so incredibly large that it could be considered virtually unlimited. In 2004, the U.S. retail industry was estimated to generate more than $3.6 trillion of sales, of which less than 2 percent was conducted online. Amazon's growth rate was slowing, but the shift from offline to online commerce was accelerating. That meant one thing: if Amazon's growth continued to decelerate, the company would become a smaller and smaller player in online commerce over time. We were determined to find a way to reverse this trend.

What would it take to get Amazon's top-line growth back on track? For a smaller business, a single action such as introducing a new feature, running a promotion, adding a product category, or expanding into a new territory might suffice to deliver an immediate and noticeable impact on sales. If we had been a small company, we might have cooked up a storewide promotion and launched it with a marketing blitz toward the end of the quarter. It might have made the financial results look better (at least on the revenue side) for the quarter, but such a one-off action wouldn't have fixed the underlying problems. We'd likely find ourselves right back in the same place in the next quarter.

A larger company might address its slowing-growth problem in a more dramatic way, perhaps by making an acquisition of another company, with the goal of creating a big jump in sales (though maybe not profit). But for Amazon at the time, there were few, if any, mergers or large acquisitions that made sense. All the e-tailers we might have bought were small, and their acquisition would not have moved our sales needle appreciably. Buying an offline retailer made no sense—although it might increase the number of customers, it would burden us with the brick-and-mortar costs and inefficiencies we wanted to avoid. Either of those actions carried the very real risk of becoming a resource-consuming internal distraction. We needed to make a move that would convince more customers to shop online with us.

One action we did briefly consider was creating a national advertising campaign to build awareness for the Amazon brand. In

2002, we ran a long-term advertising test in Portland and Minne-apolis. The campaign drove a bump-up in sales, but we ultimately decided not to fully move forward with it. The modest sales uplift was nowhere near enough to justify the $50 million per year we estimated we'd have to spend on an effective national marketing campaign. The better investment was to plow that money back into improving the customer experience.

How could we offer a shopping experience so compelling that an ever-increasing number of customers would shift their retail buying online, specifically to Amazon? Cue the well-worn scenes of C-suite drama: Faced with financial trouble, the CEO calls an emergency meeting of top brass. He leaps to his feet, slams his fists on the table, and, with reddening face, bellows, "We need to grow revenue faster! We need more urgency about driving revenue! I want each group to develop and launch an end-of-quarter market-ing promotion, so we can hit our numbers."

I have to admit that in the late 1990s, a few years before the Prime discussions started, we had a few scenes that looked a bit like that as we grappled with our growth concerns. We tried a number of initiatives, including promotions (buy five books, get one free!) and online nudges for customers to buy across categories. Eventually we realized that such actions wouldn't work, because they took precious resources away from improving the long-term customer experience.

In the end, as always, we looked to our Leadership Principles, two of which were particularly relevant at this time:

Customer Obsession. Leaders start with the customer and work backwards. They work vigorously to earn and keep customer trust. Although leaders pay attention to competitors, they obsess over customers.
Deliver Results. Leaders focus on the key inputs for their business and deliver them with the right quality and in a timely fashion. Despite setbacks, they rise to the occasion and never settle.

After all, retail customers don't care about a company's revenue— they care about what they get back in return for parting with their hard-earned dollars. Amazon customers cared about three main things that we could deliver for them:

- *Price.* Is the price low enough?
- *Selection.* Does Amazon have a wide range of products—ideally everything?
- *Convenience.* Is the product in stock, and can I get it quickly? Can I easily find or discover the product?

Price, selection, and convenience were therefore the inputs for our business. And we could control all three.

Every week the senior leaders would review detailed price, selection, and convenience metrics for each product line and challenge the teams if they were falling short along any of those dimensions. If a competitor beat us in the prior week on pricing for our top-selling items, if we did not add enough new products to the store, if we were out of stock or late on deliveries, or if our website was responding too slowly, the team would have to formulate and enact a plan to fix it. For instance, in the fourth quarter of 2003, we added over 40,000 new gourmet food items, 60,000 new jewelry items, and 70,000 unique health and personal care items in the United States. In Canada and France, we launched Marketplace, the feature that allowed independent third-party retailers to sell their products on our site. We also launched the Home and Kitchen category in Japan. We were adding new items for sale in every other product category as well.

It was not enough. The answer to our stalling growth was likely somewhere inside the triangle of price, selection, and convenience. And that's where we focused our patient but persistent search for new ways to grow. Only over time did the answer become clearer; we were driving up selection and driving down price, but we still had to do something about convenience. And that, most likely, would involve something related to shipping.

Free Shipping 1.0—Super Saver Shipping

Everyone in e-commerce knew customers were laser focused on shipping costs. At Amazon, we knew this because we collected and analyzed customer data in many ways. We conducted surveys of new customers, existing customers, people who had shopped online but had not yet done so on Amazon, and people who had never shopped online at all. We asked them for the top reasons why they didn't place an online order, and what would make them shop online more frequently. In every survey, the top answers remained the same: one of the biggest reasons people didn't order online was that they didn't want to pay for shipping.

The data we'd collected over the years through many tests just reinforced this. Shipping promotions drove significantly higher growth than any other type of promotion. The perceived value of free shipping was higher than straight discounting of product prices. Put another way, if the average discount of a free shipping promotion was 10 percent, we'd see significantly more demand lift (called elasticity) by offering free shipping than by discounting product prices by 10 percent. It wasn't even close. Free shipping drove sales. We just had to figure out a sustainable way to offer free shipping.

Relying on promotions over the long term can be a slippery slope for any retailer, especially one-off promotions. There is danger in training your customers to delay purchases until the next deal comes along.

By the time Jeff sent that October 2004 email calling us to action on Prime, we had actually been working for two and a half years to develop an array of everyday free shipping initiatives that worked for customers, without harming the financial health of the company. We had made some headway, but the results were nowhere near what we needed to revitalize our sales growth. Our first attempt was in early 2002, when we launched the Free Super Saver Shipping program for qualifying orders over $99. "Qualifying" meant products that were sold by Amazon rather than by Marketplace sellers, and also products that were not abnormally large or too heavy to ship.

Super Saver Shipping was built in much the same way that Amazon Prime was later developed. Both projects started with a decisive move, and an insanely compressed timeline, leading up to a public launch. These timelines were part of the DNA of a company whose very first employee's job description, as you may recall, made clear that the candidate would have to accomplish large and complex tasks in "one-third the time that most competent people think possible."

On a Friday evening in mid-November 2001, Sarah Spillman, a product manager in the Marketing group (and Colin's future wife) was driving from Seattle to Portland for a well-deserved long weekend after finishing a grueling period completing that year's holiday promotion plan. A few miles outside Portland, a three-hour drive from Seattle, Sarah received a call from David Risher, the SVP of Retail.

"Hello?" Sarah asked.

"Hi, Sarah. It's David Risher."

"No it's not!" Sarah assumed someone was playing a joke on her and laughed into the phone. "Who is this really? I'm just about to arrive in Portland."

"This really is David Risher." David chuckled, then moved to a casual but most definitely businesslike tone. "I'm glad I was able to catch you. About that trip to Portland . . ."

He told her that the company would be scrapping its current planned holiday promotion, the one she'd worked so hard to complete, and instead would offer something new: a free shipping promotion for orders over $25. And oh, by the way, could she turn around and come back to Seattle to get started?

They met the following morning—Saturday—to go over the details. She and her team spent most of their waking hours over the following two weeks reworking the holiday promotion with an offer of free shipping for orders over $25. Because Amazon had never done this kind of promotion, it required substantial software and site design changes. Likewise, the marketing messages—both on the website and in a mass email campaign sent to virtually every Amazon customer—had to be crafted and coordinated to launch simultaneously. Despite the last-minute time crunch, the promotion launched on time—and was such a hit with customers that we decided to turn it into a permanent program after the holidays. We formally launched Super Saver Shipping on January 22, 2002, albeit with a higher minimum order of $99. (In order to maximize attention to the new product, Jeff announced it in the same press release as the quarterly earnings results, which you'll see is a recurring pattern.)

Customers responded with such enthusiasm that in the first several months of 2002, the order threshold to qualify for Super Saver Shipping was lowered to $49, then dropped to $25 on qualifying orders. As predicted, customers who took advantage of Super Saver Shipping bought more, driving up their gross order totals.

Super Saver Shipping was meant to appeal to price-sensitive customers. In January 2005, the standard shipping charge for an order containing books was $3.00 per shipment plus $0.99 per item. If you wanted faster delivery, you could opt for two-day shipping, which cost $7.49 per shipment plus $1.99 per item, or one-day shipping, which cost $12.49 per shipment plus $2.99 per item. Shipping fees on a typical two-book order, then, could range from $4.98 for standard to $18.47 for one-day.[2] The higher price reflected our cost of expedited shipping, which usually required that the package make some of its journey aboard an airplane rather than a truck. Not surprisingly, most customers chose standard shipping. These shipping charges are cringeworthy by today's standards, but were actually quite competitive at the time.

With Super Saver Shipping, the order would leave the fulfillment center within three to five days of being placed, and would be carried to its destination by a ground delivery service. This enabled Amazon to keep its costs low, since no flights were involved. It also made it possible for Amazon to group items together—ones that might have been ordered separately or were not all immediately available from a single fulfillment center—which reduced the total number of packages shipped. So Super Saver Shipping reduced our costs and lowered prices for the customer. The program, which seems laughably primitive today, offered a valuable insight into what our customers wanted. They were delighted to be given a free shipping option, even if the trade-off was "slow and free" or "fast and expensive." And we were becoming reasonably competent at affordably and reliably delivering this customer experience.

Super Saver Shipping had set a new standard. But it would not last. Customer expectations are not static. They rise over time, which means you cannot rest on your laurels.

There Was a Catch

Two years after launch, in 2004, Super Saver Shipping appeared to be a big success. Customers were ordering more frequently each year and the average number of items per order increased. Since the $25 order threshold to qualify for free shipping was higher than the average price of a single item, customers bought more than one item just to get the free delivery—our metrics confirmed that there was an increase in the number of items per order—an obvious benefit for Amazon. And as the average order size increased, there was more product profit available to offset the cost of free shipping.

Super Saver Shipping also worked nicely with the fulfillment and delivery network, the supply chain, that we had built. At the end of 2004, Amazon had roughly 4.4 million square feet of fulfillment center space across eight U.S. facilities located in Kentucky, Pennsylvania, Kansas, Nevada, North Dakota, and Delaware. We had established operations in those locations in part because they were close to the hubs of third-party delivery services such as the U.S. Postal Service, FedEx, and UPS.

Even though Super Saver Shipping made sense for Amazon's supply chain and was a popular feature, we realized that it could not be the driver of significant growth for the retail business. First, this was because many of our heaviest buyers needed the fastest possible delivery—they were not willing to wait three to five days for an item to ship. Second, some of our price-sensitive customers were not willing to up their order to $25 just to qualify for Super Saver Shipping. It didn't make sense to them to spend more on goods just to pay less on shipping. As a result, they would do what 98 percent of other consumers did at the time—shop at a brick-and-mortar store. So, while Super Saver Shipping was popular, it did not appeal to large segments of our customer base. We realized that we needed something better, some kind of friction-free program that would appeal to our entire customer base, regardless of their time or price sensitivity.

One way in which we tracked our shipping performance was with a metric called "Click to Deliver." This was the total amount of time from the moment the customer placed an order (click) to the moment the package arrived at its final destination (deliver). We divided the process into two segments. The first—the click-to-ship time—was the amount of time required for Amazon to process the order, package it, and hand it over to a third-party delivery service. The second segment—the ship-to-deliver—was the time between the handover and the customer receiving their package.

Click-to-ship was the part of the process that we could control, and we constantly looked for ways to shorten it. If we could reduce the time it took to process and fulfill an order, we could push the order cut-off time to later in the day—such as, "orders placed by 7 p.m. will ship the same day"—which was an important customer benefit. But no matter how much we improved click-to-ship time, we did not control the ship-to-deliver segment of the process, which meant that customers had to bear the burden of the cost/speed trade-off. It became clear that, if we were to reduce the total delivery time, we would have to gain more control of the ship-to-deliver metric, which was largely determined by two things: the distance between the fulfillment center and the customer delivery location, and the shipment method. To improve total delivery time, we would need to make big changes to our supply chain. Our current fulfillment network had been built to optimize for nearby access to our third-party shippers so we could reliably and cheaply ship products to customers in three to five days. This logistics topology had been convenient for Amazon, but not for the customers who wanted products delivered fast and free. To optimize the ship-to-deliver segment, we would need many more fulfillment centers, and they would have to be located so that free, one-to-two-day delivery was both possible and cost effective. That meant a much greater presence near urban areas. Now that customers had gotten a taste of free shipping, they no longer wanted to be forced to choose between "slow and free" and "fast and expensive." Jeff exhibits discomfort when presented with an either/or proposition in which both results are mediocre. Viewed through the Customer Obsession and Insist on the Highest Standards leadership principles, the only answer to the question, "Which would you rather have, 'slow and free' or 'fast and expensive'?" is "fast and free." So the catch was that "fast and free" was where Amazon needed to go next, but our fulfillment capabilities were not up to the task.

The question was how to accomplish such a major shift. If we offered fast-and-free delivery with our current supply chain structure, the cost to Amazon would be extremely high. But it would take years to build out the new fulfillment network required to reduce delivery time affordably.

Loyalty Programs

So, we brainstormed solutions to the fundamental shipping problem. Our marketing, retail, and finance teams set three criteria that any new marketing initiative would have to meet to go forward:

1. It had to be affordable (an eye-catching but financially unsustainable approach was out of the question).
2. It had to drive the right customer behavior (that is, nudge customers to buy more from Amazon).
3. It had to be a better use of funds than the obvious alternative, which was to invest those same funds into actions that would improve the customer experience, such as lowering prices even further or improving our in-stock rate.

Crafting an affordable program that we felt would lead customers to buy more—rather than continuing on with our tried-and-true method of funneling cost savings back into lower prices—seemed difficult, if not impossible, at the time, especially given the constraints of our fulfillment and delivery supply chain.

One promising approach, however, was to create some kind of loyalty program. In 2000, Amazon had no large-scale loyalty program, which was unusual for an e-commerce company of its size. Jeff asked David Risher, Alan Brown (head of Marketing), and Jason Child (Finance) to create a loyalty program that would drive durable growth. The marketing and retail teams analyzed several variations of loyalty programs, including free standard shipping for orders over $25 (which was essentially Super Saver Shipping but without the three-to-five-day click-to-ship time), free shipping on all preorders (that is, an order placed before the item's official first ship date), paying an annual fee for free standard shipping, or free two-day shipping. We also considered an alternate form of loyalty program that would include different combinations of purchases of our "owned inventory" (items we stocked in our fulfillment centers) and those of third-party items, where we would have to subsidize shipping costs or require third-party sellers to do so. We even evaluated rebates and points-based programs similar to the airlines', but there's an important difference between airlines and retailers. Once a plane takes off, its empty seats have no value. Therefore, airlines, in exchange for loyalty, can give away marginal inventory that would otherwise go unsold. Whereas in retail, giving away either product or shipping fees always has a cost. None of the ideas made it very far because they could not meet the three essential criteria.

The proposals were not limited to the marketing and retail teams. An idea similar to Prime occurred to a principal software engineer named Charlie Ward as he described a problem at a software team meeting. Charlie had spent the better part of a year trying to untangle our ordering software into separate distributed components. Two of these components were the shipping software and the promotions software, which is where the Super Saver Shipping logic resided. Charlie said that for Super Saver Shipping orders we had invented one of the most complicated and bug-ridden ways to calculate zero. The shipping software calculated the shipping charges, and then the promotions software dutifully tried to unwind these charges until they netted to zero. He said there had to be a better way. After Charlie described the problem, another software team reported on its work building a subscription platform for an Amazon DVD rental business that would soon launch.

Charlie was intrigued. He asked, "Why couldn't we have customers pay an annual subscription fee that would include free shipping for a year? That would be a big win for customers. And we could stop spending so much effort reconciling fees." Kim Rachmeler, who ran the customer service department at the time, liked the idea. "You may have something there, Charlie," she said. "Why don't you run with it."[3]

Charlie talked with colleagues, refined the idea, wrote up a one-page narrative, and submitted it. He then left for a well-deserved vacation in Italy.

Though it's unclear whether Jeff knew about Charlie's idea before sending out his directive to launch a free shipping program in October, it doesn't really matter—the story is noteworthy for a couple of reasons. First, customer-focused ideas come from all areas within Amazon. Many companies have the "business people" tell the "technical people" what to build. There's little discussion back and forth, and the teams stay in their own lanes. Amazon is not like this at all. It's everyone's job to obsess over customers and think of inventive ways to delight them.

A second noteworthy aspect of the story is that when Charlie returned from vacation and found out we had decided to build something akin to his idea, he joined the team charged with making Prime a reality, and played a vital role on it. Once Amazon Prime launched, Charlie became its leader for technical systems, customer experience, and financial performance.

In other words, Charlie was, in Amazonian terms, a "strong general athlete" (SGA). These customer-obsessed, inventive, long-term thinkers take pride in operational excellence and embody the Amazon Leadership Principles. Amazon often puts SGAs like Charlie into leadership positions and gives them the tools to become subject matter experts. Kim Rachmeler too was an SGA. She held many leadership roles. In addition to running customer service, she led Amazon's Supply Chain Systems and the Personalization department. She was also a member of the S-Team.

Despite the many free shipping ideas circulating around the company, none of the proposals that were initially put forward met all three criteria we had established for the shipping solution. We worried that the membership programs that involved an annual fee for free standard shipping or for free two-day shipping would encourage customers to purchase fewer items per order. This would not generate enough money to cover shipping costs, which meant it would not be sustainable. Unsustainable growth at any cost was definitely not the customer behavior we were after. Review meetings often ended when someone asked, "Wouldn't the money be better spent on lowering prices and improving In Stock for customers?" We knew these actions were effective at increasing customer sales, but we weren't so sure that a subscription program would do the same.

Another concern that caused a big debate was how heavy buyers would respond to a loyalty program. Would it encourage them to place additional orders? Or would they have placed the same orders even if they had to pay for shipping? The purpose of this program was to drive incremental buying behavior, not for Amazon to pick up the shipping tab as a way of saying thanks to our big customers.

As we considered proposals, there were a number of sound arguments put forward for why we should *not* embark on a free shipping program. A big one was that it would be too expensive, largely because it would require the massive retooling of our supply chain. We couldn't even accurately estimate the cost, because our models could not really predict how customers would react, so we were relying more on judgment and educated guesses than on data. Even if our assumptions were correct, the program would take years to pay off; not a single person in the leadership team other than Jeff was pushing for Prime to launch in 2004; it was the holiday season, which meant we were already really busy! This very nearly became one of those scenarios when a company takes the seductive but ultimately wrong path of staying the course, making a serious error of omission as a result.

The "institutional no" is a big reason why Amazon could have made an error of omission in this case. Jeff and other Amazon leaders often talk about the "institutional no" and its counterpart, the "institutional yes." The institutional no refers to the tendency for well-meaning people within large organizations to say no to new ideas. The errors caused by the institutional no are typically errors of omission, that is, something a company doesn't do versus something it does. Staying the current course offers managers comfort and certainty—even if the price of that short-term certainty is instability and value destruction later on.

Moreover, the errors of omission caused by the institutional no can be notoriously tricky to spot. Most businesses don't have the tools to evaluate the cost of not doing something. And when the cost is high, they only realize when it's too late to change. The institutional no can infiltrate all levels of the organization. It's what causes a board of directors to say no to a big change of strategy (think Nokia and Microsoft missing the turn on smartphones). It's what drives frontline managers to keep their top performers working on a current project and say no to their involvement in high-risk experiments that could fail but could also pay off handsomely later—especially if that payoff is likely to be after the manager has moved on to another role.

Jeff would likely have been making just such an error of omission if his October 2004 email had read, "Let's wait to introduce free shipping and just focus on making this 2004 holiday season our best ever!" If he had stopped pressing the teams for more free shipping ideas, there would no doubt have been a sigh of relief. We would have looked at each other and said thank goodness we made the right call to pause.

Instead of marking a turning point in Amazon's history, that mid-October day might have been remarkable in another way. It might have been the moment we made a disastrous mistake, even if we didn't realize it until years later.

Walking the Store

Most retail CEOs walk the store when they have a chance, and Jeff is no exception. The typical CEO will pay a visit to a retail outlet when they're in the area—often unannounced, or even incognito—to do a bit of browsing and observe what's going on. An online retail CEO can walk the store anytime, of course, and Jeff's preferred walking-the-store time was early Saturday and Sunday mornings. It was not unusual for me to wake up at 7 a.m. on a weekend, check my email, and read five or six messages from Jeff to the relevant teams on issues he had found while walking the store that morning.

The first discussions that would shape Amazon Prime actually began in the spring of 2004, several months before Jeff's notable October email. The process started with a scattering of email exchanges between Jeff and a handful of Amazon executives. The participants usually included Greg Greeley (a finance and retail VP who would eventually own and operate the Amazon Prime program), Tom Szkutak (CFO), Diego Piacentini (SVP of Worldwide Retail), Jeff Wilke (then SVP of Worldwide Operations), and me (Colin).

As we discussed in chapter six, price, selection, and convenience are three key elements of Amazon's flywheel. And shipping is a large component of convenience. The Amazon Deliver Results leadership principle states, "Leaders focus on the key inputs for their business and deliver them with the right quality and in a timely fashion. Despite setbacks, they rise to the occasion and never settle." Shipping speed is a key input metric for Amazon. So, if you are customer obsessed, then you're also obsessed with measuring and improving the shipping experience for customers. Jeff was no exception here, and therefore it was no surprise that shipping was the main focus of these email exchanges.

One spring 2004 walking-the-store email that Jeff wrote ended up making a direct contribution to the Prime conversation, though we didn't know it at the time. It addressed an issue that was seemingly nontechnical in nature: making too much profit on an item. Jeff browsed our electronics and jewelry stores. The prices for flat-screen TVs and precious jewelry ran into the hundreds and sometimes thousands of dollars. We had little pricing flexibility on many of these items due to supplier relationships.

Since we couldn't offer lower prices, Jeff felt we should do the next best thing: offer free next-day shipping. We made quite a bit of gross profit from those items, compared to the gross profit from a $15 book or video, so we could afford to offer free expedited shipping for the same all-in price.

Jeff sent an email to the relevant category leaders and S-Team members with his suggestion to offer free shipping on selected items. When he sent a team an idea, it did not need to be implemented, but it definitely needed to be evaluated and that evaluation needed to be communicated back to him. As Jeff Holden, a former SVP and S-Team member, once told Jeff, "You have enough ideas to crush the company." (Jeff responded with his distinctive laugh.)

As counterintuitive as it may sound that a company would deliberately choose to cut into its margins, it made sense for Amazon. We had to figure out how to thrive in a world where we made a modest amount of money on each item we shipped. So it was no great surprise that the category managers responded to Jeff's email by saying that they had in fact already tried to implement this feature. The challenge was that adding this functionality would require significant resources from several software teams who already had more work than they could handle. As discussed in chapter three, we had grown so fast over the years that our software was a tangled mess, especially the promotions and shipping software. We hadn't yet removed the technical dependencies among most of our key systems. To make even a simple change was risky and expensive because it required meticulous design and testing to make sure things worked properly after the change was completed. That meant any proposed software change had to be justified by its ability to deliver a large payback. They said they'd take another look at it.

After a few weeks, I followed up on Jeff's suggestion. The teams had been thinking about it, but determined that it was a complex cross-functional project and enabling free shipping for a limited number of high-priced electronics and jewelry items would not deliver a sufficient payback. There were plans in the works that would have made promotions of that type easier to implement, but the required changes to the software would take more than a year to complete.

But the larger problem remained unsolved. The idea of free shipping on selected items was tabled that summer, but our growth rates were still decelerating, and the emails from Jeff kept coming. Every few weeks, he'd start a thread about shipping, posing questions such as, "What about an annual membership program where we charge $X and offer free standard shipping?" Or, "Can we ship all jewelry items for free?" Or, "How about all orders over $X ship immediately for free (versus the three-to-five-day delay for Super Saver Shipping)?"

If the team had already considered the idea or had a ready answer, they would respond immediately. If not, Jeff's question would trigger a group of financial analysts, category managers, and operations analysts to model the idea, project its expected cost, identify its strengths, weaknesses, and risks, and finally make a recommendation. Greg Greeley was the point person in charge of responding. At one point he had over half a dozen different scenarios to analyze. In early October, Jeff said he wanted to see a comparison of all these alternatives by the end of the month. A few days later, in the middle of the month, Jeff sent the house-on-fire email and said rather than presenting the set of ideas in three weeks, we should select the best one and launch the program by the end of the year. I think at some point he had decided that it wasn't the idea that was flawed, but the decision-making process, a process encumbered by institutional risk-aversion. The "October surprise" email arose out of his realization that you simply could not prove a priori that free shipping would work. You just had to try it.

It's Time

At this point in mid-October, the thought experiments transitioned to a "tangible project," albeit one with no dedicated resources and no definition other than "launch a shipping membership program by the end of the year." After much back and forth, by the second half of November, there was general consensus that the best option was a paid yearly membership that would offer free two-day shipping. Now we needed to find a team to build it. What came next was a clear expression of another one of Amazon's Leadership Principles in action, Have Backbone; Disagree and Commit: "Leaders are obligated to respectfully challenge decisions when they disagree, even when doing so is uncomfortable or exhausting. Leaders have conviction and are tenacious. They do not compromise for the sake of social cohesion. Once a decision is determined, they commit wholly."

As we have described, numerous leaders had disagreed with Jeff on this topic. But the time for debate on whether and when we should launch free shipping was over. It was now time to act on the second half of "disagree and commit." Everybody sprang into action. Jeff Holden was tasked with marshaling whatever resources were necessary to build and launch by the Q4 2004 earnings call scheduled for the end of January. We were going to do it well and do it quickly. Jeff scheduled a meeting for Friday, December 3, to meet with the implementation team leads, including Vijay Ravindran and Dorothy Nichols. The only problem is that Amazon started experiencing technical issues with the site and there was a significant outage. Vijay took the unusual but correct move to cancel the meeting and reschedule for another time. Jeff took it in stride and said, how about tomorrow morning at my house? That's when Jeff, Jeff Holden, Vijay, and Dorothy met to go over what would become Amazon Prime. Jeff said he wanted to build a moat around our best customers. Prime would be a premium experience for convenience-oriented customers. Jeff H., Vijay, and Dorothy could recruit whoever they needed to the team, but it had to launch concurrently with the next earnings call.

The teams involved were in a flat-out sprint with long hours for the duration of the project, which internally was called Futurama. It was only at this point in the process that the Futurama PR/FAQ was belatedly written and revised. While completing the project required heroic efforts from several dozen team members (including Charlie Ward, recently returned from his vacation), the implementation story is outside the scope of this book and has been covered in the press. The earnings call was even bumped out to February 2, 2005, to accommodate the project launch.

It's also worth pointing out that other teams had created building blocks for other purposes that could be deployed for developing Prime—and without which we would not have been able to meet the aggressive schedule. Jeff was aware of the details that would give us a head start. One building block that we took advantage of was the Fast Track program. Jeff had seen customers' positive reaction to Amazon's newly acquired capabilities with Fast Track and, as usual, he wanted to double down the bet, which in this case meant using it for Prime. Fast Track had been developed to allow the fulfillment system to make more precise estimates about shipping time—that is, we went from "Usually ships within 24 hours" to "This item will ship tonight if you order within 1 hour and 32 minutes." Fast Track took two years to complete, and had required a massive amount of software development as well as physical modifications to the fulfillment centers. So we didn't have to reinvent the wheel when it came to the accuracy and success rates of the shipping promises. A second building block, as noted, was the subscription platform for an upcoming DVD rental launch. There would have been no Amazon Prime anytime remotely near February 2005 without these two building blocks.

Indeed, on February 2, 2005, less than four months after the notorious October email from Jeff, Amazon Prime launched. The truth is, it was not an overnight success as the Kindle had been. The first customers who joined were the heavy buyers who already spent more than $79/year on expedited shipping. So we were really just subsidizing their existing habits. Though we had created a game-changing online shopping experience, shifting consumer behavior takes time. In the months and years since, it is hard to overestimate the extent to which Prime finally created a viable alternative for shoppers around the world. Prime transformed Amazon from a fairly successful company in the e-commerce space to a top player in the retail space. And Prime changed the way people think about shopping online—and shopping, period. As one journalist wrote, "Amazon single-handedly—and permanently—raised the bar for convenience in online shopping. That, in turn, forever changed the types of products shoppers were willing to buy online. Need a last-minute gift or nearing the end of a pack of diapers? Amazon was now an alternative to the immediacy of brick-and-mortar stores."[4]

As Jeff announced to shareholders in 2018, "13 years post-launch, we have exceeded 100 million paid Prime members globally."[5]

Amazon Prime is a great example of the tremendous value you can unlock by ruthlessly applying the principles of customer obsession and long-term thinking to a problem—in this case, increasing revenue growth. To do so, we had to accept the fact that the current logistics infrastructure we had painstakingly built over the years, though doing reasonably well at the time, wouldn't cut it in the long run. We had to change the expected payback period of our decision from the next quarter or two to five or even seven years ahead. Given that focus on the customer experience and our willingness to think long term, doing Amazon Prime made perfect sense. We were able to give customers what they had long wanted while generating free cash flow for Amazon that was dramatically higher than if we had tried to squeeze as much as possible from the status quo.

9
Prime Video

A disastrous Unboxing. The Howard Hughes model. The problem of digital rights management. Seeking a path to the living room. Netflix changes the game. Prime Instant Video as an Amazon Prime benefit. The development of Amazon Studios.

* * *

It was August 2006. The staff of Amazon's Seattle headquarters had assembled in the 5th Avenue Theater for the quarterly All Hands Meeting. The day would be the trial run for a project that I (Bill) had been working on furiously for the past 12 months. As Roy Price and Ethan Evans, co-leaders of the Amazon digital video business, came onstage to introduce everyone to Amazon's first digital movie and TV show service, Amazon Unbox, I sat nervously with my team and about two thousand other Amazonians.

We were excited to have reached the finish line on Unbox. The public launch was just a week away.

Roy and Ethan explained to the audience how Unbox would work. The customer would go online and browse through tens of thousands of movie and TV show titles. They'd buy or rent whatever they wanted to watch. Download it to their PC. Hit play. Sit down and enjoy the show. As simple as that.

After the introduction, it was time for the dramatic reveal on the big screen. Ethan approached the laptop. We held our breath.

He clicked play. The screen lit up and the video started playing . . . upside down. The crowd emitted a sound that was part nervous laughter and part howl of pain.

That disastrous live demo was a harbinger of what was to come. In just a few weeks, we would be receiving feedback from customers that mirrored that audience reaction: empathy, groans, pain, bewilderment. I had hoped and expected the launch of Unbox to be one of the greatest achievements of my Amazon career. Instead, it turned out to be my single biggest failure.

This is the story of how we began by getting something terribly wrong, but learned from our mistakes and, in the end, got it fantastically right.

* * *

Cut to February 22, 2011: Amazon Prime users who visited the site discovered a new benefit of membership. We (Bill and team) had launched Prime Instant Video that morning.[1] It offered streaming of five thousand movies and TV shows as part of the Amazon Prime membership, at no extra charge. Until that moment, the Amazon Prime brand had meant one thing to subscribers: fast, free shipping. Millions of customers had subscribed. Tens of millions of customers knew what Prime stood for. But now Amazon Prime meant streaming video too?

To us, the vision was clear: to add more benefits that had broad, global appeal in order to make Prime earth's most compelling and irresistible value for customers. As Jeff would say in his 2016 shareholder letter, "We want Prime to be such a good value, you'd be irresponsible to not be a member." Five thousand titles was just the beginning. In the coming months and years we planned to add thousands of must-see movies and TV series to make watching Prime Video a daily habit. Today, Amazon Prime Video is an integral component of Prime, with more than 100 million subscribers globally, and tens of thousands of titles available for streaming. Among those titles are shows and movies such as *Transparent*, *The Marvelous Mrs. Maisel*, *Mozart in the Jungle*, and *Manchester by the*

Sea—winners of prestigious awards, including Golden Globes and Emmys.

Once again, getting to this point involved significant hurdles, among them making the right investments in streaming technology and applications for mobile and TV devices, overcoming resistance from reluctant device manufacturers, creating our own line of successful devices, and making the right eight- and nine-figure investments in movies and TV shows. We achieved this by combining a long-term perspective with continuous improvement in our digital video customer experience over more than ten years.

The journey to that 2011 launch took more than six years of work and a string of missteps, challenges, and, yes, outright failures. The process began in early to mid-2004, even before Prime, when we embarked on Amazon's first video initiative, which had a brand name that has been long since forgotten by Amazon customers and recalls bad memories for those of us who built it: Amazon Unbox.

Unbox was Amazon's first digital video service. Jeff Bezos and I landed on that name after countless brainstorming sessions. The "Un" part was meant to convey that it was counter to or unlike the way people watched movies and TV shows in those days. The problem was the name was neither fish nor fowl. It wasn't quite an "empty vessel" name, like Hulu, that didn't mean anything but sounded distinctive and memorable; nor was it a name whose meaning was instantly understandable, like Netflix.

The Unbox customer experience was a failure. My team and I were new at this—we hadn't launched a digital media service before. Also, we had no track record at setting high standards when developing a new customer experience. Further, we were limited by technical constraints (internet bandwidth, hardware, software), by what movies and TV shows the studios were willing to offer, by how customers would be allowed to watch them and at what prices. Finally, Amazon didn't have a hardware and software ecosystem that would enable us to control the end-to-end customer experience—Apple was way ahead of us on this and jumped out to a big lead in 2007, outselling us by more than ten times.

Unbox: A Misstep on the Long and Winding Road to the Living Room

It's hard to remember what it was like to watch a movie before streaming. In those days, people who wanted to watch movies at home basically had two alternatives: drive to the video store (remember those?) and rent a movie or receive a red envelope in the mail from Netflix. We were offering one of the first services that would enable customers to buy movies and TV shows online and download them to their computer. We believed that we were creating a service that would instigate a new and valuable customer experience. After all, how great would it be to have access to a huge selection of popular movies and television shows and be able to download them to your computer or laptop so you could watch them at home or on the go, with complete control over when and how you watched them, and to have access to them forever?

Netflix DVD service was growing fast at the time, but we made a bet that downloading would eventually be more attractive to the customer than DVD rental, and it would certainly be a whole lot better than the Blockbuster brick-and-mortar model. Blockbuster was then at its peak, but the customer experience they offered was, in our view, pretty much the pits. Although Blockbuster introduced a DVD online subscription service in 2006, the typical customer throughout the United States, and indeed all over the world, still went through the dismal Friday-evening drill. They'd leave work and schlep to their local Blockbuster store in hopes of finding a good movie to watch that evening. The good titles and the latest releases were always gone, so they'd settle for something the whole family could at least tolerate. Often, they returned the title late and had to pay dreaded late fees that could double or triple the cost of a rental.

We thought Unbox could change all that.

Let me explain how our service worked, or, I should say, sort of worked. First, you would go to the Amazon website to get the Amazon Unbox application, download it, and install it on your PC. I say PC because if you were a Mac user, you were out of luck—Unbox only ran on Windows machines, and only on Windows machines less than three years old. And even if you had a PC, the installation process was frustratingly slow. However, if you got the app installed, you could then go on the Amazon website and select a movie for download.

That was where Unbox ran into more trouble.

In 2005, because streaming high-quality video was not yet possible, you had to download the movie to your hard drive before you could start watching. How long did that take? Well, a clever customer would take their personal laptop to the office where they would have access to what was then considered a "high-speed" network. Even with that, it would take an hour or two to download a two-hour movie. For those who forgot to do an office download, or didn't have access to a high-speed network, the process would take considerably longer. With a DSL connection, the standard of the day, it could take as long as four hours to get the job done.

We knew that could in no way be considered an appealing customer experience, so we spent a lot of time coming up with potential solutions.

One idea was to create a dedicated DVD burner that the customer would install at home. When they purchased the movie, it would automatically start downloading to the burner, and the DVD would pop out as soon as it was done, ready to watch on your TV. This would solve one Unbox problem—namely, if you downloaded the movie onto your computer, there was no way to transfer it to your TV, unless you were geeky enough to be able to kludge a connection.

We abandoned the burner approach and developed a feature called RemoteLoad. It enabled you to browse the Amazon site on any computer—it didn't have to be the one you were going to watch it on—purchase a title, and initiate the download so the movie would be available for viewing on your computer of choice whenever you were ready. The shortcoming was, if you wanted to watch the movie on, say, your home PC, that PC had to be pow-ered up, the Unbox app had to be open, and the machine had to be connected to the internet. Very few customers would take the trouble to do all that.

We also wanted to include one other innovative feature—the capability for the customer to download the movie or TV show multiple times to different devices at no additional charge. On Ap-ple's iTunes music app, the customer would download songs to their computer. They could listen on their Mac, but they had to "sideload" songs to their iPod, using a cable. If you lost a song, or your entire music library, from the computer, you were out of luck. You might have spent hundreds of dollars building up your music collection only to see it vanish thanks to a faulty hard drive, an ac-cidental deletion, or some other mishap.

We knew from our research that this drove customers crazy, but the solution was not a technical one, because the problem was about rights. The studios earned 70 percent of the revenue on each purchase and considered every download to be a new sale. They did not think of themselves as being in the customer experience business—they simply wanted to extract as many royalty payments as they could from their distributors (e.g., Apple and Amazon) and their distributors' customers.

In an effort to rectify the problem, we entered into negotiations with the movie studios. This took time and was not a great deal of fun, but we succeeded. We were proud to launch Unbox with a "Whispernet-like" feature that no other service offered: your per-sonal library of videos—called "your video library" (internally we called it YVL, pronounced "whyvull")—stored on the Amazon site, that you could download multiple times onto multiple devices, at no additional fee. That's standard today, but it was a breakthrough at the time.

This kind of thinking and work on behalf of the customer would pay off for Amazon in the long term, but in the short term, this feature wasn't significant enough to help Unbox overcome its shortcomings.

As we soon found out, there were too many other customer

experience problems for Unbox to succeed. Not only was the download ridiculously slow, but the Microsoft Windows Media digital rights management software that we relied on was so buggy that a large percentage of customers couldn't play the videos at all. Our commitment to deliver a great viewing experience, with DVD-quality picture and sound, made the download slower and more likely to fail.

As it turned out, download speed was much more important to customers than image quality. Remember that in December 2005, YouTube had burst onto the scene. It offered user-generated content, no popular movies or TV shows. The video was low-resolution and played in a small frame on your PC. Consumers were not bothered by the low-quality video, and YouTube began to attract tens of millions of viewers. Weeks after our launch, Apple launched the capability to watch movies and shows on an iPod screen, even tinier than the YouTube frame. Customers ate that up, too. Fast. Easy. iPod compatible. Everything that Unbox was not.

A few days after launch Jeff called Steve Kessel, me, and Neil Roseman into his office. He was disappointed that we hadn't set high enough standards for the quality of the customer experience, and he was frustrated that we had let our customers down.

In retrospect, it is easy to see the mistakes. We had rushed Unbox out the door before it was ready. In the weeks leading up to launch, rumors had been swirling around Hollywood and in the press that Apple was close to launching a digital video service. We didn't want to come in second to Apple so we were in a frenzy to ship Unbox and ship it fast. This was directly antithetical to the notion of focusing on the customer, not the competitor. We had conducted an internal employee-only beta test, but we failed to use the results as an opportunity to slow down, carefully review the customer feedback, and take the time needed to make real changes to improve the quality of the customer experience. We were just focused on shipping. We had prioritized speed, press coverage, and *competitor* obsession over the customer experience. We had been decidedly un-Amazonian.

This is my self-assessment that I wrote in my performance review that year:

Overall, my performance was dreadful in 2006. In Unbox, our launch was poorly received, partly due to DRM [digital rights management] and licensing issues that restrict content usage, and selection, partly due to bad product choices we made for consumers (erring on the side of quality over download speed) and partly due to engineering defects. In any case, I didn't manage these issues appropriately and the result was a weak launch with weak consumer response and negative press reaction.

Net my performance versus goals can be summarized by a poor execution percentage in terms of projects completed and the main project that is complete (Unbox Video) is not a compelling customer experience (yet) and the rate of sales is pitiful. I think a grade of 'D' for my performance vs. goals would be generous.

Painful to read! At least I can say it embodied the "vocally self-critical" aspect of the Earn Trust leadership principle. In any other company, I probably would have been fired. Fortunately for me, Amazon's commitment to long-term thinking includes its investment in people. They understand that when you innovate and build new things, you will frequently fail. If you fire the person, you lose the benefit of the learning that came along with that experience. Jeff would say something like this to a leader who had just laid an egg: "Why would I fire you now? I just made a million-dollar investment in you. Now you have an obligation to make that investment pay off. Figure out and clearly document where you went wrong. Share what you have learned with other leaders throughout the company. Be sure you don't make the same mistake again, and help others avoid making it the first time."

I learned a lot from what went wrong with the launch of Unbox, and I was able to share my knowledge with others at Amazon. That knowledge stayed with me and has informed how I think about every new product and feature I have been involved with in the years since that brutal self-assessment.

Not long after the Unbox launch, my boss, Steve Kessel, took me aside. He told me that he had had an interesting meeting with Jeff, who had made it very clear that setting and insisting on high standards for the digital media organization was an essential part of Steve's job. To make his point, Jeff asked Steve if he had ever seen the movie *The Aviator*, the story of Howard Hughes, the business tycoon, aviator, and film director. Jeff described a scene in which Hughes, played by Leonardo DiCaprio, visits one of his aircraft manufacturing facilities to check on the progress of his latest project—the Hughes H-1 Racer, a sleek single-passenger plane designed to set new speed records. Hughes examines the plane closely, running his fingers along the surface of the fuselage. His team watches anxiously. Hughes is not satisfied. "Not enough," he says. "Not enough. These rivets have to be completely flush. I want no air resistance on the fuselage. She's got to be cleaner. Cleaner! You understand?"

The team leader nods. Back to the drawing board.

Jeff had told Steve that it was his job to be like Howard Hughes. From then on, Steve had to run his fingers over each new Amazon product, checking for anything that might reduce the quality, insisting that his team maintain the highest standards. My sense was that Steve was telling me the story for two reasons. First, it was a kind of heads-up. He wanted me to know, as one of his senior team members, that he would be sending me and my team back to the drawing board if a product didn't measure up. Second, he was telling me indirectly that I too was responsible for setting higher standards for our products. I had to be more like Howard Hughes.

The Issue of Rights

Now we had to figure out how to fix what we had so poorly wrought.

The fact of the matter was that Unbox was boxed in on all sides: by our competitors, particularly Apple; by our reliance on Microsoft for media playback and PCs running Windows; and by our suppliers, the movie studios. A key issue was the use of digital rights management software, or DRM, to control the download of proprietary content and prevent theft, sharing, and reuse by customers. Apple had developed its proprietary DRM software, called FairPlay, that ensured secure content download, and Apple had deals in place with the major content producers. The only way for us to enable our customers to download and play movies on Macs and iPods was to use FairPlay DRM.

We needed DRM software for Unbox, but there was no way Apple would license FairPlay to us, and no way the studios could force Apple to do so. Unless we built our own DRM, we had to go with Microsoft's Windows Media DRM, which only worked on Windows devices, and there not very well.

If these hurdles weren't difficult enough to surmount, we were further frustrated by a little clause buried deep in decades-old contracts between the motion picture studios and the major pay TV channels such as HBO, Showtime, and Starz—the "blackout window" clause. The clause stated that when a new movie became available on DVD from a studio, we had a clearly defined window—usually 60 to 90 days—during which we could digitally sell or rent the title. After that came the blackout window, a period usually lasting three years, during which the pay TV channels had the exclusive rights to air the movies, and we were not allowed to digitally rent or sell them on our service.

The studios were nervous and uncertain about the new digital download services being offered by Amazon and Apple, which they referred to as transactional video on demand, or TVOD. Yes, they could see that TVOD was growing fast and held enormous promise, but the revenue stream was still just a trickle—tens of millions of dollars a year—and it looked like a risky bet, so they were reluctant to change their contracts.

For us, it meant that we had a very short sales window for our digital movie service. Two to three months after the release of the DVD, then nothing for three years, the period of greatest demand.

We knew that we had to change this if we expected video streaming to become a great customer experience and a big business for us in the long term. But I would quickly learn that this was not within our control. When I met with studio executives, I would explain that the TVOD business was going to take off and would one day be much more valuable to them than their pay-TV deals. The executives nodded, said they understood, agreed that this needed to change, but told me their bosses didn't see it that way. As with all media companies, the decisions made by top Hollywood brass were then, and still are, all about achieving short-term financial goals.

Fast-forward ten years, and thanks to their short-term thinking, the studios were scrambling to launch their own streaming video services like Disney+, Warner's HBO Max, and NBC's Peacock in a bid to fight for their survival and compete with Amazon and Netflix.

At Amazon, our compensation wasn't tied to financial results. As we mentioned in chapter one, the maximum base salary at Seattle headquarters was $160,000 per year, and there was no bonus system at all. Additional compensation was in Amazon stock. If you got a raise, it was completely in stock, which wouldn't begin vesting for 18 to 24 months.

My incentives were very different from those of my counterparts at the movie studios and record companies. To benefit financially, I needed Amazon to grow over the long term. I can't say that everyone at Amazon was always pleased with this compensation philosophy. We all have a need to be rewarded for an important accomplishment, and we want to receive our reward in a timely fashion. But for those who thought and acted long term, and hung around, it paid off.

We weren't about to bring the studios around to Amazon's way of operating, so for Unbox this was a battle we couldn't and didn't win. In fact, it wasn't until 2013 that the blackout clause was removed.

Given all these challenges, it was hard to see how we could fix Unbox. We were a distant number two in the business to Apple, who had launched their digital video service just a few days after we did. It was super frustrating for me and the team to be looking up at Apple in those days. They had the iPod and iTunes, the most popular media device and application, respectively. The two worked seamlessly together and inspired customer love, so it was extremely difficult to identify any vulnerability in their product that would enable us to catch or pass them.

Seeking a Path to the Living Room

In the late autumn of 2006 I held a two-day offsite meeting with the Amazon Unbox team to develop plans for 2007. If we had worked at many other companies of our size, we might have flown the team to some fabulous location like Sun Valley, Sedona, or Napa, stayed in a five-star hotel, had meetings in the morning and spent the afternoon playing golf, followed by the sipping of wine. But one implication of being at the earth's most customer-centric company is that you don't spend money on things that don't benefit customers. Not only did we stay in Seattle, we didn't even spend money to book a conference room at a local hotel. We made our way from 605 5th Avenue South to another Amazon office building next to Seattle's Union Station. I don't think we even paid for lunch.

We devoted two days to discussions about how to fix Unbox. The team had spent two weeks writing PR/FAQs and narratives describing various product ideas and solutions to make our video service a success. Some focused on how to improve the user interface. Others thought a big marketing campaign was the solution. But none would solve the fundamental problems of Mac access or studio blackout. My frustration grew as I rejected one proposal after another.

Then a new business development guy on the team, Josh Kramer, spoke up.

Josh, unlike the rest of us MBAs and engineers, had actual experience in Hollywood. He had co-produced the movie *Death and the Maiden*, directed by Roman Polanski, starring Sigourney Weaver and Ben Kingsley. But Josh was not your typical Gucci-loafer-wearing, Porsche-driving Hollywood guy. Somehow, he managed to stain his perpetually untucked shirt (before untucking was cool) with coffee or ketchup every day. His shoes were always untied, his glasses held together with tape. His desk was an OSHA violation of half-consumed coffee cups, food, and stacks of stained papers. Josh was a creative and brilliant guy who had majored in sound as art medium at Brown and also had an MBA from Wharton. Not only did he understand the inner workings of Hollywood, he had also taught himself to write code as a hobby. So he understood business, tech, and content.

In the few months that Josh had been on the team, he had been meeting with many potential partners, one of which was TiVo—the pioneer in digital video recording devices, or DVRs. Typically, a biz dev guy like Josh will come back from third-party meetings spouting seemingly great ideas for partnerships that end up being technically impossible. Josh, on the other hand, came back from his meetings with an idea that might actually work—Amazon movies could be downloaded to a TiVo set-top box. He had vetted the idea with our engineering team before pitching it at the onsite offsite.

This offered a win for both companies and our mutual customers. For TiVo, they added a broad selection of movies and TV shows to buy and rent on demand from a trusted brand. And for us, TiVo would provide us with a "path to the living room"—more specifically a route to the television set. In those days, most people wanted to watch movies with their butt planted firmly on their living room couch, gazing at their 48-inch flat-screen TV, not with their nose glued to the computer screen.

In March 2007 we launched Unbox on TiVo,[2] and just like that, we were delivering a customer experience we could be proud of, at least once you got it set up. You could browse and shop for movies and shows on the Amazon site, and they would be downloaded automatically to your TiVo. The download still took time, but it had a feature called progressive download. As soon as the runtime of the downloaded content exceeded the time it would take to download the rest of the movie, you could start watching. It wasn't real streaming, but it did speed things up. Amazon customers who already owned a TiVo device were delighted and sang our praises. TiVo became our best source of growth for revenue and new customers.

Unfortunately, though, our competitors hadn't been idle.

A Massive Disruption

Two months earlier, in January 2007, Netflix launched its video streaming service, then called Watch Now, inaugurating one of the most profound changes in the history of the entertainment industry. In those days the Netflix streaming service offered a pretty paltry selection, about a thousand movies and TV shows, mostly classics like *Casablanca*, cult films, foreign titles, and a few TV series such as the original BBC series *House of Cards*—no recent releases or big hits. But they'd made significant breakthroughs that would stand them in good stead as they improved their content.

The two big, revolutionary breakthrough features of the Netflix service were subscription and streaming. Amazon and Apple were the leaders in premium movie and TV distribution, but we offered downloads only (and you had to purchase or rent each movie or show). We thought of streaming as a low-quality phenomenon— the domain of YouTube, with its videos of dancing cats that you watched on your PC for a couple of minutes between meetings. So when Netflix launched Watch Now, we took note and discussed the service in detail, but the prevailing wisdom inside our team and among others in the industry was that it was a half-baked test, not a serious offering.

The other noteworthy feature of the Netflix streaming service was that it was free. Actually, as my mother used to say when trying to teach me good fiscal sense, "It isn't free. It's *included*." It came at no extra cost with most of the Netflix DVD rental-by-mail subscription plans.

In retrospect, it seems obvious that the Netflix launch was a significant threat, because streaming plus subscription would prove to be the magic combination in the digital video business. And they were smart and savvy about how they launched it by including the streaming titles as free/included for DVD subscribers. This eliminated the major hurdle of getting people to pay for a subscription service from a cold start. But we were hardly the only company not to understand the threat. Jeff Bewkes famously said that the Netflix threat to Warner Bros., where he was chairman at the time, was about the same as the threat of the Albanian army to the U.S. armed forces. "[I]s the Albanian Army going to take over the world? . . . I don't think so," he told the *New York Times*.[3] Oh the delicious irony that, ten years later, Jeff Bewkes and the CEO of AT&T were in the midst of a public relations campaign to convince the Justice Department that the merger of their two companies was necessary because the roles had reversed—Netflix was now the U.S. Army, and Warner had become the Albanians! It turns out that, like Amazon, Netflix has a track record of long-term thinking and willingness to be misunderstood for long periods of time, both of which have contributed to their great success.

Another reason we didn't take the Netflix streaming service seriously was that it had no immediate, perceptible impact on Unbox. But when Hulu launched in October 2007, the impact *was* perceptible. Unlike Netflix streaming, Hulu offered some of the most popular TV shows in the United States—the latest shows from Fox and NBC the day after they aired on TV. Not only that, Hulu was free (with advertising), and not the included-kind-of-free that my mom taught me about—just plain free. We had been selling these same TV shows on Unbox for $2.99 an episode, which was cheaper than buying a DVD, and making them available the day after broadcast. Now, with Hulu, you could watch many of the same shows, just as soon, and for free. Suddenly our $2.99 was a lousy deal, and a bunch of our top-selling TV shows were not selling at all. (Maybe the Hulu launch was also a bit painful because it was led by my [Bill's] first Amazon manager, and good friend, Jason Kilar, the first CEO of Hulu.)

We had no ability to influence the studios on this matter because two of them—News Corp and NBC Universal—owned Hulu. They had created the service in response to the growth of YouTube and its sale, in 2006, just six months after its launch, to Google for $1.65 billion. The studios figured they could create a similar service, offering Hollywood content, and sell it for even bigger bucks, just as fast.

Except it didn't turn out that way. Although Hulu attracted a lot of viewers, the potential buyers—including Apple, Amazon, and Google—realized that the studios would never sell their content along with Hulu and, without it, Hulu was not worth nearly as much. Eventually, Hulu went to a subscription model and is now controlled by Disney. It did not fade away, however. It continued to gain viewers and also got into production, creating such hits as *The Handmaid's Tale*. It has become an important long-term asset for Disney in their bid to compete with Netflix and Amazon.

Connected TVs

In 2008, further developments showed that the path to the living room had more twists and turns that would have to be negotiated. We decided it was time for Amazon to add streaming video to our download service and saw the shift as an opportunity to dump the name Unbox, which had accumulated a lot of negative baggage.[4] We relaunched the service in September 2008 with the name Amazon Video On Demand (VOD). No, it wasn't particularly creative—we were a bit gun-shy after our creative flop with the Unbox branding—but it was accurate and, best of all, it wasn't Unbox. We also launched our streaming application on TV sets offered by many manufacturers, including Sony, Vizio, Samsung, LG, and Panasonic, as well as a new streaming device from a company called Roku, which is now in more than 20 million homes.[5]

With streaming on demand, Amazon customers could at last watch their favorite movies and TV shows on their television set rather than on the small screens of their computers and phones. But because the speed of internet connection varied from home to home, and because there were so many different kinds of hardware and software involved, the viewing experience varied from device to device and customer to customer. Some were delighted; some tore their hair out. The hair-tearers typically suffered from a phenomenon known as "rebuffering," which is what happens when the downloading speed lags behind the viewing: the picture freezes, and you get to watch the "spinning wait cursor," more commonly referred to as the "wheel of death." This was a common enough occurrence that I made the decision to provide customers with an automatic refund if they had to suffer through three or more re-bufferings while watching a movie rental. We would still have to pay the studio their share of the purchase, but I felt we had to make it clear that Amazon understood that this was not acceptable.

I hadn't checked with Jeff on the refund, but I guess he agreed. In his shareholder letter he wrote:

> We build automated systems that look for occasions when we've provided a customer experience that isn't up to our standards, and those systems then proactively refund customers. One industry observer recently received an automated email from us that said, "We noticed that you experienced poor video playback while watching the following rental on Amazon Video On Demand: Casablanca. We're sorry for the inconvenience and have issued you a refund for the following amount: $2.99. We hope to see you again soon." Surprised by the proactive refund, he ended up writing about the experience: "Amazon 'noticed that I experienced poor video playback . . .' And they decided to give me a refund because of that? Wow . . . Talk about putting customers first."[6]

Netflix remained the streaming leader. They had recognized the promise of streaming to living room devices early on and created a dedicated engineering team to develop proprietary streaming technology. By 2008, Netflix was available on an impressive array of devices including TVs, Blu-ray players, and game consoles from many manufacturers. They also kept adding to their library of titles. Netflix's business was exploding.

At that time, gaming console use was also growing fast with Microsoft Xbox, Sony PlayStation, and Nintendo Wii. There were tens of millions of game consoles in U.S. households, and nearly all of them were connected to HDTVs and the internet. Gamers pounded on their consoles for hours every day but they needed to take a break now and again, so watching a movie or TV show was an obvious and easy value proposition for them. We wanted to make Amazon VOD available on game consoles, too.

But our business development team had some bad news for us. Neither Microsoft nor Sony would allow us to put the Amazon streaming app on their gaming devices, because they had their own à la carte digital video stores and wanted to build those businesses. They did not ban Netflix, however, because it was a subscription service, and they did not see it as directly competitive. We were seriously disadvantaged by our exclusion from those devices in those first two or three years. One alarming statistic shows why: we estimated that 95 percent of Netflix's streams came either through their website, the three main game consoles (Xbox, PlayStation, and Nintendo Wii), or through the iPad and iPhone.

We also got pushback from some retailers. At the time, Walmart and Best Buy sold the most TVs to consumers, but Amazon's retail business was a growing threat to them. Starting in 2007, they had employed a number of tactics to slow us down, such as declining to carry Amazon gift cards in their stores. Now their buyers warned some of the electronics manufacturers that any devices loaded with Amazon Video On Demand would not make it to their shelves. Walmart and Best Buy were such dominant players in the sale of electronic devices that many manufacturers wouldn't work with us. When we convinced Sony to add Amazon's streaming service to their Bravia TVs and Blu-ray players in September 2008, the logjam started to break. But it would take another four long years for us to convince the PlayStation team to play along with Amazon so we could finally tap into the 20 million–strong PlayStation user base.

The delays prevented faster growth, and it became increasingly clear to us that the digital media business was very different from our online physical goods retail business. We did not have full control of the content (movies and TV shows) we were selling. We did not have proprietary or unique content, as Netflix did. Nor did we have control of the devices people used to play and display content, as Microsoft, Sony, and Apple did.

The inputs to the Amazon flywheel of growth—low prices, faster delivery, lower cost structure—were not dimensions along which we could differentiate from our competitors if we only offered an à la carte digital video store. There was one aspect of the process, however, that did require technical skill: building applications that functioned well on a range of TVs and set-top devices and delivered high-quality video without crashing or constant re-buffering. That's why we eventually purchased a small London-based software engineering shop called Pushbutton.

Even our great asset, the Amazon website, wasn't quite as important to the sale of digital media as it was to physical goods. Yes, it attracted lots of customers who were looking to buy media products, but applications on Macs, PCs, tablets, phones, and TVs were more and more important than our website for delivering a high-quality digital media experience. Apple, for example, sold all their digital media through an application running on Macs and PCs (iTunes) rather than on their website. And, unlike Amazon, Apple had control over their own devices. The combination of application and device delivered a high-quality streaming (or download) and playback experience and therefore delivered tremendous value to the consumer.

When it came to content controlled by the studios, nothing much had changed. Content creators like HBO had an advantage because they had a unique and exclusive content offering—shows like *The Sopranos* and later *Game of Thrones*—and had exclusive movie licensing deals with the studios. At that time, no other company was in the internet-delivered subscription business, so HBO had the field mostly to themselves. They could license and accumulate a lot of great movies and TV shows with very little competition.

But as the Apple and HBO business models demonstrate, there was one important way that the world of digital media was the same as the old, analog media world: there was still a great advantage to be had in control. In the old media world, you could control one of two things: the method of distribution of the content or the content itself (or in some cases both). Broadcast networks like NBC and CBS controlled their networks and also developed exclusive content such as TV shows, sports events, and news broadcasts. Studios like Warner and Disney created movies and shows. In the new digital media world, broadcast networks and studios would lose their control on distribution, to be replaced by applications on internet-connected devices.

As time went on, we realized that Amazon Video On Demand was stuck in the middle of the value chain—the valley, really. We didn't control the upstream end of content development. We didn't control the downstream end of playback devices. We were essentially a digital distribution system, with nothing unique or proprietary about it. No wonder we kept slamming into barriers on both ends of the value chain—content development and distribution on devices.

As we discussed in the Kindle chapter, years earlier, probably in 2004, Jeff and Steve had drawn a simple diagram of the value chain. Here it is again:

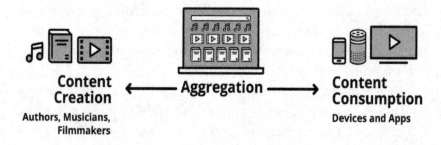

Content Creation ← **Aggregation** → **Content Consumption**

Authors, Musicians, Filmmakers

Devices and Apps

It was this insight into the value chain that led us to create Kindle. Since we didn't do content creation via developing or publishing books (although we would do that later), we made the move to control consumption, that is, the reading experience. In digital movies and TV, we were still stuck in the aggregation role. The retail business input metrics of price and selection did not differentiate us in this digital business, and our output metrics—number of video buyers and revenue—showed that this strategy was a failure. So, beginning in 2010, we put our resources into a number of new initiatives designed to get us out of the middle: Prime Instant Video, Amazon Studios, and new Amazon devices—Fire Tablet, Fire Phone,

Fire TV, and Echo/Alexa. We also made an acquisition that enabled us to increase our capabilities and expand our geographic reach.

Prime Instant Video: An Oh-by-the-Way Benefit

In 2010, we held a series of meetings with Jeff to discuss ideas and options for moving us toward the lucrative ends of the value chain. It was clear that consumers loved the all-you-can-eat, fee-based subscription model of Netflix, but we learned that Netflix was probably pouring between $30 and $40 million annually into licensing deals. While today, $40 million does not seem like a lot of money for Amazon to invest, believe me, this was not the case at the much smaller and leaner Amazon of 2010. That number shocked us. It seemed like a crazy big commitment.

Not to Jeff. In one meeting he said something like, "In case it isn't clear enough, I want to see the plan for how we are going to make a similar investment to get going in subscription video." Jeff also made it clear that we should explore other big, digital-media ideas, including the creation of hardware devices.

Wisely, I took Jeff's not-so-subtle hint that it was time for my team and me to get going on it.

I tasked Cameron Janes to lead the effort, with Josh Kramer taking point on working with studios. The two had been key leaders in my organization for several years and were veterans of the digital entertainment business. Cameron had joined the team in July 2007 after having spent the prior few years working on the e-commerce business at Walmart.com. He was a well-rounded business athlete with an MBA from Kellogg who could tackle any problem whether it pertained to content, finance, product, or otherwise. Whatever it was, if I gave it to Cameron, he would grab hold of it and figure it out.

So began weeks and weeks of effort, meetings, and idea iteration. Three of the ideas we pursued were for hardware devices. One was a universal remote control that would make it easy to play Amazon video on your TV. Another was for a puck-shaped device that was connected to your home AV system. It would learn the preferences of each member of the household through voice detection and commands, enabling personalized video playback for each customer. This was a variant on the puck idea first conceived by Jeff years earlier as a shopping device (mentioned in chapter five), and it would later morph again to become the Amazon Echo. A third idea was for a set-top device that was preloaded with the most popular movies and shows and would be updated wirelessly. We spent weeks researching, writing, and rewriting PR/FAQs for these ideas, but there were technical licensing or pricing problems with all of them. After several weeks, we shifted our focus exclusively to subscription content ideas.

Josh led the information-gathering part of the effort. He worked the phones, took in-person meetings with people he already knew at the major studios, and also established new relationships.

What we learned in the process was disheartening. Netflix had such a big head start that, even with a similar budget, there was no way we could put together a catalog with the kind of selection they offered. We also learned that the $30–40 million figure we had heard was off. By the time we got started, Netflix was spending twice that on content.

In the subscription business, it's no good to come out second with a copycat offering. We had to offer movies and shows that Netflix didn't have available. We also had to have a different offering from Hulu, which had a lock on most of the best series from Fox and NBC. In the TVOD business, differentiation based on selection wasn't possible—Amazon, Apple, Microsoft, and Sony all had the same titles—but in the subscription business, a unique catalog was key.

We brainstormed countless concepts. One approach was to go deep in specific genres like horror or documentaries. Another was to attract customers by offering one free movie per week in hopes they would be enticed to sign up for the subscription. We talked about starting at a low price, maybe $3.99 a month, in recognition that our selection of quality titles was pretty slim. But we wouldn't make much money at that price. And we would want to raise the price as soon as we could and that was not very Amazonian.

In our fourth or fifth meeting with Jeff, it was painfully obvious that we were getting nowhere with hardware or subscription. A small group of the leaders of the digital video team sat around the table in his small conference room on the sixth floor of the Day One North building in South Lake Union. Just as we had in previous meetings, we reviewed a bunch of ideas, talked about movie genres, and considered pricing and budget options.

At some point, Jeff came up with a simple idea: "Let's make videos free for Prime members."

This had not been on anybody's list of ideas. How would that work? Jeff reminded us of how Netflix got started by offering Watch Now streaming videos to its DVD subscription service—free. I mean included. "It's an 'oh-by-the-way' offering," he said. When Netflix started, they didn't have a great selection of movies and TV shows either, not good enough that customers would pay extra for them. Instead, Netflix gave their customers additional value as part of their existing subscription. Netflix was essentially saying, "The service you pay for is great and, oh, by the way, here is something extra for you to watch." As we spoke, three years later, most Netflix customers were exclusively streamers. They never rented a DVD. The transition might not have been as smooth and seamless if Netflix had started the streaming offering as a separate subscription service from launch. Actually, it's unlikely that many consumers would have been willing to pay a subscription fee at all.

There is a difficult chicken-and-egg problem with a subscription service. You need to have a great offering to attract paying subscribers. To be able to afford a great offering, you need a lot of paying subscribers. It's a challenging cold-start problem that generally requires a large up-front investment, which you can hopefully pay back with subscriber growth in future years. Jeff argued that even if we offered streaming videos to Prime members at no additional cost, the business could still be profitable in the long run. (Long-term thinking = *being Amazonian*.)

How? A streaming subscription service is a fixed-cost business. When Netflix licensed a movie or TV series from a studio, they paid a fixed fee. The amount was not based on usage. Netflix customers could watch the video once or ten million times, the costs were the same. Yes, there were some variable costs involved, for bandwidth and servers, but these costs amounted to pennies per view. And, as with most technology, those costs declined over time. The cost structure is very different from the DVD rental-by-mail business, where the costs—warehouses, wages, shipping, replacement discs—are variable. The major benefit of establishing a popular subscription service with a fixed-cost base is that once you exceed a certain number of subscribers, every new dollar of subscription revenue is pure profit. The hard parts of pulling off this strategy are (a) acquiring a large number of subscribers, and (b) building a catalog of must-see movies and TV series. By integrating Prime Video into the already large and growing Prime customer base we had a leg up on solving the first problem. We were less concerned about the poor initial selection because our time horizon for success was measured in years. We were confident that, given time, we could make the right investments and assemble a great selection of movies and TV series. If we did this well, customers would eventually be attracted to Prime, not only for the fast free shipping but also for the streaming videos included in the fee.

The "oh-by-the-way" addition would become a "gotta-have" benefit.

Jeff also argued that Prime, with streaming video, would be a unique offering and competitive differentiator. Amazon was an increasingly complex company, competing in multiple markets and territories around the world. To establish Amazon as a distinct product in every business category and every market was incredibly difficult to do. But he saw Prime as a tantalizing way to do just that. Any competitor might launch a Prime shipping clone, or they could potentially build a new Netflix-type service, but it was unlikely that any one of them would be able to do both.

Prime Video was a go, and we had only a few months to get it ready for launch—scheduled for February 2011.

LOVEFiLM: Not Actually

During that same period, we were pursuing another initiative: the acquisition of a European movie and TV subscription service called LOVEFiLM. It was essentially the Netflix of Europe, offering DVD rental by mail as well as streaming films and TV shows. LOVEFiLM would help us get a jump on Netflix, which had not launched in Europe at the time. After the acquisition, we entered quickly into negotiations with several studios for long-term exclusive licenses to some of the best movies and TV series from Hollywood. If all went as we expected, our selection in the United Kingdom and Germany would be better than that of either Amazon or Netflix in the United States.

Then, in early 2011, the floor fell out from under our feet. The key studios—including Sony, Warner, and others—informed us that Netflix had entered the bidding for the same titles we wanted and had offered twice the money for them. Out of the blue, we found ourselves in a bidding war. Who won? The studios. Their fees skyrocketed while we duked it out with Netflix, all to win the eyes, ears, and hearts of UK and German customers.

This experience crystallized our thinking about the value chain. It seemed to me that going forward we had to get out of the never-ending cycle of bidding against Netflix and, later, Hulu. We didn't want to pay studios additional fees for each and every country we entered. We had to control our own destiny. That led me to a startling conclusion: we had to create our own content. It was time to make our own movies and TV shows.

At the Delivery End: Devices

Meanwhile, as we were figuring out how to navigate to the upstream end of the value chain and finding our way through the LOVEFiLM acquisition, we were also working to establish a presence at the other end—consumption and playback. For that, we needed to create our own hardware offerings, devices that would enable consumers to access Amazon content within the context of the entire Amazon experience. Because, years earlier, Steve Kessel had established an organization and capability to design and develop our own devices, beginning with Kindle, we were positioned to innovate and build a variety of devices that could also support video, music, apps, and more.

The first device out of the gate was the Kindle Fire Tablet, launched in November 2011. It had much of the capability of the iPad and sold for $199—hundreds less than the iPad. Launching Amazon Video on Fire Tablet was a scramble that involved overcoming all kinds of security and rights challenges, especially because it was our first time enabling HD video on a mobile device.

Kindle Fire Tablet quickly gained a meaningful share of the market and got Amazon a secure toehold at the video playback end of the value chain. Just shy of a year after launch, in September 2012, Kindle Fire Tablet had sold millions of units and was the second-bestselling tablet after the iPad.[7] We dropped the Kindle name in 2014, and Amazon has continued to improve and add capability to the Fire Tablet, such that today it is a staple of the Amazon device offering.

After the success of Fire Tablet, the Amazon Devices organization, now led by Dave Limp, began to develop so many new offerings that they just identified them with letters, which made them easier to talk about and keep track of. It also helped keep the name and nature of the project confidential. If an unauthorized person happened into a discussion about Project A, they wouldn't have much to go on. Fire TV was project B, code-named "Bueller" after *Ferris Bueller's Day Off*.

Fire TV launched in April 2014 at $99, with a number of features that improved the customer experience. In particular, we put our years of app-building experience to work to design a fluid and intuitive user interface. It enabled viewers to bridge what we thought of as the ten-foot user interface gap—the 10' UI, for short—meaning the distance between the couch and the TV set. Fire TV had voice search capability built into the remote control, which made it much easier for viewers to find, select, and play the show they wanted to see.

The results speak for themselves. As of this writing, there are millions of Fire TVs in homes around the globe—it is one of the top-selling TV-connected video streaming devices in the world.

Amazon, Hollywood Producer

We'd known since our first experiments began in 2010 that we wanted our own TV series and movies. And we saw just how competitive and expensive it was—and would continue to be—to purchase content from a multitude of studios and other parties. We had to create our own if we wanted to control our costs and enjoy the benefits of having exclusive, first-run TV shows and movies that we could stream to customers worldwide.

Despite the false start, getting Amazon Studios off the ground was one of the fastest new business creation tasks I had during my time at Amazon. This is largely because of the particular and distinct nature of the entertainment industry. Unlike the software and hardware engineering talent pool, which is limited and in high demand, there is a large talent pool of producers, directors, actors, and craftspeople. A small percentage of them are full-time employees in any kind of organization. Most are independent, freelance contractors. Engagements are relatively short term. Scripts too are in virtually endless supply, although, as we'd learned, the percentage of great ones is small.

All it really takes to get a production going is commitment and, most important of all, capital. Amazon had the cash. The hard part was finding, selecting, and sometimes competing for, the best scripts to greenlight. To solve that challenge, we opened an office in Santa Monica and hired a team of development executives, each of whom had a focus on a specific content genre: comedy, drama, kids. We made no exceptions for the fact that this was Hollywood. We used the Bar Raiser process to hire each member of the Studios team, and they would have to get accustomed to our frugal ways, including working in small, shared offices or open workspaces, a base salary capped at $160K, no cash bonus program, and riding in coach, not first class. This made for some hard conversations.

It's important to say that changes in the environment had also made the new initiative easier and, in fact, possible. Streaming had become ubiquitous. We had the hardware in place. And there was one other significant development: the Netflix original series *House of Cards*, which first aired in February 2013. It was a 13-episode political thriller starring big Hollywood names Kevin Spacey and Robin Wright. The show was a sensation, a hit, and a game-changer. Before *House of Cards*, most A-list Hollywood players wanted nothing to do with online productions. Such things were beneath them, just as appearing in advertising had once been seen as low class. But Spacey was willing to take that risk, and he and Netflix broke through the barrier. Though his career has since cratered after allegations of sexual misconduct, he was then an unquestioned star: an Academy Award winner, with a long and respected career onstage, in television, and in the movies. Not only did he agree to do the show, but *House of Cards* won multiple awards. Spacey himself became the first actor in a web TV series to be nominated for an Emmy, and he won a Golden Globe for his performance as the anything-goes politician who becomes president, Frank Underwood.

A door had opened.

Now we began to operate like a Hollywood studio, with the continuing and important difference that we compensated our team in the same way we compensated all Amazon leaders: no short-term performance targets. The development team was smart and focused in their pursuit of the best scripts that would appeal to Amazon viewers based on years of viewership data. We green-lighted five comedies and five kids shows for pilots (Jeff was involved in the selection). That meant we would produce ten pilot shows, most of them costing several million dollars to create. We did add one interesting new wrinkle. We made all the pilots available to view for free on Amazon before making a decision as to which to greenlight. Through this process, we were able to gather viewership data and ratings and reviews from real customers in order to make better-informed decisions about which shows would attract the most viewers. So, after all, we did find a way to make the process more customer centric than the studios', and therefore more Amazonian.

For kids, we greenlit *Creative Galaxy* and *Tumbleleaf*, series that would receive audience and critical acclaim and live on for three and six seasons, respectively. Of the five comedies we produced, we selected two for full-season production. *Alpha House* was developed by *Doonesbury* cartoonist Garry Trudeau, and it told the stories of three Republican senators living together in a row house in Washington, D.C. It premiered in April 2013. The second was *Betas*, our take on the Silicon Valley culture, which aired the following year. Both shows were solid efforts but did not become major hits.

In 2014 and early 2015, we premiered new Amazon Studios series *Transparent*, *Mozart in the Jungle*, and *The Man in the High Castle*. These series gained a great deal of attention and put Amazon on the map as a producer of high-quality, distinctive content.

* * *

We entered the world of subscription service in 2004 and digital media in 2006, with the goal of generating growth. Both were long-term efforts that took time to develop and more time to realize their objectives. There were some real setbacks—most notably, Unbox. But with digital media, all four initiatives—Prime Video, devices, the LOVEFiLM acquisition, and Amazon Studios—succeeded in their own ways and to different degrees.

Throughout the development of these projects, we adhered to Amazon's distinctive management practices. Above all, they are examples of Amazonian long-term thinking, customer obsession, willingness to invent, and operational excellence. Throughout, we were stubborn on the vision and flexible on the details.

10

AWS

A new class of customers. The origins of AWS in data sharing with affiliates. Colin gets "the call" from Jeff, who comes on board. Eight people attend the first software developer conference. How the Invent and Simplify leadership principle enabled Amazon to become the leader in web services. How we used the Working Backwards process to create AWS.

* * *

Scene: Colin's office. His phone rings. Caller ID displays "Jeff Bezos."

COLIN: Hi, Jeff.

JEFF: Hi, Colin. I'm getting up to speed on what we are doing with web services and your name came up. Can you tell me what you are doing, if anything, with web services?

COLIN: Sure. It's probably easiest to show you. When is a good time for you?

JEFF: How about now?

COLIN *(while canceling the next two meetings and tucking his laptop under his arm)*: Now is great. I'll be right down.

As we've already seen, in the early 2000s, the transformation from physical media to digital media posed an existential threat to Amazon's business. Roughly 75 percent of Amazon's business at that time consisted of selling physical books, CDs, and DVDs to customers. We had to invent or risk becoming an irrelevant has-been in media sales. Also, while hugely successful, Amazon Prime was essentially an extension (albeit a very large one) of our existing online physical media retail business.

Unlike Digital or Prime, however, Amazon Web Services had nothing to do with the core business. The term "cloud computing"— the on-demand delivery of IT resources such as computing power and data storage over the internet with pay-as-you-go pricing without having to buy, own, and maintain physical data centers and servers[1]—wasn't widely used in the early 2000s, and Amazon was likely not on many people's list of companies that were well positioned to offer it. Further, it involved an entirely new class of customer for Amazon: software developers.

In this chapter we will not provide a comprehensive story about the origins and history of AWS. That subject could fill a whole book in itself. Instead, we will attempt to answer the following two questions, which can help you incorporate key elements of *being Amazonian* into your organization:

1. What elements of *being Amazonian* enabled Amazon to move into this completely separate line of business?
2. Why was Amazon able to master cloud computing well before its potential competitors, including entrenched companies with large businesses to protect and well-capitalized web-based tech companies?

The answers to both questions come down to single-threaded teams ruthlessly iterating with the Working Backwards process, and obsessing over the customer experience, in order to discover the fundamental needs of the software developer in the new paradigm of cloud computing.

Influences

Web Services Proof of Concept

It was 2001, and I (Colin) was managing the affiliates business called Amazon Associates. This program allowed third parties, commonly referred to as affiliates, to place links to Amazon products on their websites. For example, as we mentioned before, a site about mountain climbing might include a curated list of recommended mountain climbing books with links to Amazon. When a visitor clicked on one of the links on the affiliate website, they were taken to the book detail page on the Amazon site. If the visitor bought a product with Amazon, the owner of the affiliate website would earn a referral fee. Up until this point, affiliates could choose which Amazon products they wanted to feature along with a few parameters to determine how they would be displayed on their website, similar to how an ad server works today. The program was wildly popular. Over the four years I was involved with the program, the number of affiliates grew from 30,000 to roughly one million. But, as Jeff often mentions, customers are divinely discontented, and "yesterday's 'wow' quickly becomes today's 'ordinary.'"[2] And we simply didn't have enough design resources to seamlessly integrate Amazon products into each of our affiliate's websites.

That's when we took a step back, placed ourselves in our affiliates' shoes, and looked at the problem from their perspective. We'd been operating on the correct assumption that the big attraction of the program for affiliates was the Amazon products themselves, but in so doing we'd overlooked their desire to have choices around the look and feel of the display—for instance, the font size, color palette, or image size. Turns out they didn't want to settle for the "best available" Amazon format.

So, in March 2002, we decided to take a chance and launch an experimental feature that changed the way we shared information with the affiliates. Instead of receiving a fully formed product display, the affiliates could choose to receive the product data in a text format called XML. The affiliates would then take that XML product data and write their own software code to incorporate it into their websites according to their own design standards. The goal was for us to get out of the design business so they could innovate without us holding them back.

This feature was novel and risky in two ways. First, since we began the Associates Program, our core customer had been the owner of a website. To be an affiliate, it was not necessary to be a software developer, or even to be able to understand or write basic computer code. That meant we had to keep things very simple. We would generate the code for the affiliate. Just a few mouse clicks were all that was needed to be up and running. No software programming was necessary.

This new feature was different. It was aimed at a technical audience, affiliates who had software developers on their teams who knew how to write code that transforms the product data XML into something that looks good on their website. We had to create new elements such as user manuals, technical specifications, and sample code all rolled into a software developer kit (SDK) to show them how the system worked. We also created a discussion board where developers could post details about their experience with the services and ask each other questions. We didn't really know how our affiliates would react to this more complicated but also more powerful and flexible feature.

The second way this feature was novel, and even controversial, was that it was a lot more than just a tool that allowed website owners to design their own links to Amazon products. As the name suggests, the product data XML service contained rich information about Amazon products, such as "customers who bought this product also bought X." We had painstakingly built our catalog of tens of millions of products, which also contained valuable data about consumer behavior toward those products, and many in the company viewed this catalog as a competitive asset not to be shared. On the Associates team, however, we felt that the benefits of letting hundreds of thousands of developers build commerce solutions on top of this data outweighed the potential risks. We did place some restrictions on what the affiliate could do with the data in an attempt to mitigate our risk. They could only use it for selling Amazon products, and they couldn't store the data permanently. Beyond that, although we were excited to see the creative ways in which affiliates would use this data, no amount of analysis could predict what they would do.

Here's another example of where a single-threaded leader and team helps. I was accountable for the financial performance and overall health of the affiliates business. Our team had virtually all the resources required to launch this feature: we had software engineers and product managers to build the feature; and we had our own customer service representatives armed with specialized knowledge and tools to field questions from affiliates. We knew our customers well, had conviction that the experiment was worth doing, and were willing to be misunderstood as we tried something new. We also had a rollback plan in the unlikely event that the experiment failed.

We decided to launch the feature and see what happened. We issued no press release and made no big public announcement. We simply sent an email to our affiliates that explained the new feature and its potential benefits and pointed them to the SDK we had created for them. We made it clear that the feature wasn't for everyone. They'd have to write some code to get it to work for them.

Whenever we sent an email like this one to our affiliates, I made it a habit to monitor how they responded. I would look at a dashboard that displayed such information as how many people had read the email, how many had clicked on the links in the email, and how many incremental referral fees were generated as a result of the email. I'd also check in with our customer service group for any anecdotal data they might have collected about contacts with affiliates, and I'd also read the comments and questions on the discussion board. I must admit, I had been a little anxious after hitting the proverbial send button for this particular email—the list of possible outcomes ranged from promising to a very long day reacting to bad news. That anxiety turned into excitement very quickly. Literally hours after releasing this feature, I knew that we were onto something big and that our experiment would far exceed our expectations. On the discussion boards, affiliates were posting links to web pages they had created with this new service along with the code they used to do it. They were proud of what they had created and wanted to share it with others. They were enthusiastically answering questions posted by other affiliates, even before we could respond. And they immediately started suggesting new features that would make the service even better.

Over the next several days I compiled a list of websites that were using the service in surprising and innovative ways. One developer created an addictive game where visitors would race against the clock and each other to see how fast they could name the author, artist, or movie based on the cover art flashed on the screen. Another developer made it easy for people to create a web page containing a virtual bookshelf of their personal media collections. Finally, there were two examples that essentially tried to re-create the shopping experience of Amazon but with completely different user interfaces than that found on the Amazon site. The first case we informally called Amazon Lite. It was a simple, stripped-down, text-heavy version of the site. Not flashy, but it worked especially well on small screens and feature phones. (The first iPhone was still five years out in the future.) The second case we labeled Amazon Graph, and it looked nothing like a website. It was an app that displayed a network graph with nodes and lines connecting the nodes. Each node represented a single product, and the lines pointed to other products based on our similarities data. It was a fascinating representation of our product catalog. These types of web applications simply could not have been created before we released this feature.

And then I got "the call" mentioned at the top of the chapter, when Jeff summoned me to his office. I grabbed my laptop and hurried out of my office in the 1930s Art Deco building that used to be part of the Marine Hospital Service, descended one flight of stairs, and went into Jeff's office. We sat around a conference table next to his door desk where I briefly explained the new feature. I told him the most interesting insight was not what Amazon was doing with web services; rather, it was what *our affiliates* were doing with them. I proceeded to show him some of the more interesting sites and applications, including some of the ones mentioned above, along with numbers showing the traffic and sales generated by them.

I told Jeff that every day since the launch, software developers were creating applications that used the features in ways we had never imagined.

After we finished the virtual tour, Jeff commented that this adoption rate and level of innovation from a single feature was unusual and that we needed to double down on our activities in this area. I responded that we were looking at ways to roll it out to a wider audience with a much richer feature set in July, three months away. From that day, Jeff was an avid supporter.

Jeff was not the only one who saw promise in what we were doing. Asking for additional software engineers to work on your project at Amazon is akin to looking for loose change someone left in a vending machine. It almost never happens. But when I approached Neil Roseman, my manager, to see whether anyone was available, he immediately got back to me and said that a group headed by Rob Frederick had just finished a project called Amazon Anywhere, which used XML to enable Amazon commerce on mobile devices. Rob and his team were just as passionate about web services as we were and enthusiastically joined the effort. Sarah Spillman headed up the product management team. We also had quite a bit of support from Rick Dalzell, the CIO, and a senior technologist and VP, Al Vermeulen, who would go on to play an instrumental role in designing and building many of the key components of AWS. Rob and Sarah rolled up their sleeves and led the technology and business teams in the race to launch the next full-featured version. Al and Rick helped spread the news not only within Amazon but also among several influential early adopters in the software industry.

The next three months were a blur. We felt we were pioneers creating something truly special for our new customers, the software development community.

Since we did not have much experience creating programs for software developers, we sought in-person feedback from heavy users of the service. We decided to host an Amazon software developer conference in our Seattle headquarters. The first one attracted a grand total of eight people. We flew two of them in from Europe. I discovered, just a week before the conference, that one of the

European attendees was a teenager. I had to check with our legal department if that was okay—fortunately we didn't need permission from his parents, and he was able to join us at the conference.

We worked out the logistics and set up a full day of sessions. Tim O'Reilly and Rael Dornfest from the O'Reilly Media, who were both avid supporters of the web services movement and taught us a lot about this new field, were there too. Another attendee was an avid customer who happened to live in Seattle. His name was Jeff Barr. He commented:

> The attendees were outnumbered by the Amazon employees. We sat and listened as the speakers talked about their plans to build on their success and to expand their web service offering over time. One speaker (it may have been Colin Bryar but I am not sure) looked to the future and said that they would be looking around the company for other services to expose in the future.
>
> This was the proverbial light-bulb moment for me! It was obvious that they were thinking about developers, platforms, and APIs and I wanted to be a part of it.[3]

Jeff Barr joined Amazon a few weeks later and is still with the company, serving as VP and chief evangelist for AWS.

For those in attendance, the final session of the day was probably the most memorable—a Q&A with Jeff Bezos. Needless to say, many of those eight attendees were thrilled and surprised at the chance for this intimate meeting with Jeff, as well as by the depth of his knowledge about the service. In his 2006 shareholder letter, Jeff made his reasons clear:

> Like any company, we have a corporate culture formed not only by our intentions but also as a result of our history. For Amazon, that history is fairly fresh and, fortunately, it includes several examples of tiny seeds growing into big trees. We have many people at our company who have watched multiple $10 million seeds turn into billion dollar businesses. That first-hand experience and the culture that has grown up around those successes is, in my

opinion, a big part of why we can start businesses from scratch. The culture demands that these new businesses be high potential and that they be innovative and differentiated, but it does not demand that they be large on the day that they are born.

I remember how excited we were in 1996 as we crossed $10 million in book sales. It wasn't hard to be excited—we had grown to $10 million from zero. Today, when a new business inside Amazon grows to $10 million, the overall company is growing from $10 billion to $10.01 billion. It would be easy for the senior executives who run our established billion dollar businesses to scoff. But they don't. They watch the growth rates of the emerging businesses and send emails of congratulations. That's pretty cool, and we're proud it's a part of our culture.[4]

I opened this chapter with a question: How was it that Amazon got to cloud computing first and became the largest provider of web services? Jeff provides the answer in his letter: it is because of Amazon's innovative spirit combined with the patience that comes with long-term thinking. Even when the business was brandnew and very small, we realized it had high potential, that it was an area where we could innovate and differentiate, and we had the patience to stick with it.

In July 2002, we launched the very first version of Amazon Web Services. If the product data XML we had sent to affiliates a few months earlier was the beta, AWS was the 1.0. It included some search and shopping capabilities and a full software development kit, and it was available to anyone, not just affiliates. Also, it was still free. For this one, we did issue a press release, in which Jeff said:

We're putting out a welcome mat for developers—this is an important beginning and new direction for us. . . . Developers can now incorporate Amazon.com content and features directly onto their own websites. We can't wait to see how they're going to surprise us.[5]

Up until this point Amazon had two sets of customers—buyers and sellers. Now we had a new customer set—the software developer.

After the launch, as we monitored the response, we had another surprise. Some of our biggest customers were not affiliates and not outsiders of any kind. They were Amazon software engineers. They found Amazon Web Services easier to use than some of our existing internal software tools they had been working with to build amazon.com. At this point there was little doubt that web services were going to become a new way of building things. We just didn't know how big it could be or how quickly developers would adopt it. Within a year, we had a pretty good idea—over 25,000 developers enrolled in the program[6] and were constantly surprising us with what they built.

Though this program was called Amazon Web Services, it bears little resemblance to today's AWS. In fact, the service we launched in 2002 was renamed the Amazon Product API and had a significant limitation—it had to be used to market Amazon products and therefore was solely focused on improving the Amazon retail ecosystem.

There were other projects that also helped us realize how big web services could be. Also in 2001, we embarked on a project called the "3-Ring Binder," which was an attempt to create and document a set of APIs that would allow partners to quickly add their product selection to the Amazon site and to create websites powered by Amazon's technology, but at their own URLs, under their control. This project eventually allowed us to create websites for partners such as Target and other retailers. Additionally, we developed a program called Seller Central, which provided web services that Amazon's third-party sellers could use to manage their businesses. The Amazon Associates Product API, Amazon Anywhere, the 3-Ring Binder, and Seller Central all reinforced our hypothesis that a seismic shift was happening in the way software was built.

In the summer of 2003, just as Web Services was taking off, I lost my job. Or rather, I switched to a different job. As I mentioned in the introduction, Jeff asked if I would like to become his technical advisor—his shadow—an offer I could not refuse. Andy Jassy had been Jeff's technical advisor for the previous 18 months and was ready for a new role. He could have taken virtually any job in the company, including a leadership role in any of its largest businesses. Fortunately for us, he decided to start and lead a new team that would build on our experiment. Andy and his team envisioned and created a much more robust set of products that would usher in the era of cloud computing and become the massive hit that AWS is today. While the explosive growth of AWS and its sophisticated suite of product offerings all came after I had moved on to other projects, it serves as a vivid example of *being Amazonian*.

It's worth noting that we had competition. Several other companies were offering web services–based developer programs at the time. Like the Amazon Product API, their programs were intended to enhance their own ecosystem. For example, eBay's developer API provided developers with tools to build applications to buy and sell products on eBay. Google had a search API, which launched the same week as Amazon Product API. Amazon had a second web services program that Marketplace sellers could use to manage the products they sold on Amazon. These programs generated quite a bit of buzz in the developer community.

The one thing all these programs had in common was that their ultimate goal was to have their parties build new software that would in some way accrue benefit to their core business—such as Amazon affiliate sales, more eBay transactions, more Google searches, and more Amazon Marketplace seller transactions. All of us, leaders and developers from these companies, were looking at similar data and trends. We ran into each other at developer conferences, participated on panels together, and shared customers who were using our developer programs. We were all swimming in the same primordial soup. Yet it was Amazon who took the first step in web services and said, "Why don't we build a set of tools that any developer can use to build anything they want, even if it has nothing to do with our core business?" As mentioned earlier, it was largely because of the Amazon focus on invention. Part of the Invent and

Simplify leadership principle states, "As we do new things, we accept that we may be misunderstood for long periods of time." Despite skeptics saying Amazon didn't belong in this space, we'd experienced firsthand the enthusiasm of the developer community, and we doubled down on that enthusiasm.

There were two additional factors that influenced the decision to make a bet on web services.

The Primitives Are Known, They Just Haven't Been Exposed as Web Services

For several decades, well-established hardware and software companies had built and sold capable solutions for a well-known set of problems inherent in building commercial software—storage (databases used to save and retrieve data), message queueing, and notifications (the latter two are different methods computer processes use to communicate with one another). If a software developer needed to implement one of these building blocks, they would have to buy a software license that would typically incur a nontrivial one-time cost plus yearly maintenance fees for however long the product was in use. Moreover, they would either have to buy hardware and run it in their own data center or pay a partner to do it.

We didn't have to invent these building blocks—or "primitives" as they have been called—we just had to figure out how to offer them in the cloud as a web service. For instance, if you want to use Amazon's S3 storage service, all you need to do is sign up for a free account and provide a credit card. After a few lines of code to set up your own storage area (called provisioning), you can start storing and retrieving data. You then pay only for what you use, which means there is no time-consuming vendor-selection process and no cost negotiation (the list prices of many corporate software licenses were just the starting point in a negotiation). And you don't have to secure computers and a data center to run your new database. The cloud provider, in this case Amazon, handles all that.

I kept my eye on these developments even as I shifted to being

Jeff's shadow. Jeff and I attended an O'Reilly Emerging Technology conference shortly after I moved jobs, and we went to a panel featuring Stewart Butterfield, who co-founded Flickr, the popular photo-sharing site, and later Slack. Someone asked Stewart to describe a typical day at Flickr. His answer was surprising. He said that about half the day was probably the same as it was for many of the people in the audience—scrambling to keep their technology platform one step ahead of the rapid growth of their business. They worked on scaling their databases, web servers, software, and hardware. Stewart said they did not spend as much time as he would like on innovating things that were unique to Flickr.

After the meeting, Jeff and I had a brief chat about Stewart's comments. We'd both noticed the same thing—a phenomenon that Amazon would later refer to as "undifferentiated heavy lifting," that is, the tasks that we could do for companies that would enable them to focus on what made them unique. This was an opportunity.

Server-Side Was Easy for Us and Hard for Most Everyone Else

Another factor that influenced our decision to offer a broader set of services was that, in building and operating one of the world's largest websites, we had acquired a core competency only a few companies could match. We had the capability to store massive amounts of data, perform computations on that data, and then quickly and reliably deliver the results to end users, be they humans or computers.

Suppose, for example, that you want to build a service that stores millions of photos to be searched and queried by millions of customers. In 2002, that would have been a reasonably large but very doable project for Amazon. That pretty much describes, in fact, our Search Inside the Book capability. For most companies, however, such a project would have been cost and time prohibitive. But it was clear that more and more companies would develop or acquire these capabilities, and they eventually would become an undifferentiated commodity.

That is exactly what happened. Today, building the capability to store and retrieve millions of photos could well be a homework assignment for a college student taking a computer science class. In several of the Working Backwards documents for the early AWS products, the PR/FAQ stated that we wanted the student in a dorm room to have access to the same world-class computing infrastructure as any Amazon software engineer. That powerful metaphor in the PR/FAQ document really helped crystallize the thoughts and ideas of the AWS product development teams.

There were a number of factors that influenced Amazon's decision to start the foray into web services that would ultimately become AWS. We had several proofs of concept in the Amazon Product API and the Amazon Seller API demonstrating that the area was worthy of attention. It was simply a better way to build software than the traditional methods used at that time. There was a relatively clear roadmap on what was needed since the software building blocks were known, but hadn't yet been offered as web services. We also knew our unique capabilities would not be unique for very long, which provided a sense of urgency. (The first company to offer a robust set of general-purpose web services wouldn't be guaranteed to win in the long run, but the head start sure would help.)

That sense of urgency is codified in Amazon's Bias for Action leadership principle. It states, "Speed matters in business. Many decisions and actions are reversible and do not need extensive study. We value calculated risk-taking." It wasn't unusual for a senior leader like Andy Jassy to choose to start a new business from scratch rather than to assume leadership of an established business. Just as it wasn't unusual for Steve Kessel and Bill to move from Amazon's then-largest business to one of its smallest, or for Colin and team to take a chance with releasing a new but controversial web service.

We also had some luck. In the 2015 shareholder letter, Jeff states, "Luck plays an outsized role in every endeavor, and I can assure you we've had a bountiful supply."[7] We were lucky that it took much longer than we expected for the pre-cloud incumbents or web tech companies to mobilize and start offering their own set of cloud services. By the time they realized the potential of cloud computing, Amazon had a several-year head start.

AWS as It Started

So what happened next? Basically, the first part of the race consisted of many months of iterating on the Working Backwards PR/FAQ process and going through the Bar Raiser process one candidate at a time as fast as we could to start building out the teams. As usual, we avoided shortcuts. It's also notable that only two out of the first set of about a half-dozen services were runaway successes—Amazon S3 (Simple Storage Service) and Amazon EC2 (Elastic Compute Cloud). Jeff and I would meet with Andy and the leaders of these teams every two weeks, sometimes more often. There was also a large team that was building out the infrastructure that all these services would use. This infrastructure consisted of components such as metering, billing, reporting, and other shared functions.

Though the initial roadmap of primitives was relatively straightforward, what wasn't so easy was figuring out how to build them so that they could operate on a scale several orders of magnitude greater than what we were doing for the Amazon retail business. There were many thorny technical issues and some truly astounding engineering work done by the teams to solve them. A full account is outside the scope of this book, but to give you an idea, the following is a description of one key issue we discussed and refined.

The Working Backwards process is all about starting from the customer perspective and following a step-by-step process where you question assumptions relentlessly until you have a complete understanding of what you want to build. It's about seeking truth. Sometimes the Working Backwards process can uncover some surprising truths. Some companies, in a rush to get a project to market, ignore that truth and keep building according to the original plan. In their attachment to the modest gains of that plan, they motivate the team to pursue it aggressively, only to realize much later that there was a much bigger gain to be had if they'd taken the time to question their own assumptions. The cost of changing course in the PR/FAQ writing stage is much lower than after you've launched and have an operating business to manage. The Working Backwards process tends to save you from the expensive proposition of making a significant course change after you've launched your product. One example that illustrates this point is an issue that came up with S3.

In the FAQ there was a simple question that read something like, "How much does S3 cost?" One of the first versions of the answer was that S3 would be a tiered monthly subscription service based on average storage use, with a possible free tier for small amounts of data. Customers would choose a monthly subscription rate based on how much data they typically needed to store—Simple Storage Service with simple pricing. We hadn't worked out the exact details of the tiers and the prices for each tier, but you don't have to do that in early iterations of the Working Backwards process. The engineering team was ready to move on to the next question.

Except that day we never got to the next question. We kept discussing this question. We really did not know how developers would use S3 when it launched. Would they store mostly large objects with low retrieval rates? Small objects with high retrieval rates? How often would updates happen versus reads? How many customers would need simple storage (can easily be re-created, stored in only one location, not a big deal if you lose it) and how many would need complex storage (bank records, stored in multiple locations, a very big deal if you lose it)? All those factors were unknown yet could meaningfully impact our costs. Since we didn't know how developers would use S3, was there a way to structure our pricing so that no matter how it was used, we could ensure that it would be affordable to our customers and to Amazon?

Thus, the discussion moved away from a tiered subscription pricing strategy and toward a cost-following strategy. "Cost following" means that your pricing model is driven primarily by your costs, which are then passed on to your customer. This is what construction companies use, because building your customer's gazebo out of redwood will cost you a lot more than building it out of pine. If we were to use a cost-following strategy, we'd be sacrificing the simplicity of subscription pricing, but both our customers and Amazon would benefit. With cost following, whatever the developer did with S3, they would use it in a way that would meet their requirements, and they would strive to minimize their cost and, therefore, our cost too. There would be no gaming of the system, and we wouldn't have to estimate how the mythical average customer would use S3 to set our prices.*

Would the most important cost drivers for S3 be the cost of storing data on the disk? The bandwidth costs of moving the data? The number of transactions? Electrical power? We finally settled on storage and bandwidth. As we discovered after S3 launched, our prediction was a little off. As Werner Vogels, the CTO of AWS, puts it,

> An example in the early days where we did not know the resources required to serve certain usage patterns was with S3: We had assumed that the storage and bandwidth were the resources we should charge for; after running for a while, we realized that the number of requests was an equally important resource. If customers have many tiny files, then storage and bandwidth don't amount to much even if they are making millions of requests. We had to adjust our model to account for all the dimensions of resource usage so that AWS could be a sustainable business.[8]

However, crucially, our decision to use the cost-following strategy allowed us to correct our mistake and adjust our pricing relatively easily. Having already determined in our PR/FAQ process

---

* A few years before Amazon Prime launched, we tested a promotion where if you ordered two books, shipping would be free. We immediately noticed that a $0.49 book shot to the top of the bestseller chart. It didn't take long to figure out that enterprising customers would choose the book they wanted, then add this $0.49 book to their shopping cart to get free shipping. We called this the "Book of Hope." Cost following would make gaming the system in this way impossible.

what all the possible cost drivers for the service would be, we could now adjust our pricing to conform to what they actually were. The adjustment would have been much larger and more costly if we'd stayed with our original idea of subscription pricing.

Amazon was just starting to use the Working Backwards process in those days when we were developing this early version of AWS. And many teams were frustrated by how slow it was to do things this way. The software engineers in the PR/FAQ meeting where we discussed pricing were getting antsy. One of them pulled me aside afterward and said, "We're software engineers, not pricing specialists with MBAs. We want to write software, not more Word documents." Painstakingly following the Working Backwards process meant we didn't even get to the rest of the PR/FAQ document in that meeting. And it meant the engineers now had to do a bunch of research, testing, and measurement on the relative costs of the service before the next meeting. I asked them to trust the process even though it seemed painful in the moment.

Jeff was insistent that we follow the process until we uncovered the truth and were crystal clear on what we were trying to build. He said that with the volume of scale we wanted to achieve, unless the service was built right with the initial release, teams would spend all their time keeping the system running and would not be able to develop any new features. And as it turns out, if you take a look at the first PR/FAQ for any of these services and compare them to the PR/FAQ at launch, they all evolved quite a bit for the better.

You can't wind the clock back, replay the experiment, and see what would have happened if we had built and launched these services quickly without knowing some of the truths we discovered using Working Backwards. However, though there were still some post-launch maintenance issues and outages, the performance and rapid customer adoption speak for themselves. Based on my experience of going through the Working Backwards process with Jeff for well over a dozen different product teams across AWS, Digital, and other services, I can say confidently that the extra time we spent slowing down to uncover the necessary truths was ultimately a faster path to a large and successful business. The results speak for themselves. Amazon has large viable digital devices and media businesses. And, as mentioned in the introduction, AWS reached the $10 billion annual revenue milestone faster than Amazon the online retailer.

* * *

The launch of this early version of AWS is a particularly good case study of some of the fundamental Amazonian principles and processes. Bias for Action is an important leadership principle at Amazon, and with AWS we were certainly under time pressure to launch this product before our competitors did. But Bias for Action does not obviate the need for the painstaking aspects of the Working Backwards process. We did not allow ourselves to be so driven by what our competitors might do that we would launch a product without first having thought very carefully about how our customers would use it and benefit from it. To put it another way, Working Backwards was the process that enabled us to put into action the principle of Customer Obsession.

AWS today is much, much bigger and quite different from the version I worked on in the early 2000s, thanks to the visionary work of AWS CEO Andy Jassy and his team. But that is exactly what makes AWS so Amazonian. What began as a little experiment of sending out product data XML to our affiliates has grown into one of the major divisions of the Amazon business, one that brought in $35 billion in revenue in 2019. In recognizing the potential of this little seed to become the mighty oak of AWS, Jeff and others at Amazon embodied the Amazonian principles of Ownership, Invent and Simplify, and Think Big.

Conclusion

Being Amazonian Beyond Amazon

Being Amazonian in your business. Being Amazonian means having to change habits and ways of doing things, deferring gratification, and persisting through challenging times, but also reaping distinct rewards. How to start being Amazonian wherever you are.

* * *

Both of us learned a great deal at Amazon. It was a defining period in our careers. And we've both since moved on to other ventures. But *being Amazonian* remains part of our DNA, and it always will. It affects how we think, make decisions, act, and view business and the world at large.

What's most fascinating to us, and the reason we have written this book, is that the elements of *being Amazonian* are so applicable to other companies, businesses, industries, and endeavors—as well as endeavors outside business, such as not-for-profit or community organizations. Defining the basics of the culture, articulating leadership principles, regularizing essential practices—Bar Raiser hiring, teams with single-threaded leaders, written narratives, Working Backwards, focusing on input metrics—all these things have proved to be essential to us in other endeavors. Indeed, we can't imagine doing business without them.

It is true that the Amazonian Day One mentality does not always produce results as intended. Some Amazonians go on to leadership roles in other companies and try to implement Amazonian practices without success. It may be that the timing isn't right, or that the senior-most executive, usually the CEO, does not support the approach. Far more often, however, the "Amazon Way" has been successfully adopted by other organizations. And, as we've said, it is wonderfully fractal, applicable at any scale and scope.

We do not suggest that becoming Amazonian is easy—for an entire organization or for the individuals within it. Working in separable, single-threaded teams can be intense, and the organization has to be constructed in a way that allows for autonomy. The Working Backwards process requires the individual to present ideas in a narrative form and to accept the critique of anyone in the room. Focusing on input metrics is unfamiliar to those schooled in traditional evaluation methods. Making a commitment to long-term "return on work" investment—through equity ownership—is hardly the norm for Western companies that link compensation to the achievement of short-term goals.

The rewards, however, are clear and distinct for both the company and the person. Amazon is clear up front about seeking people who obsess over the customer experience and who value long-term success and continuous innovation over making a quick buck or earning a fancy title. It offers a context that supports risk-taking and openness to ideas from people at any level of the business; it also provides the fulfillment that comes from taking on difficult challenges under daunting time constraints and wrangling them to the best outcome possible. Most often, this brings superior results for the company.

Even when a project does not achieve its goals or is deemed a failure, if the effort was admirable and adherent to Amazon practices and principles, the result for the individual is neither dismissal nor shame. Failure is almost always understood as the failure of a group, a process, a system, as much as that of a single person—many people have been involved, made comments, shaped the idea, and given approvals along the way. For the company, then, failure is typically viewed as an experiment from which a great deal can be learned that can lead to change and improvement. Very often, failure is temporary and eventually gives birth to success.

As we personally experienced it, *being Amazonian* can bring the satisfaction, even pride, that comes with creating products and services that change an industry, deliver exceptional customer experiences, and—as we hope this book can do—even make a contribution to management practice.

* * *

The questions that typically follow a presentation of the ideas in this book are, "How do I start? Where do I start? What do I actually do to bring some of the aspects of *being Amazonian* into my business?"

Here are a few suggestions:

- *Ban PowerPoint* as a tool to discuss complicated topics and start using six-page narratives and PR/FAQ documents in your leadership team meetings. This can be implemented almost instantly. There will be pushback and grumbling, but we've found it produces results swiftly, and eventually your leaders will say to themselves, "We can never go back to the old way."
- *Establish the Bar Raiser hiring process.* This approach is no longer unique to Amazon and we have seen it work in many companies. It too can be established relatively quickly, once a training process is in place. It also delivers short-term results by improving the quality of the process and enabling learning for everyone involved in the loop. It should reduce the number of poor hires and, in the long run, improve the overall quality of thinking and performance in each team, and in the company as a whole.
- *Focus on controllable input metrics.* Amazon is relentless about identifying metrics that can be controlled and have the greatest impact on outputs such as free cash flow per share. This is not an easy process, because it requires patient trial and error as you seek the input metrics that best allow you to assume control of your desired results. Note too that this is not an argument for abandoning output metrics. Amazon *does* care a great deal about free cash flow per share.
- *Move to an organizational structure that accommodates autonomous teams with single-threaded leaders.* As noted in chapter three, this takes time and requires careful management, as it invariably raises questions about authority and power,

jurisdiction, and "turf." You'll also have to be on the lookout for dependencies and roadblocks that are preventing autonomy in your organization. But it can be done. Start with your product development group, and then see what other areas, if any, work better in teams.

- *Revise the compensation structure for leaders* so that it encourages long-term commitment and long-term decision-making. Avoid making too many exceptions for "special cases." Make sure that leaders in all areas of the company are compensated with the same basic approach.
- *Articulate the core elements of the company's culture*, as Amazon did with long-term thinking, customer obsession, eagerness to invent, and operational excellence. Then build these into every process and discussion. Do not assume that simply stating them and displaying them will have any significant effect.
- *Define a set of leadership principles*. These must be developed with participation from many contributors. Don't assign the task to a single group or outsource it to a consultant or service provider. Do it yourselves. Hash out the details. Revisit the principles from time to time and revise if and as necessary. Then, as with the aspects of the culture, bring the principles into every process, from hiring to product development.
- *Depict your flywheel*. What are the drivers of growth for your company? Make a picture of them that shows how they act upon the flywheel. Evaluate everything you do in light of its positive or negative effect on one or more drivers of the flywheel.

Finally, keep in mind what we said at the beginning: we don't claim that the Amazon approach is the only right one. Many successful, high-performing companies operate differently than Amazon does. But, then again, there aren't many companies that have achieved the level of growth, the record of invention, the ability to move into new businesses beyond the core, and the amount of influence that Amazon has. So, at the very least, it's worth considering how *being Amazonian* might benefit your company and, even more important, your company's customers.

If you would like to learn more about how to apply the Amazon processes and principles and get your organization to start working backwards, visit our website at www.workingbackwards.com.

Appendix A

Interview Feedback Examples

Below are examples of weak and strong feedback. Note how the weak feedback focuses extensively on the candidate's work experience, passion, and strategic thinking (good that the interviewer asked about thinking) but doesn't give specific examples of actual work the candidate has accomplished. (In the strong feedback example, the candidate's answer about his actual work proved to be the reason we didn't hire him.) There is also no verbatim Q&A—we don't know what questions the interviewer asked or what the candidate's answers were. There is no data from the interview that a hiring manager can use to assess the candidate.

Read the second example of feedback to see how much easier it is to form your own opinion of the candidate based on the questions and answers. The feedback is a combination of objective data and subjective analysis.

Weak Feedback

I am inclined to hire Joe for a product management position on our team. He has a solid background owning and driving strategy for Red Corp. and two other relevant companies. He came across as having a good understanding of the unique challenges that face our space, and his experience would be an asset to our company as we craft the various ways in which to enter this market segment. In discussing the challenges that face our company, he was articulate and demonstrated a firm grasp on the ways that our company should enter a market segment that is quickly evolving. His experience at Red Corp. will be useful in the context of evaluating/analyzing companies to partner with or acquire to further our strategy. I liked his demonstrated passion for the media industry throughout his career.

Good Feedback

I interviewed Joe both for his biz dev abilities and his product management skills. I was left flat on both. I thought his strategic thinking and business judgment were weak and that his examples from work lacked specificity as to his own contributions—too much about "what we did" as opposed to "what I did"—too hard to get him to clearly articulate his own contributions. He was a passenger, not a driver.

Q: *Why do you want to work for our company?*
A: *You're focused on customer experience. The trajectory of the company is favorable. I like the idea of getting involved while your company is this size and at this stage of growth.*

Okay, I guess this answer is reasonable, but the reasoning didn't seem particularly solid or compelling.

Q: *What is your most significant professional accomplishment?*
A: *Biz dev deal that we did with Blue Corp. while I was at Red Corp. While I was too junior to lead the strategy elements for the deal, the strategic output of the deal was really big for us—brought several other players like Yellow.com to our doorstep to do similar deals.*
Q: *So what was your role?*
A: *I was one of three members of the deal team; me, the VP of Product Development, and a guy from legal. My role was relationship manager, so when business owners had specific needs, they would bring them to me and I would execute them with Blue Corp.*
Q: *So what was your big accomplishment in this deal?*
A: *It was my job on this deal to work with the biz dev guy at Blue Corp. to turn our needs for the deal into a contract. The contract was two hundred pages long.*

While I probed multiple times here, he didn't give me any evidence of something substantial that he had personally done on this deal. He was proud of the strategic import of the deal, but admitted at the outset that he had nothing to do with setting deal strategy. I was then looking for him to give me specific evidence of tough hurdles or negotiation tactics that he had employed in cranking out this huge agreement (or at least evidence of really hard work), but he didn't volunteer anything. I was psyched when he first started to tell me about this, thinking that he has great experience in putting together big deals, but it sounded like the VP and legal team members did all the driving.

Q: *If you could add or change anything about our website to improve customer experience, what would it be and why?*

A: *I would make Category X more prominent. It is buried on the site today and people don't know that it's available.*

Q: *Really? Why do you think it is strategically important for us to surface Category X more prominently?*

A: *Well actually, Category Y is probably a better example of something that I would add to the website and make more prominent.*

Q: *Okay, so then why should we make Category Y more prominent? Of all the products we sell, why is that one strategically important to surface?*

A: *Because competitor A is running away with the business and competitor B is in the business now too, and because it is something customers would want to buy from us.*

Q: *Okay, forget about these categories for a minute, what should we change in our website with respect to Category Z?*

A: *I would create a daily goods checklist that lets people buy goods like Z1, which they need regularly, and which we would ship to them at regular intervals before they run out. This would save people a trip to Competitor C.*

He failed miserably on this question. Not only did he waffle on his original answer, but he showed really poor innovation and strategic thinking here by honing in on smaller concepts that failed to tie back to big meaty customer experience or competitive issues (selection, price, customer experience).

Appendix B

Sample Narrative Tenets and FAQs

Dave Glick, a former Amazon VP, was the first person to use tenets in the six-pager. Dave had a series of narrative review meetings with Jeff that did not go well. Dave said,

> We had gotten through those bad meetings and to a place where we could have a discussion about our strategy. At the end of the discussion, we had agreement on the strategy, and we summarized it in five bullet points. Jeff said, "You should write these down and put them at the top of your document every month, so we remember what we decided last time." And thus, tenets were born. The next month I showed up with my document with the tenets front and center. It helped us all reload the cache, and made the rest of the meeting productive since we didn't have to rehash our previous decisions.[1]

One of the many benefits tenets can bring is strong alignment among everyone involved. They also provide a set of guiding principles to rely on to help with decision-making. Jeff liked the tenets so much that he asked other teams to incorporate them into their narratives. Formulating a tenet is difficult, and subtle nuances of meaning can sometimes have a large downstream impact on a project.

Tenets help organizations make hard choices and trade-offs. A tenet breaks the tie between two benefits, values, or outcomes where there is a natural tension between them. It is often the case that individuals or departments find themselves in conflict over the two outcomes because there is a legitimate argument for both outcomes. A simple example is speed vs. quality. Obviously both are desirable, and certain teams or individuals may be more focused on speed while others are more focused on quality.

Sample Tenets

Simple example tenet (this is not an Amazon tenet): Speed and quality are always important, but, when forced to make a choice between the two, we will always prioritize quality.

In this tenet, either answer (speed or quality) is valid. When the leadership team of your company aligns on a tenet like this one, refers to it consistently in meetings, and insists that it appear in relevant six-pagers, you will be amazed by how effective this is in aligning and enabling your organization.

Amazon had been working with tenets before we adopted the six-pager narrative approach. Jeff, for example, often discussed the following tenet with various internal audiences.

Tenet: We don't make money when we sell things. We make money when we help customers make purchase decisions.[2]

This guided some challenging and controversial decisions in Amazon's early days, one of which was about product reviews posted on our website. Negative reviews could potentially discourage a customer from buying a product and thus reduce revenue. So, if we are in the business to make money, why would we post negative reviews? But the tenet states that we make money not by selling things, but by helping customers make purchase decisions. The tenet instantly makes our obligation obvious. The customer needs information, positive and negative, to make an informed decision. We continued to post negative customer reviews.

Tenet: When forced to choose between building something that's convenient for customers or convenient for ourselves, we'll choose the former.

Seems like an obvious one, but companies don't always follow this tenet. Packaging, for example. Have you ever experienced the joy of opening a box that contains that product you've desperately been waiting for, only to have your joy turn to despair because the product is encased in a clamshell container of military-grade plastic? That packaging was most definitely created for the convenience of the company—easier to ship, easier to display in a store, harder for customers to steal.

Before we articulated this tenet, Amazon made this very mistake. We developed packaging designed to make it cheap and easy to wrap our books and sturdy enough to prevent damage in shipping. In 1999, Jeff received an email from an elderly woman who wrote that she loved Amazon's service, except for one problem: she had to wait for her nephew to come over to break through the packaging.[3] After receiving that email, Jeff asked the team to invent a new design that would have all the characteristics the company needed and that would also be easy for customers to open. Amazon extended that concept ten years later to other product lines with its Frustration-Free Packaging Initiative.[4]

Tenet: We don't let defects travel downstream. When we notice a defect, we will not rely on good intentions to solve the problem. We'll invent and build systematic methods to eliminate that defect.

This tenet is useful in any continuous improvement environment such as the fulfillment centers and the customer service operation. In order to prevent a defect from traveling downstream, you may need to build systems to detect and measure the defect and create a feedback loop to make sure the defect doesn't happen again. The problem will not be solved by encouraging people to try harder or relying on the good intentions of customer service people. The heartfelt "I'm sorry you had this problem, we will try harder to meet your needs in the future" does not result in the improvement of a flawed system.

One well-known defect in a fulfillment center is the "switcheroo"—when the actual weight of a package ready for loading onto a delivery truck does not match the expected weight of the products that should be in the box (plus the weight of the packaging). This is an indication that something is wrong with the order—maybe the wrong item was packed or the order is incomplete. When the weights don't match, the package is flagged and a person has to open it and inspect what's inside. This sounds pretty simple, but, in aggregate, it's a massive endeavor. You have to have precise data on the weight of tens of millions of items from millions of manufacturers, merchants, and sellers. Your weighing scales have to be extremely accurate, or they may detect a mismatch when there isn't one.

But what happens if a package goes out with the defect undetected? The customer may get something different from what was ordered. This does not make for a good customer experience.

The tenet says that we will "eliminate the defect." That's an aggressive goal, and it cannot be achieved immediately. It serves as a powerful advocate for the customer, and it has led to the development of many systems and processes to prevent and eliminate defects. As we've described, one of the best-known of these processes is the Andon Cord, which was adapted from the Toyota Production System: factory workers can pull a physical cord to halt the assembly line when they spot a defect. At Amazon, the customer service people have a virtual cord—actually a button—that they can push when a defect is noticed. It instantly prevents Amazon from selling any more of the affected product until the customer issue is resolved.

This tenet appeared in so many narratives and was so useful in advocating for the customer that Amazon incorporated it into the Leadership Principles as Insist on the Highest Standards.

Sample FAQs

An FAQ is a good way to tee up issues for discussion or highlight important points or risks in your argument. Such FAQs allow the author to take control over the discussion and steer it to productive areas for dialogue. An honest, objective, and nonemotional tone tends to work best when answering these questions. There's no point in sugarcoating things, and it helps to state the tough issues up front. Amazon's Earn Trust leadership principle states, "Leaders listen attentively, speak candidly, and treat others respectfully. They are vocally self-critical, even when doing so is awkward or embarrassing. Leaders do not believe their or their team's body odor smells of perfume. They benchmark themselves and their teams against the best." Here are some FAQs that we have found useful:

What were the biggest mistakes we have made last period, and what have we learned from them?

What are the key inputs for this business?

What is the single biggest thing we can do to move the needle in this business, and how will we organize to do just that?

What are the top reasons we should not do what we're proposing today?

When push comes to shove, what are the things we won't compromise on?

What's hard about the problem we are trying to solve?

If our team had X more people or Y more dollars, how would we deploy those resources?

What are the top three new initiatives, products, or experiments our team has launched in the past X months, and what did we learn from them?

What dependencies do we have in our area today over which we wish we had control?

Appendix C

Timeline of Events in the Book

1998
Colin joins Amazon

1999
Bill joins Amazon
Bar Raiser program launched

2001
Formal Weekly Business Review
(WBR) established

2002
Amazon Product API launches
First two-pizza teams created

2003
Colin starts as Jeff's shadow
Amazon Web Services (AWS) group
is formed

2004
Working Backwards PR/FAQ pro-
cess formalized
Use of PowerPoint at S-Team meet-
ings is banned (June 9)
Digital Media organization formed
(Bill owns business team)
First version of Amazon Leadership
Principles distributed to company

2005
Amazon Prime launch
(February 2)
Colin ends role as Jeff's shadow
to become COO of IMDb
(July)

2006
AWS Simple Storage Service (S3)
launch (March 14)
AWS Elastic Compute Cloud (EC2)
Public Beta launch
(August 25)
Unbox public launch
(September 7)
Fulfillment by Amazon launch
(September 19)

2007
Kindle launch (November 9)

2008
Amazon Video On Demand launch
(September)

2011
Prime Video launch and rebranding
(February)

Acknowledgments

This book would not have been possible without the help of many Amazonians past and present who were so generous with their time, allowing us to interview them or agreeing to review drafts of the manuscript. Without them we would have never been able to get all the facts and stories straight. Our thanks to Robin Andrulevich, Felix Anthony, Charlie Bell, Jason Child, Cem Sibay, Rick Dalzell, Ian Freed, Mike George, Dave Glick, Drew Herdener, Cameron Janes, Steve Kessel, Jason Kilar, Tom Killalea, Jonathan Leblang, Chris North, Laura Orvidas, Angie Quennell, Diego Piacentini, Kim Rachmeler, Vijay Ravindran, Neil Roseman, Dave Schappell, Jonathan Shakes, Joel Spiegel, Tom Szkutak, Sean Vegeler, John Vlastelica, Charlie Ward, Eugene Wei, and Gregg Zehr.

In addition to the list of Amazonians above, we would like to thank and acknowledge all the Amazonians who we worked with during our combined 27 years with the company. Working long, hard, and smart with all of you challenged and stretched us in ways that are hard to put in words. You all brought a level of smarts, passion, energy, and electricity that made Amazon so special.

We would like to offer a special thank-you to Jeff Bezos. The opportunity to work alongside Jeff was a transformative experience for both of us, not to mention a highlight of our careers.

We wish to acknowledge many others who read the manuscript and provided us with valuable feedback from an unbiased (non-Amazonian) perspective, including Joe Belfiore, Kristina Belfiore, Patti Brooke, Ed Clary, Roger Egan, Brian Fleming, Robert Goldbaum, Danny Limanseta, Jan Miksovsky, Sui Riu Quek, Brian Richter, Vikram Rupani, Marni Seneker, Marcus Swanepoel, John Tippett, and Jon Walton.

At St. Martin's Press/Macmillan, we owe thanks to Alan Bradshaw and Ryan Masteller, who copyedited the book. Jonathan Bush created a cover design that captured the essence of our book. Assistant Editor Alice Pfeifer kept us on task and helped with innumerable details large and small. Associate Publisher Laura Clark understood our book from the first meeting and championed it every step of the way. Publicist Gabi Gantz helped us hone our pitch and bring the book out to the world. And Joe Brosnan and Mac Nicholas were crucial to all marketing efforts.

As first-time authors we were fortunate to have Tim Bartlett as our editor. Tim was always generous with his time. He gave us valuable guidance and challenged us to think about the book in new ways. He scoured every sentence in the manuscript to help us shape it into what you are reading today.

To our agent, Howard Yoon, who patiently coached us through the process, beginning with the new experience of writing our first book. As rookie authors, we made a lot of mistakes in the beginning of this project. Howard engaged with us in countless discussions and debates on the central theme and architecture of the book. He also served as our part-time writing instructor and guide to the world of publishing from the author side of the fence.

Thanks to Sean Silcoff for helping us with our book proposal. We didn't even know we needed one when this project started. Many thanks to our writing partners John Butman, Matthew Sharpe, and Tom Schonhoff, who helped us transform our sometimes balky sentences, paragraphs, and chapters into what we hope is an enjoyable and cogent read. John, though you won't get to see the final product, your wisdom and song are present throughout the book. Matt, thanks for jumping in at the last minute and helping us. We were amazed how quickly you got up to speed on the material and improved the book. Tom, thanks for the many, many patient hours you spent listening to our grandiose plans for each chapter and providing keen insights on how to turn them into a coherent message. You were always willing to roll up your sleeves and do whatever it took to produce a polished final product.

We would like to acknowledge our families. We love you all and you were a constant source of feedback and inspiration. To our children, Phoebe, Finn, Evan, and Maddox: your curiosity and insightful questions forced us to hone our message until it was concise and clear. And thanks for letting us use more than our fair share of the family computer at the expense of your *Minecraft* time. A special thanks to our parents, George and Cicely, Betty and Bill Sr. We would not be where we are today without your constant love and support along the way. You've been telling us since we were young that we could make a difference in the world and could do anything if we put our minds to it. Your support is one of the main reasons why it was not a big leap for us to attempt something as crazy as writing our first book thirty years into our careers. To Colin's sister, Jessica, who sadly left this world all too soon. You are my hero. Your compassion, selflessness, and determination to help others in need are awe inspiring. The memory of your smile and laugh still brightens my day whenever I need an extra boost. And finally, to Colin's wife, Sarah, and Bill's wife, Lynn. Thanks for your love, encouragement, and all the sacrifices you made throughout this journey. We have been fortunate in many ways, none more so than having you as partners for life.

Notes

Introduction

1 "Surf's Up," *Forbes*, July 26, 1998, https://www.forbes.com/forbes/1998/0727/6202106a.html#71126bc93e25 (accessed June 2, 2020).

2 Jeff Bezos, "Letter to Shareholders," 2010, https://www.sec.gov/Archives/edgar/data/1018724/000119312511110797/dex991.htm.

3 Jeff Bezos, "Letter to Shareholders," 2015, https://www.sec.gov/Archives/edgar/data/1018724/000119312516530910/d168744dex991.htm.

4 Ibid.

Chapter 1: Building Blocks

1 Kif Leswing and Isobel Asher Hamilton, "'Feels Like Yesterday': Jeff Bezos Reposted Amazon's First Job Listing in a Throwback to 25 Years Ago," *Business Insider*, August 23, 2019, https://www.businessinsider.com/amazon-first-job-listing-posted-by-jeff-bezos-24-years-ago-2018-8.

2 Jeff Bezos, "Letter to Shareholders," April 2013, https://www.sec.gov/Archives/edgar/data/1018724/000119312513151836/d511111dex991.htm.

3 876,800 in Q2 2020 per the quarterly earnings announcement at https://ir.aboutamazon.com/news-release/news-release-details/2020/Amazon.com-Announces-Second-Quarter-Results/default.aspx.

4 Jeff Bezos, "Letter to Shareholders," 2015, https://www.sec.gov/Archives/edgar/data/1018724/000119312516530910/d168744dex991.htm.

5 "Leadership Principles," Amazon Jobs, https://www.amazon.jobs/en/principles (accessed May 19, 2019).

6 About Amazon Staff, "Our Leadership Principles," Working at Amazon, https://www.aboutamazon.com/working-at-amazon/our-leadership-principles (accessed June 2, 2020).

Chapter 2: Hiring

1 Team Sequoia, "Recruit Engineers in Less Time," Sequoia, https://www.sequoiacap.com/article/recruit-engineers-in-less-time/ (accessed May 19, 2019).

2   Brent Gleeson, "The 1 Thing All Great Bosses Think About During Job Interviews," *Inc.*, March 29, 2017, https://www.inc.com/brent-gleeson/how-important-is-culture-fit-for-employee-retention.html (accessed May 19, 2019).

Chapter 3: Organizing

1   Jeff Dyer and Hal Gregersen, "How Does Amazon Stay at Day One?" *Forbes*, August 8, 2017, https://www.forbes.com/sites/innovatorsdna/2017/08/08/how-does-amazon-stay-at-day-one/#efef8657e4da.
2   Statistics derived from Amazon public financial statements 1997 and 2001, https://press.aboutamazon.com/news-releases/news-release-details/amazoncom-announces-financial-results-fourth-quarter-and-1997; https://press.aboutamazon.com/news-releases/news-release-details/amazoncom-announces-4th-quarter-profit-exceeds-sales-and-profit.
3   Jim Gray, "A Conversation with Werner Vogels," *acmqueue* 4, no. 4 (June 30, 2006): https://queue.acm.org/detail.cfm?id=1142065.
4   Tom Killalea, "Velocity in Software Engineering," *acmqueue* 17, no. 3 (July 29, 2019): https://queue.acm.org/detail.cfm?id=3352692.
5   Jeff Bezos, "Letter to Shareholders," 2016, Day One, https://www.sec.gov/Archives/edgar/data/1018724/000119312517120198/d373368dex991.htm.
6   Dyer and Gregersen, "How Does Amazon Stay at Day One?"
7   Jeff Bezos, "Letter to Shareholders," 2011, https://www.sec.gov/Archives/edgar/data/1018724/000119312512161812/d329990dex991.htm.
8   Taylor Soper, "Leadership Advice: How Amazon Maintains Focus While Competing in So Many Industries at Once," Geek Wire, July 18, 2017, https://www.geekwire.com/2017/leadership-advice-amazon-keeps-managers-focused-competing-many-industries/.

Chapter 4: Communicating

1   Edward R. Tufte, "The Cognitive Style of PowerPoint: Pitching Out Corrupts Within," https://www.edwardtufte.com/tufte/powerpoint (accessed May 19, 2019).
2   The text is taken from a redacted version of the email that Colin saw some 14 years later, when advising another company. Madeline Stone, "A 2004 Email from Jeff Bezos Explains Why PowerPoint Presentations Aren't Allowed at Amazon," *Business Insider*, July 28, 2015, https://www.businessinsider.com/jeff-bezos-email-against-powerpoint-presentations-2015-7 (accessed May 19, 2019).
3   Ibid.

Chapter 6: Metrics

1   "What Is Six Sigma?" https://www.whatissixsigma.net/what-is-six-sigma/.
2   Donald J. Wheeler, *Understanding Variation: The Key to Managing Chaos* (Knoxville, TN: SPC Press, 2000), 13.
3   XMR or individual/moving-range charts are a type of control chart used to monitor process quality and the limits of variability. See more at https://en.wikipedia.org/wiki/Control_chart.

Introduction to Part Two

1   Jeff Bezos, "Letter to Shareholders," 2015, https://www.sec.gov/Archives/edgar/data/1018724/000119312516530910/d168744dex991.htm.

2   Jeff Bezos, "Letter to Shareholders," 2008, https://www.sec.gov/Archives /edgar/data/1018724/000119312509081096/dex991.htm.

3   "Introducing Fire, the First Smartphone Designed by Amazon," press release, Amazon press center, June 18, 2014, https://press.aboutamazon.com/news-releases /news-release-details/introducing-fire-first-smartphone-designed-amazon.

4   Washington Post Live, "Jeff Bezos Wants to See an Entrepreneurial Explosion in Space," *Washington Post*, May 20, 2016, https://www.washingtonpost.com /blogs/post-live/wp/2016/04/07/meet-amazon-president-jeff-bezos/.

5   Jeff Bezos, "Letter to Shareholders," 1999, https://www.sec.gov/Archives /edgar/data/1018724/000119312519103013/d727605dex991.htm.

Chapter 7: Kindle

1   "Amazon.com Announces Record Free Cash Flow Fueled by Lower Prices and Year-Round Free Shipping," press release, Amazon press center, January 27, 2004, https://press.aboutamazon.com/news-releases/news-release -details/amazoncom-announces-record-free-cash-flow-fueled-lower-prices.

2   E Ink technology was commercialized by the E Ink Corporation, co-founded in 1997 by MIT undergraduates J. D. Albert and Barrett Comiskey, MIT Media Lab professor Joseph Jacobson, Jerome Rubin, and Russ Wilcox.

3   "Introducing Amazon Kindle," press release, Amazon press center, November 19, 2007, https://press.aboutamazon.com/news-releases/news-release-details /introducing-amazon-kindle/ (accessed May 19, 2019).

4   Jesus Diaz, "Amazon Kindle vs Sony Reader Bitchfight," Gizmodo, November 19, 2007, https://gizmodo.com/amazon-kindle-vs-sony-reader-bitchfight -324481 (accessed May 19, 2019).

5   Rick Munarriz, "Oprah Saves Amazon," Motley Fool, October 27, 2008, https://www.fool.com/investing/general/2008/10/27/oprah-saves-amazon .aspx (accessed June 30, 2020).

Chapter 8: Prime

1   "Amazon.com Announces 76% Free Cash Flow Growth and 29% Sales Growth—Expects Record Holiday Season with Expanded Selection, Lower Prices, and Free Shipping," press release, Amazon press center, October 21, 2004, https://press.aboutamazon.com/news-releases/news-release-details/amazoncom -announces-76-free-cash-flow-growth-and-29-sales-growth.

2   Amazon shipping rates: https://web.archive.org/web/20050105085224 /http://www.amazon.com:80/exec/obidos/tg/browse/-/468636.

3   Colin Bryar, interview with Charlie Ward, August 12, 2019.

4   Jason Del Rey, "The Making of Amazon Prime, the Internet's Most Successful and Devastating Membership Program," Vox, May 3, 2019, https://www.vox .com/recode/2019/5/3/18511544/amazon-prime-oral-history-jeff-bezos-one -day-shipping.

5   Jeff Bezos, "Letter to Shareholders," 2018, https://www.sec.gov/Archives /edgar/data/1018724/000119312518121161/d456916dex991.htm.

Chapter 9: Prime Video

1   The word "Instant" was dropped in 2015.

2   Rob Beschizza, "Amazon Unbox on TiVo Goes Live," *Wired*, March 7, 2007, https://www.wired.com/2007/03/amazon-unbox-on/.

3   Tim Arango, "Time Warner Views Netflix as a Fading Star," *New York Times*,

December 12, 2010, https://www.nytimes.com/2010/12/13/business/media/13bewkes.html (accessed July 1, 2020).

4   Mike Boas, "The Forgotten History of Amazon Video," Medium, March 14, 2018, https://medium.com/@mikeboas/the-forgotten-history-of-amazon-video-c030cba8cf29.

5   Paul Thurrott, "Roku Now Has 27 Million Active Users," Thurrott, January 7, 2019, https://www.thurrott.com/music-videos/197204/roku-now-has-27-million-active-users.

6   Jeff Bezos, "Letter to Shareholders," 2012, https://www.sec.gov/Archives/edgar/data/1018724/000119312513151836/d511111dex991.htm.

7   "Amazon Fire Tablet," Wikipedia, https://en.wikipedia.org/wiki/Amazon_Fire_tablet (accessed June 30, 2020).

Chapter 10: AWS

1   "What Is Cloud Computing?" AWS, https://aws.amazon.com/what-is-cloud-computing/.

2   Jeff Bezos, "Letter to Shareholders," 2017, Day One, April 18, 2018, https://www.sec.gov/Archives/edgar/data/1018724/000119312518121161/d456916dex991.htm.

3   Jeff Barr, "My First 12 Years at Amazon.com," Jeff Barr's Blog, August 19, 2014, http://jeff-barr.com/2014/08/19/my-first-12-years-at-amazon-dot-com/.

4   Jeff Bezos, "Letter to Shareholders," 2006, https://www.sec.gov/Archives/edgar/data/1018724/000119312507093886/dex991.htm.

5   "Amazon.com Launches Web Services; Developers Can Now Incorporate Amazon.com Content and Features into Their Own Web Sites; Extends 'Welcome Mat' for Developers," press release, Amazon press center, July 16, 2002, https://press.aboutamazon.com/news-releases/news-release-details/amazoncom-launches-web-services.

6   "Amazon.com Web Services Announces Trio of Milestones—New Tool Kit, Enhanced Web Site and 25,000 Developers in the Program," press release, Amazon press center, May 19, 2003, https://press.aboutamazon.com/news-releases/news-release-details/amazoncom-web-services-announces-trio-milestones-new-tool-kit.

7   Jeff Bezos, "Letter to Shareholders," 2015, https://www.sec.gov/Archives/edgar/data/1018724/000119312516530910/d168744dex991.htm.

8   Werner Vogels, "10 Lessons from 10 Years of Amazon Web Services," All Things Distributed, March 11, 2016, https://www.allthingsdistributed.com/2016/03/10-lessons-from-10-years-of-aws.html.

Appendix B

1   David Glick, "When I was at #Amazon, one of my monikers was 'Godfather of Tenets,'" LinkedIn, edited March 2020, https://www.linkedin.com/posts/davidglick1_amazon-tenets-jeffbezos-activity-6631036863471849472-IO5E/.

2   "Jeff Bezos on Leading for the Long-Term at Amazon," HBR IdeaCast, https://hbr.org/podcast/2013/01/jeff-bezos-on-leading-for-the (accessed May 19, 2019).

3   Peter de Jonge, "Riding the Wild, Perilous Waters of Amazon.com," New York Times, March 14, 1999, https://archive.nytimes.com/www.nytimes.com/library/tech/99/03/biztech/articles/14amazon.html.

4   "Amazon Certified Frustration-Free Packaging Programs," https://www.amazon.com/b/?&node=5521637011#ace-5421475708 (accessed June 30, 2020).

Index